A Developer's Guide to Amazon SimpleDB

A Developer's Guide to Amazon SimpleDB

Mocky Habeeb

Addison-Wesley

Upper Saddle River, NJ • Boston • Indianapolis • San Francisco
New York • Toronto • Montreal • London • Munich • Paris • Madrid
Cape Town • Sydney • Tokyo • Singapore • Mexico City

The publisher offers excellent discounts on this book when ordered in quantity for bulk purchases or special sales, which may include electronic versions and/or custom covers and content particular to your business, training goals, marketing focus, and branding interests. For more information, please contact:

U.S. Corporate and Government Sales
(800) 382-3419
corpsales@pearsontechgroup.com

For sales outside the United States, please contact:

International Sales
international@pearson.com

Visit us on the Web: informit.com/aw

Library of Congress Cataloging-in-Publication Data

Habeeb, Mocky, 1971-
A Developer's Guide to Amazon SimpleDB / Mocky Habeeb.
p. cm.
ISBN 978-0-321-62363-8 (pbk. : alk. paper) 1. Web services. 2. Amazon SimpleDB (Electronic resource) 3. Cloud computing. 4. Database management. I. Title.
TK5105.88813.H32 2010
006.7'8—dc22

2010016954

Pearson Education, Inc
Rights and Contracts Department
501 Boylston Street, Suite 900
Boston, MA 02116
Fax: (617) 671 3447

ISBN-13: 978-0-321-62363-8
ISBN-10: 0-321-62363-0

Text printed in the United States on recycled paper at RR Donnelley Crawfordsville in Crawfordsville, Indiana.

First printing, July 2010

To Jamie, My Soul Mate

Contents at a Glance

Contents

Preface

This book is a detailed guide for using Amazon SimpleDB. Over the years that I have been using this web service, I have always tried to contribute back to the developer community. This primarily involved answering questions on the SimpleDB forums and on stackoverflow.com. What I saw over time was a general lack of resources and understanding about the practical, day-to-day use of the service. As a result, the same types of questions were being asked repeatedly, and the same misconceptions seemed to be held by many people.

At the time of this writing, there are no SimpleDB books available. My purpose in writing this book is to offer my experience and my opinion about getting the most from SimpleDB in a more structured and thorough format than online forums. I have made every attempt to avoid rehashing information that is available elsewhere, opting instead for alternate perspectives and analysis.

About This Book

SimpleDB is a unique service because much of the value proposition has nothing to do with the actual web service calls. I am referring to the service qualities that include availability, scalability, and flexibility. These make great marketing bullet points, and not just for SimpleDB. You would not be surprised to hear those terms used in discussions of just about any server-side product. With SimpleDB, however, these qualities have a direct impact on how much benefit you get from the service. It is a service based on a specific set of tradeoffs; many features are specifically absent, and for good reason. In my experience, a proper understanding of these tradeoffs is essential to knowing if SimpleDB will be a good fit for your application.

This book is designed to provide a comprehensive discussion of all the important issues that come up when using SimpleDB. All of the available web service operations receive detailed coverage. This includes code samples, notes on how to solve common problems, and warnings about many pitfalls that are not immediately obvious.

Target Audience

This book is intended for software developers who want to use or evaluate SimpleDB. Certain chapters should also prove to be useful to managers, executives, or technologists who want to understand the value of SimpleDB and what problems it seeks to solve.

There is some difficulty in audience targeting that comes from the nature of the SimpleDB service. On the one hand, it is a web-based service that uses specific message formats over standard technologies like HTTP and XML. On the other hand, application developers, and probably most users, will never deal directly with the low-level wire protocol, opting instead for client software in his or her chosen programming language.

This creates (at least) two separate perspectives to use when discussing the service. The low-level viewpoint is needed for the framework designers and those writing a SimpleDB client, whereas a higher-level, abridged version is more suitable for application developers whose view of SimpleDB is strictly through the lens of the client software. In addition, the app developers are best served with a guide that uses a matching programming language and client.

The official Amazon documentation for SimpleDB is targeted squarely at the developers writing the clients. This is by necessity—SimpleDB is a web service, and the details need to be documented.

What I have tried to accomplish is the targeting of both groups. One of the most visible methods I used is splitting the detailed API coverage into two separate chapters.

Chapter 3, "A Code-Snippet Tour of the SimpleDB API," presents a detailed discussion of all the SimpleDB operations, including all parameters, error messages, and code examples in Java, C#, and PHP. This is fully suitable for both groups of developers, with the inclusion of practical advice and tips that apply to the operations themselves.

Chapter 10, "Writing a SimpleDB Client: A Language-Independent Guide," offers a guide and walkthrough for creating a SimpleDB client from scratch. This adds another layer to the discussion with much more detail about the low-level concerns and issues. This is intended for the developers of SimpleDB clients and those adding SimpleDB support to existing frameworks. Apart from Chapter 3, the remainder of the examples in the book are written in Java.

Code Examples

All of the code listings in this book are available for download at this book's website at http://www.simpledbbook.com/code.

Acknowledgments

I would like to thank my family for their love, support, and inspiration. Thanks to my mom for teaching me to love books and for getting me that summer job at the college library back in '89. Thanks to Mikki and Keenan for their understanding while I was spending evenings and weekends locked away.

I'm pleased to thank Kunal Mittal for the insightful reviews and for the enthusiasm. Thanks to Trina MacDonald at Pearson for her patience and for bringing me the idea for this book in the first place.

Most of all, I want to thank my amazing wife, Jamie. She made many sacrifices to make this book possible. I offer my deepest thanks to her for consistently helping me become more than I ever could have become on my own.

About the Author

Mocky Habeeb is the head of web architecture and development for Infrawise Inc., where he leads development on the web side of the house for the company's flagship product suite. He is actively involved in SimpleDB application development, and in his spare time, he puts that expertise to work by providing answers and guidance to developers who visit the official SimpleDB web forums. Over the past 13 years, he has worked in various software development positions, as a Java instructor for Sun Microsystems, and before that as a tank driver in the United States Marine Corps. Mocky studied Computer Science at SUNY, Oswego.

1

Introducing Amazon SimpleDB

Amazon has been offering its customers computing infrastructure via Amazon Web Services (AWS) since 2006. AWS aims to use its own infrastructure to provide the building blocks for other organizations to use. The Elastic Compute Cloud (EC2) is an AWS offering that enables you to spin up virtual servers as you need the computing power and shut them off when you are done. Amazon Simple Storage Service (S3) provides fast and unlimited file storage for the web. Amazon SimpleDB is a service designed to complement EC2 and S3, but the concept is not as easy to grasp as "extra servers" and "extra storage." This chapter will cover the concepts behind SimpleDB and discuss how it compares to other services.

What Is SimpleDB?

SimpleDB is a web service providing structured data storage in the cloud and backed by clusters of Amazon-managed database servers. The data requires no schema and is stored securely in the cloud. There is a query function, and all the data values you store are fully indexed. In keeping with Amazon's other web services, there is no minimum charge, and you are only billed for your actual usage.

What SimpleDB Is Not

The name "SimpleDB" might lead you to believe that it is just like relational database management systems (RDBMS), only simpler to use. In some respects, this is true, but it is not just about making simplistic database usage simpler. SimpleDB aims to simplify the much harder task of creating and managing a database cluster that is fault-tolerant in the face of multiple failures, replicated across data centers, and delivers high levels of availability.

One misconception that seems to be very common among people just learning about SimpleDB is the idea that migrating from an RDBMS to SimpleDB will automatically solve your database performance problems. Performance certainly is an important part of the equation when you seek to evaluate databases. Unfortunately, for some people, speed is the beginning and the end of the thought process. It can be tempting to view any of the new hosted database services as a silver bullet when offered by a mega-company like Microsoft, Amazon, or Google. But the fact is that SimpleDB is not going to solve your existing speed issues. The service exists to solve an entirely different set of problems. Reads and writes are not blazingly fast. They are meant to be "fast enough." It is entirely possible that AWS may increase performance of the service over time, based on user feedback. But SimpleDB is never going to be as speedy as a standalone database running on fast hardware. SimpleDB has a different purpose.

Robust database clusters replicating data across multiple data centers is not a data storage solution that is typically easy to throw together. It is a time consuming and costly undertaking. Even in organizations that have the database administrator (DBA) expertise and are using multiple data centers, it is still time consuming. It is costly enough that you would not do it unless there was a quantifiable business need for it. SimpleDB offers data storage with these features on a pay-as-you-go basis.

Of course, taking advantage of these features is not without a downside. SimpleDB is a moderately restrictive environment, and it is not suitable for many types of applications. There are various restrictions and limitations on how much data can be stored and transferred and how much network bandwidth you can consume.

Schema-Less Data

SimpleDB differs from relational databases where you must define a schema for each database table before you can use it and where you must explicitly change that schema before you can store your data differently. In SimpleDB, there is no schema requirement. Although you still have to consider the format of your data, this approach has the benefit of freeing you from the time it takes to manage schema modifications.

The lack of schema means that there are no data types; all data values are treated as variable length character data. As a result, there is literally nothing extra to do if you want to add a new field to an existing database. You just add the new field to whichever data items require it. There is no rule that forces every data item to have the same fields.

The drawbacks of a schema-less database include the lack of automatic integrity checking in the database and an increased burden on the application to handle formatting and type conversions. Detailed coverage of the impact of schema-less data on queries appears in Chapter 4, "A Closer Look at Select," along with a discussion of the formatting issues.

Stored Securely in the Cloud

The data that you store in SimpleDB is available both from the Internet and (with less latency) from EC2. The security of that data is of great importance for many applications, while the security of the underlying web services account should be important to all users.

To protect that data, all access to SimpleDB, whether read or write, is protected by your account credentials. Every request must bear the correct and authorized digital signature or else it is rejected with an error code. Security of the account, data transmission, and data storage is the subject of Chapter 8, "Security in SimpleDB-Based Applications."

Billed Only for Actual Usage

In keeping with the AWS philosophy of pay-as-you-go, SimpleDB has a pricing structure that includes charges for data storage, data transfer, and processor usage. There are no base fees and there are no minimums. At the time of this writing, Amazon's monthly billing for SimpleDB has a free usage tier that covers the first gigabyte (GB) of data storage, the first GB of data transfer, and the first 25 hours of processor usage each month. Data transfer costs beyond the free tier have historically been on par with S3 pricing, whereas storage costs have always been somewhat higher. Consult the AWS website at https://aws.amazon.com/simpledb/ for current pricing information.

Domains, Items, and Attribute Pairs

The top level of data storage in SimpleDB is the domain. A domain is roughly analogous to a database table. You can create and delete domains as needed. There are no configuration options to set on a domain; the only parameter you can set is the name of the domain.

All the data stored in a SimpleDB domain takes the form of name-value attribute pairs. Each attribute pair is associated with an item, which plays the role of a table row. The attribute name is similar to a database column name but unlike database rows that must all have identical columns, SimpleDB items can each contain different attribute names. This gives you the freedom to store different data in some items without changing the layout of other items that do not have that data. It also allows the painless addition of new data fields in the future.

Multi-Valued Attributes

It is possible for each attribute to have not just one value, but an array of values. For example, an application that allows user tagging can use a single attribute named "tags" to hold as many or as few tags as needed for each item. You do not need to change a schema definition to enable multi-valued attributes. All you need to do is add another attribute to an item and use the same attribute name with a different value. This provides you with flexibility in how you store your data.

Queries

SimpleDB is primarily a key-value store, but it also has useful query functionality. A SQL-style query language is used to issue queries over the scope of a single domain. A subset of the SQL select syntax is recognized. The following is an example SimpleDB select statement:

```
SELECT * FROM products WHERE rating > '03' ORDER BY rating LIMIT 10
```

You put a domain name—in this case, `products`—in the `FROM` clause where a table name would normally be. The `WHERE` clause recognizes a dozen or so comparison operators, but an attribute name must always be on the left side of the operator and a literal value must always be on the right. There is no relational comparison between attributes allowed here. So, the following is not valid:

```
SELECT * FROM users WHERE creation-date = last-activity-date
```

All the data stored in SimpleDB is treated as plain string data. There are no explicit indexes to maintain; each value is automatically indexed as you add it.

High Availability

High availability is an important benefit of using SimpleDB. There are many types of failures that can occur with a database solution that will affect the availability of your application. When you run your own database servers, there is a spectrum of different configurations you can employ.

To help quantify the availability benefits that you get automatically with SimpleDB, let's consider how you might achieve the same results using replication for your own database servers. At the easier end of the spectrum is a master-slave database replication scheme, where the master database accepts client updates and a second database acts as a slave and pulls all the updates from the master. This eliminates the single point of failure. If the master goes down, the slave can take over. Managing these failures (when not using SimpleDB) requires some additional work for swapping IP addresses or domain name entries, but it is not very difficult.

Moving toward the more difficult end of the self-managed replication spectrum allows you to maintain availability during failure that involves more than a single server. There is more work to be done if you are going to handle two servers going down in a short period, or a server problem and a network outage, or a problem that affects the whole data center.

Creating a database solution that maintains uptime during these more severe failures requires a certain level of expertise. It can be simplified with cloud computing services like EC2 that make it easy to start and manage servers in different geographical locations. However, when there are many moving parts, the task remains time consuming. It can also be expensive.

When you use SimpleDB, you get high availability with your data replicated to different geographic locations automatically. You do not need to do any extra work or become an expert on high availability or the specifics of replication techniques for one vendor's database product. This is a huge benefit not because that level of expertise is not worth attaining, but because there is a whole class of applications that previously could not justify that effort.

Database Consistency

One of the consequences of replicating database updates across multiple servers and data centers is the need to decide what kind of consistency guarantees will be maintained. A database running on a single server can easily maintain strong consistency. With strong consistency, after an update occurs, every subsequent database access by every client reflects the change and the previous state of the database is never seen.

This can be a problem for a database cluster if the purpose of the cluster is to improve availability. If there is a master database replicating updates to slave databases, strong consistency requires the slaves to accept the update at the same time as the master. All access to the database would then be strongly consistent. However, in the case of a problem preventing communication between the master and a slave, the master would be unable to accept updates because doing so out of sync with a slave would break the consistency guarantee. If the database rejects updates during even simple problem scenarios, it defeats the availability. In practice, replication is often not done this way. A common solution to this problem is to allow only the master database to accept updates and do so without direct contact with any slave databases. After the master commits each transaction, slaves are sent the update in near real-time. This amounts to a relaxing of the consistency guarantee. If clients only connect to the slave when the master goes down, then the weakened consistency only applies to this scenario.

SimpleDB sports the option of either eventual consistency or strong consistency for each read request. With eventual consistency, when you submit an update to SimpleDB, the database server handling your request will forward the update to the other database servers where that domain is replicated. The full update of all replicas does not happen before your update request returns. The replication continues in the background while other requests are handled. The period of time it takes for all replicas to be updated is called the eventual consistency window. The eventual consistency window is usually small. AWS does not offer any guarantees about this window, but it is frequently less than one second.

A couple things can make the consistency window larger. One is a high request load. If the servers hosting a given SimpleDB domain are under heavy load, the time it takes for full replication is increased. Additionally a network or server failure can block replication until it is resolved. Consider a network outage between data centers hosting your data. If the SimpleDB load-balancer is able to successfully route your requests to both data centers, your updates will be accepted at both locations. However, replication will fail between the two locations. The data you fetch from one will not be consistent with updates you have applied to the other. Once the problem is fixed, SimpleDB will complete the replication automatically.

Using a consistent read eliminates the consistency window for that request. The results of a consistent read will reflect all previous writes. In the normal case, a consistent read is no slower than an eventually consistent read. However, it is possible for consistent read requests to display higher latency and lower bandwidth on occasion.

Sizing Up the SimpleDB Feature Set

The SimpleDB API exposes a limited set of features. Here is a list of what you get:

- You can create named domains within your account. At the time of this writing, the initial allocation allows you to create up to 100 domains. You can request a larger allocation on the AWS website.
- You can delete an existing domain at any time without first deleting the data stored in it.
- You can store a data item for the first time or for subsequent updates using a call to `PutAttributes`. When you issue an update, you do not need to pass the full item; you can pass just the attributes that have changed.
- There is a batch call that allows you to put up to 25 items at once.
- You can retrieve the data with a call to `GetAttributes`.
- You can query for items based on criteria on multiple attributes of an item.
- You can store any type of data. SimpleDB treats it all as string data, and you are free to format it as you choose.
- You can store different types of items in the same domain, and items of the same type can vary in which attributes have values.

Benefits of Using SimpleDB

When you use SimpleDB, you give up some features you might otherwise have, but as a trade-off, you gain some important benefits, as follows:

- **Availability—** When you store your data in SimpleDB, it is automatically replicated across multiple storage nodes and across multiple data centers in the same region.
- **Simplicity—** There are not a lot of knobs or dials, and there are not any configuration parameters. This makes it a lot harder to shoot yourself in the foot.
- **Scalability—** The service is designed for scalability and concurrent access.
- **Flexibility—** Store the data you need to store now, and if the requirements change, store it differently without changing the database.
- **Low latency within the same region—** Access to SimpleDB from an EC2 instance in the same region has the latency of a typical LAN.
- **Low maintenance—** Most of the administrative burden is transferred to Amazon. They maintain the hardware and the database software.

Database Features SimpleDB Doesn't Have

There are a number of common database features noticeably absent from Amazon SimpleDB. Programs based on relational database products typically rely on these features. You should be aware of what you will not find in SimpleDB, as follows:

- **Full SQL support—** A query language similar to SQL is supported for queries only. However, it only applies to "select" statements, and there are some syntax differences and other limitations.
- **Joins—** You can issue queries, but there are no foreign keys and no joins.
- **Auto-incrementing primary keys—** You have to create your own primary keys in the form of an item name.
- **Transactions—** There are no explicit transaction boundaries that you can mark or isolation levels that you can define. There is no notion of a commit or a rollback. There is some implicit support for atomic writes, but it only applies within the scope of each individual item being written.

Higher-Level Framework Functionality

This simplicity of what SimpleDB offers on the server side is matched by the simplicity of what AWS provides in officially supported SimpleDB clients. There is a one-to-one mapping of service features to client calls. There is a lot of functionality that can be built atop the basic SimpleDB primitives. In addition, the inclusion of these advance features has already begun with a number of third-party SimpleDB clients. Popular persistence frameworks used as an abstraction layer above relational databases are prime candidates for this.

Some features normally included within the database server can be written into SimpleDB clients for automatic handling. Third-party client software is constantly improving, and some of the following features may be present already or you may have to write it for yourself:

- **Data formatting—** Integers, floats, and dates require special formatting in some cases.
- **Object mapping—** It can be convenient to map programming language objects to SimpleDB attributes.
- **Sharding—** The domain is the basic unit of horizontal scalability in SimpleDB. However, there is no explicit support for automatically distributing data across domains.
- **Cache integration—** Caching is an important aspect of many applications, and caching popular data objects is a well-understood optimization. Configurable caching that is well integrated with a SimpleDB client is an important feature.

Service Limits

There are quite a few limitations on what you are allowed to do with SimpleDB. Most of these are size and quantity restrictions. There is an underlying philosophy that small and quickly serviced units of work provide the greatest opportunity for load balancing and maintaining uniform service levels. AWS maintains a current listing of the service limitations within the latest online SimpleDB Developer Guide at the AWS website. At the time of this writing, the limits are as follows:

- Max storage per domain: 10GB
- Max attribute values per domain: 1 billion
- Initial max domains per account: 100
- Max attribute values per item: 256
- Max length of item name, attribute name, or value: 1024 bytes
- Max query execution time: 5 seconds
- Max query results: 2500
- Max query response size: 1MB
- Max comparisons per query: 20

These limits may seem restrictive when compared to the unlimited nature of data sizes you can store in other database offerings. However, there are two things to keep in mind about these limits. First, SimpleDB is not a general-purpose data store suitable for everything. It is specifically designed for storing small chunks of data. For larger data objects that you want to store in the cloud, you are advised to use Amazon S3. Secondly, consider the steps that need to be taken with a relational database at higher loads when performance begins to degrade. Typical recommendations often include offloading processing from the database, reducing long-running queries, and applying selective de-normalization of the data. These limits are what help enable efficient and automatic background replication and high concurrency and availability. Some of these limits can be worked around to a degree, but no workarounds exist for you to make SimpleDB universally appropriate for all data storage needs.

Abandoning the Relational Model?

There have been many recent products and services offering data storage but rejecting the relational model. This trend has been dubbed by some as the NoSQL movement. There is a fair amount of enthusiasm both for and against this trend. A few of those in the "against" column argue that databases without schemas, type checking, normalization, and so on are throwing away 40 years of database progress. Likewise, some proponents are quick to dispense the hype about how a given NoSQL solution will solve your problems. The aim of this section is to present a case for the value of a service like SimpleDB that addresses legitimate criticism and avoids hype and exaggeration.

A Database Without a Schema

One of the primary areas of contention around SimpleDB and other NoSQL solutions centers on the lack of a database schema. Database schemas turn out to be very important in the relational model. The formalism of predefining your data model into a schema provides a number of specific benefits, but it also imposes restrictions.

SimpleDB has no notion of a schema at all. Many of the structures defined in a typical database schema do not even exist in SimpleDB. This includes things such as stored procedures, triggers, relationships, and views. Other elements of a database schema like fields and types do exist in SimpleDB but are flexible and are not enforced on the server. Still other features, like indexes, require no formal definition because the SimpleDB service creates and manages them behind the scenes.

However, the lack of a schema requirement in SimpleDB does not prevent you from gaining the benefits of a schema. You can create your own schema for whatever portion of your data model that is appropriate. This allows you to cherry-pick the benefits that are helpful to your application without the unneeded restrictions.

One of the most important things you gain from codifying your data layout is a separation between it and the application. This is an enabling feature for tools and application plug-ins. Third-party tools can query your data, convert your data from one format to another, and analyze and report on your data based solely on the schema definition. The alternative is less attractive. Tools and extensions are more limited in what they can do without knowledge of the formats. For example, you cannot compute the sum of values in a numeric column if you do not know the format of that column. In the degenerate case, developers must search through your source code to infer data types.

In SimpleDB, many of the most common database features are not available. Query, however, is one important feature that is present and has some bearing on your data formatting. Because all the data you store in SimpleDB is variable length character data, you must apply padding to numeric data in order for queries to work properly. For example, if you want to store an attribute named "price" with a value of "269.94," you must first add leading zeros to make it "00000269.94." This is required because greater-than and less-than comparisons within SimpleDB compare each character from left to right. Padding with zeros allows you to line up the decimal point so the comparisons will be correct for all possible values of that attribute. Relational database products handle this for you behind the scenes when you declare a column type is a numeric type like int.

This is a case in SimpleDB where a schema is beneficial. The code that initially imports records into SimpleDB, the code that writes records as your app runs, and any code that uses a numeric attribute in a query all need to use the exact same format. Explicitly storing the schema externally is a much less error-prone approach than implicitly defining the format in duplicated code across various modules.

Another benefit of the predefined schema in the relational model is that it forces you to think through the data relationships and make unambiguous decisions about your data layout. Sometimes, however, the data is simple, there are no relationships, and creating a data model is overkill. Sometimes you may still be in the process of defining the data model. SimpleDB can be used as part of the prototyping process, enabling you to evolve your schema dynamically as issues surface that may not otherwise have become known so quickly. You may be migrating from a different database with an existing data model. The important thing to remember is that SimpleDB is simple by design. It can be useful in a variety of situations and does not prevent you from creating your own schema external to SimpleDB.

Areas Where Relational Databases Struggle

Relational databases have been around for some time. There are many robust and mature products available. Modern database products offer a multitude of features and a host of configuration options.

One area where difficulty arises is with database features that you do not need or that you should not use for a particular application. Applications that have simple data storage requirements do not benefit from the myriad of available options. In fact, it can be detrimental in a couple different ways. If you need to learn the intricacies of a particular database product before you can make good use of it, the time spent learning takes away from time you could have spent on your application. Knowledge of how database products work is good to have. It would be hard to argue that you wasted your time by learning it because that information could serve you well far into the future. Similarly, if there is a much simpler solution that meets your needs, you could choose that instead. If you had no immediate requirement to gain product specific database expertise, it would be hard to insist that you made the wrong choice. It is a tough sell to argue that the more time-consuming, yet educational, route is always better than the simple and direct route. This is a challenge faced by databases today, when the simple problems are not met with simple solutions.

Another pain point with relational databases is horizontal scaling. It is easy to scale a database vertically by beefing up your server because memory and disk drives are inexpensive. However, scaling a database across multiple servers can be extremely difficult. There is a whole spectrum of options available for horizontal scaling that includes basic master-slave replication as well as complicated sharding strategies. These solutions each require a different, and sometimes considerable, amount of expertise. Nevertheless, they all have one thing in common when compared to vertical scaling solutions. On top of the implementation difficulty, each additional server results in an additional increase in ongoing maintenance responsibility. Moreover, it is not merely the additional server maintenance of having more servers. I am referring to the actual database administration tasks of managing additional replicas, backups, and log shipping. It also includes the tasks of rolling out schema changes and new indexes to all servers in the cluster.

If you are in a situation where you want a simple database solution or you want horizontal scaling, SimpleDB is definitely a service to consider. However, you may need to be prepared to defend your decision.

Scalability Isn't Your Problem

Around every corner, you can find people who will challenge your efforts to scale horizontally. Beyond the cost and difficulty, there is a degree of resistance to products and services that seek to solve these problems.

The typical, and now clichéd, advice tends to be that scalability is not your problem, and trying to solve scalability at the outset is a case of premature optimization. This is followed by a discussion of how many daily page views a single high-performance database server can support. Finally, it ends by noting that it is really just a problem for when you reach the scale of Google or Amazon.

The premise of the argument is actually solid, although not applicable to all situations. The premise is that when you are building a site or service that nobody has heard of yet, you are more concerned about handling loads of people than about making the site remarkable. It is good advice for these situations. Moreover, it is especially timely considering that there is a small but religious segment of Internet commentators who eagerly chime, "X doesn't scale," where X is any alternative to the solution the commenter uses. Among programmers, there is a general preoccupation with performance optimization that seems somewhat out of balance.

The fact is that for many projects, scalability really is not your problem, but availability can be. Distributing your data store across servers from the outset is not a premature optimization when you can quantify the cost of down time. If a couple hours of downtime will have an impact on your business, then availability is something worth thinking about. For the IT department delivering a mission-critical application, availability is important. Even if only 20 users will use it during normal business hours, when it provides a competitive advantage, it is important to maintain availability through expected outages. When you have a product launch, and your credibility is at stake as much as your revenue, you are not putting the cart before the horse when you protect yourself against hardware failures.

There are many situations where availability is an important system quality. Look at how common it is for a multi-server web cluster to host one website. Before you can add a second web server, you must first solve a small set of known problems. User sessions have to be managed properly; load balancing has to be in place and routing around unresponsive servers. However, web server clusters are useful for more than high-traffic load handling. They are also beneficial because we know that hardware will fail, and we want to maintain service during the failure. We can add another web server because it is neither costly nor difficult, and it improves the availability. With the advent of systems designed to provide higher database availability that are not costly nor hard, availability becomes worth pursuing for less-critical projects.

Avoiding the SimpleDB Hype

There are many different application scenarios where SimpleDB is an interesting option. That said, some people have overstated the benefits of using SimpleDB specifically and hosted NoSQL databases in general. The reasoning seems to be that services running on the infrastructure of companies like Amazon, Google, or Microsoft will undoubtedly have nearly unlimited automatic scalability. Although there is nothing wrong with enthusiasm for products and services that you like, it is good to base that enthusiasm on reality.

Do not be fooled into thinking that any of these new databases is going to be a panacea. Make sure you educate yourself about the pros and cons of each solution as you evaluate it. The majority of services in this space have a free usage tier, and all the open-source alternatives are completely free to use. Take advantage of it, and try them out for yourself. We live in an amazing time in history where the quantity of information available at our fingertips is unprecedented. Access to web-based services and open-source projects is a huge opportunity. The tragedy is that in a time when it has never been easier to gain personal experience with new technology, all too often we are tempted to adopt the opinions of others instead of taking the time to form our own opinions. Do not believe the hype—find out for yourself.

Putting the DBA Out of Work

One of the stated goals of SimpleDB is allowing customers to outsource the time and effort associated with managing a web-scale database. Managing the database is traditionally the world of the DBA. Some people have assumed that advocating the use of SimpleDB amounts to advocating a world where the DBA diminishes in importance. However, this is not the case at all.

One of the things that have come about from the widespread popularity of EC2 has been a change in the role of system administrators. What we have found is that managing EC2 virtual instances is less work than managing a physical server instance. However, the result has not been a rash of system administrator firings. Instead, the result has been that system administrators are able to become more productive by managing larger numbers of servers than they otherwise could. The ease of acquisition and the low cost to acquire and release the computing power have led, in many cases, to a greater and more dynamic use of the servers. In other words, organizations are using more server instances because the various levels of the organization can handle it, from a cost, risk, and labor standpoint.

SimpleDB and its cohorts seem to facilitate a similar change but on a smaller scale. First, SimpleDB has less general applicability than EC2. It is a suitable solution for a much smaller set of problems. AWS fully advocates the use of existing relational database products. SimpleDB is an additional option, not a replacement. Moreover, SimpleDB finds good usage in some areas where a relational database might not normally be used, as in the case of storing web user session data. In addition, for those projects that choose to use SimpleDB instead of, or along with, a relational database, it does not mean that there is no role for the DBA. Some tasks remain similar to EC2, which can result in a greater capacity for IT departments to create solutions.

Dodging Copies of C.J. Date

There are database purists who wholeheartedly try to dissuade people from using any type of non-relational database on principle alone. Not only that, but they also go to great lengths to advocate the proper use of relational databases and lament the fact that no current database products correctly implement the relational model. Having found the one-true data storage paradigm, they believe that the relational model is "right" and is the only one that will last. The purists are not wrong in their appreciation for the relational model and for SQL. The relational model is the cornerstone of the database field, and more than that, an invaluable contribution to the world of computing. It is one of the two best things to come out of 1969. Invented by a mathematician and considered a branch of mathematics itself, there is a solid theoretical rigor that underlies its principles. Even though it is not a complete or finished branch, the work to date has been sound.

The world of mathematics and academic research is an interesting place. When you have spent large quantities of your life and career there, you are highly qualified to make authoritative comments on topics like correctness and provability. Nevertheless, being either a relational model expert or merely someone who holds them in high regard does not say anything about your ability to deliver value to users. It is clearly true that modeling your data "correctly" can provide measurable benefits and that making mistakes in your model can lead to certain classes of problems. However, you can still provide significant user value with a flawed model, and correctness is no guarantee of success.

It is like perfectly generated XHTML that always validates. It is like programming with a functional style (in any programming language) that lets you prove your programs are correct. It is like maintaining unit tests that provide 100% test coverage for every line of code you write. There is nothing inherently bad you can say about these things. In fact, there are plenty of good things to say about them. The problem is not a technical problem—it is a people problem. The problem is when people become hyper-focused on narrow technological aspects to the exclusion of the broader issues of the application's purpose.

The people conducting database research and the ones who take the time to help educate the computing industry deserve our respect. If you have a degree in computer science, chances are you studied C.J. Date's work in your database class. Among professional programmers, there is no good excuse for not knowing data and relational fundamentals. However, the person in the next row of cubicles who is only contributing condescending criticism to your project is no C.J. Date. In addition, the user with 50 times your stackoverflow.com reputation who ridicules the premise of your questions without providing useful suggestions is no E.F. Codd. Understanding the theory is of great importance. Knowing how to deliver value to your users is of greater importance. In the end, avoid vociferous ignorance and don't let anyone kick copies of C.J. Date in your face.

Other Pieces of the Puzzle

In the world of cloud computing, there are a growing number of companies and services from which to choose. Each service provider seeks to align its offerings with a broader strategy. With Amazon, that strategy includes providing very basic infrastructure building blocks for users to assemble customized solutions. AWS tries to get you to use more than one service offering by making the different services useful with each other and by offering fast and free data transfer between services in the same region. This section describes three other Amazon Web Services, along with some ways you might find them to be useful in conjunction with SimpleDB.

Adding Compute Power with Amazon EC2

AWS sells computing power by the hour via the Amazon Elastic Compute Cloud (Amazon EC2). This computing power takes the form of virtual server instances running on top of physical servers within Amazon data centers. These server instances come in varying amounts of processor horsepower and memory, depending on your needs and budget. What makes this compute cloud elastic is the fact that users can start up, and shut down, dozens of virtual instances at a moment's notice.

These general-purpose servers can fulfill the role of just about any server. Some of the popular choices include web server, database server, batch-processing server, and media server. The use of EC2 can result in a large reduction in ongoing infrastructure maintenance when compared to managing private in-house servers. Another big benefit is the elimination of up-front capital expenditures on hardware in favor of paying for only the compute power that is used.

The sweet spot between SimpleDB and EC2 comes for high-data bandwidth applications. For those apps that need fast access to high volumes of data in SimpleDB, EC2 is the platform of choice. The free same region data transfer can add up to a sizable cost savings for large data sets, but the biggest win comes from the consistently low latency. AWS does not guarantee any particular latency numbers but typically, round-tripping times are in the neighborhood of 2 to 7 milliseconds between EC2 instances and SimpleDB in the same region. These numbers are on par with the latencies others have reported between EC2 instances. For contrast, additional latencies of 50 to 200 milliseconds or more are common when using SimpleDB across the open Internet. When you need fast SimpleDB, EC2 has a lot to offer.

Storing Large Objects with Amazon S3

Amazon Simple Storage Service (Amazon S3) is a web service that enables you to store an unlimited number of files and charges you (low) fees for the actual storage space you use and the data transfer you use. As you might expect, data transfer between S3 and other Amazon Web Services is fast and free. S3 is easy to understand, easy to use, and has a multitude of great uses. You can keep the files you store in S3 private, but you can also make them publicly available from the web. Many websites are using S3 as a media-hosting service to reduce the load on web servers.

EC2 virtual machine images are stored and loaded from S3. EC2 copies storage volumes to and loads storage volumes from S3. The Amazon CloudFront content delivery network can serve frequently accessed web files in S3. The Amazon Elastic MapReduce service runs MapReduce jobs stored in S3. Publicly visible files in S3 can be served up via the BitTorrent peer-to-peer protocol. The list of uses goes on and on.... S3 is really a common denominator cloud service.

SimpleDB users can also find good uses for S3. Because of the high speed within the Amazon cloud, S3 is an obvious storage location choice for SimpleDB import and export data. It is also a solid location to place SimpleDB backup files.

Queuing Up Tasks with Amazon SQS

Amazon Simple Queue Service (Amazon SQS) is a web service that reliably stores messages between distributed computers. Placing a robust queue between the computers allows them to work independently. It also opens the door to dynamically scaling the number of machines that push messages and the number that retrieve messages.

Although there is no direct connection between SQS and SimpleDB, SQS does have some complementary features that can be useful in SimpleDB-based applications. The semantics of reliable messaging can make it easier to coordinate multiple concurrent clients than when using SimpleDB alone. In cases where there are multiple SimpleDB clients, you can coordinate clients using a reliable SQS queue. For example, you might have multiple servers that are encoding video files and storing information about those videos in SimpleDB. SimpleDB makes a great place to store that data, but it could be cumbersome for use in telling each server which file to process next. The reliable message delivery of SQS would be much more appropriate for that task.

Comparing SimpleDB to Other Products and Services

Numerous new types of products and services are now available or will soon be available in the database/data service space. Some of these are similar to SimpleDB, and others are tangential. A few of them are listed here, along with a brief description and comparison to SimpleDB.

Windows Azure Platform

The Windows Azure Platform is Microsoft's entry into the cloud-computing fray. Azure defines a raft of service offerings that includes virtual computing, cloud storage, and reliable message queuing. Most of these services are counterparts to Amazon services. At the time of this writing, the Azure services are available as a Community Technology Preview. To date, Microsoft has been struggling to gain its footing in the cloud services arena.

There have been numerous, somewhat confusing, changes in product direction and product naming. Although Microsoft's cloud platform has been lagging behind AWS a bit, it seems that customer feedback is driving the recent Azure changes. There is every reason to suspect that once Azure becomes generally available, it will be a solid alternative to AWS.

Among the services falling under the Azure umbrella, there is one (currently) named Windows Azure Table. Azure Table is a distributed key-value store with explicit support for partitioning across storage nodes. It is designed for scalability and is in many ways similar to SimpleDB. The following is a list of similarities between Azure Table and SimpleDB:

- All access to the service is in the form of web requests. As a result, any programming language can be used.
- Requests are authenticated with encrypted signatures.
- Consistency is loosened to some degree.
- Unique primary keys are required for each data entity.
- Data within each entity is stored as a set of properties, each of which is a name-value pair.
- There is a limit of 256 properties per entity.
- A flexible schema allows different entities to have different properties.
- There is a limit on how much data can be stored in each entity.
- The number of entities you can get back from a query is limited and a query continuation token must be used to get the next page of results.
- Service versioning is in place so older versions of the service API can still be used after new versions are rolled out.
- Scalability is achieved through the horizontal partitioning of data.

There are also differences between the services, as listed here:

- Azure Table uses a composite key comprised of a partition key followed by a row key, whereas SimpleDB uses a single item name.
- Azure Table keeps all data with the same partition key on a single storage node. Entities with different partition keys may be automatically spread across hundreds of storage nodes to achieve scalability. With SimpleDB, items must be explicitly placed into multiple domains to get horizontal scaling.
- The only index in Azure Table is based on the composite key. Any properties you want to query or sort must be included as part of the partition key or row key. In contrast, SimpleDB creates an index for each attribute name, and a SQL-like query language allows query and sort on any attribute.
- To resolve conflicts resulting from concurrent updates with Azure Table, you have a choice of either last-write-wins or resolving on the client. With SimpleDB, last-write-wins is the only option.

- Transactions are supported in Azure Table at the entity level as well as for entity groups with the same partition key. SimpleDB applies updates atomically only within the scope of a single item.

Windows Azure Table overall is very SimpleDB-like, with some significant differences in the scalability approach. Neither service has reached maturity yet, so we may still see enhancements aimed at easing the transition from relational databases.

It is worth noting that Microsoft also has another database service in the Windows Azure fold. Microsoft SQL Azure is a cloud database service with full replication across physical servers, transparent automated backups, and support for the full relational data model. This technology is based on SQL Server, and it includes support for T-SQL, stored procedures, views, and indexes. This service is intended to enable direct porting of existing SQL-based applications to the Microsoft cloud.

Google App Engine

App Engine is a service offered by Google that lets you run web applications, written in Java or Python, on Google's infrastructure. As an application-hosting platform, App Engine includes many non-database functions, but the App Engine data store has similarities to SimpleDB. The non-database functions include a number of different services, all of which are available via API calls. The APIs include service calls to Memcached, email, XMPP, and URL fetching.

App Engine includes an API for data storage based on Google Big Table and in some ways is comparable to SimpleDB. Although Big Table is not directly accessible to App Engine applications, there is support in the data store API for a number of features not available in SimpleDB. These features include data relations, object mapping, transactions, and a user-defined index for each query.

App Engine also has a number of restrictions, some of which are similar to SimpleDB restrictions, like query run time. By default, the App Engine data store is strongly consistent. Once a transaction commits, all subsequent reads will reflect the changes in that transaction. It also means that if the primary storage node you are using goes down, App Engine will fail any update attempts you make until a suitable replacement takes over. To alleviate this issue, App Engine has recently added support for the same type of eventual consistency that SimpleDB has had all along. This move in the direction of SimpleDB gives App Engine apps the same ability as SimpleDB apps to run with strong consistency with option to fall back on eventual consistency to continue with a degraded level of service.

Apache CouchDB

Apache CouchDB is a document database where a self-contained document with metadata is the basic unit of data. CouchDB documents, like SimpleDB items, consist of a group of named fields. Each document has a unique ID in the same way that each SimpleDB item has a unique item name. CouchDB does not use a schema to define or validate documents. Different types of documents can be stored in the same database. For querying, CouchDB uses a system of JavaScript views and map-reduce. The loosely structured data in CouchDB documents is similar to SimpleDB data but does not place limits on the amount of data you can store in each document or on the size of the data fields.

CouchDB is an open-source product that you install and manage yourself. It allows distributed replication among peer servers and has full support for robust clustering. CouchDB was designed from the start to handle high levels of concurrency and to maintain high levels of availability. It seeks to solve many of the same problems as SimpleDB, but from the standpoint of an open-source product offering rather than a pay-as-you-go service.

Dynamo-Like Products

Amazon Dynamo is a data store used internally within Amazon that is not available to the public. Amazon has published information about Dynamo that includes design goals, runtime characteristics, and examples of how it is used. From the published information, we know that SimpleDB has some things in common with Dynamo, most notably the eventual consistency.

Since the publication of Dynamo information, a number of distributed key-value stores have been developed that are in the same vein as Dynamo. Three open-source products that fit into this category are Project Voldemort, Dynomite, and Cassandra. Each of these projects takes a different approach to the technology, but when you compare them to SimpleDB, they generally fall into the same category. They give you a chance to have highly available key-value access distributed across machines. You get more control over the servers and the implementation that comes with the maintenance cost of managing the setup and the machines. If you are looking for something in this class of data storage, SimpleDB is a likely touch-free hosted option, and these projects are hands-on self-hosted alternatives.

Compelling Use Cases for SimpleDB

SimpleDB is not a replacement for relational databases. You need to give careful consideration to the type of data storage solution that is appropriate for a given application. This section includes a discussion of some of the use cases that match up well with SimpleDB.

Web Services for Connected Systems

IT departments in the enterprise are tasked with delivering business value and support in an efficient way. In recent years, there has been movement toward both service orientation and cloud computing. One of the driving forces behind service orientation is a desire to make more effective use of existing applications. Simple Object Access Protocol (SOAP) has emerged as an important standard for message passing between these connected systems as a means of enabling forward compatibility. For new services deployed in the cloud, SimpleDB is a compelling data storage option.

Data transfer between EC2 instances and the SimpleDB endpoint in the same region is fast and free. The consistent speed and high availability of SimpleDB are helpful when defining a Service Level Agreement (SLA) between IT and business units. All this meshes with the ability of EC2 to scale out additional instances on demand.

Low-Usage Application

There are applications in the enterprise and on the open web that do not see a consistent heavy load. They can be low usage in general with periodic or seasonal spikes—for instance, at the end of the month or during the holidays. Sometimes there are few users at all times by design or simply by lack of popularity.

For these types of applications, it can be difficult to justify an entire database server for the one application. The typical answer in organizations with sufficient infrastructure is to host multiple databases on the same server. This can work well but may not be an option for small organizations or for individuals. Shared database hosting is available from hosting companies, but service levels are notoriously unpredictable. With SimpleDB, low-usage applications can run within the free tier of service while maintaining the ability to scale up to large request volumes when necessary. This can be an attractive option even when database-sharing options are available.

Clustered Databases Without the Time Sink

Clustering databases for scalability or for availability is no easy task. If you already have the heavy data access load or if you have the quantifiable need for uptime, it is obviously a task worth taking on. Moreover, if you already have the expertise to deploy and manage clusters of replicated databases, SimpleDB may not be something you need. However, if you do have the experience, you know many other things as well: you know the cost to roll the clusters into production, to roll out schema updates, and to handle outages. This information can actually make it easier to decide whether new applications will provide enough revenue or business value to merit the time and cost. You also have a great knowledge base to make comparisons between in-house solutions and SimpleDB for the features it provides.

You may have a real need for scalability or uptime but not the expertise. In this case, SimpleDB can enable you to outsource the potentially expensive ongoing database maintenance costs.

Dynamic Data Application

Rigid and highly structured data models serve as the foundation of many applications, while others need to be more dynamic. It is becoming much more important for new applications to include some sort of social component than it was in the past. Along with these social aspects, there are requirements to support various types of user input and customization, like tagging, voting, and sharing. Many types of social applications require community building, and can benefit from a platform, which allows data to be stored in new ways, without breaking the old data. Customer-facing applications, even those without a social component, need to be attentive to user feedback.

Whether it is dynamic data coming from users or dynamic changes made in response to user feedback, a flexible data store can enable faster innovation.

Amazon S3 Content Search

Amazon S3 has become a popular solution for storing web-accessible media files. Applications that deal with audio, video, or images can access the media files from EC2 with no transfer costs and allow end users to download or stream them on a large scale without needing to handle the additional load. When there are a large number of files in S3, and there is a need to search the content along various attributes, SimpleDB can be an excellent solution.

It is easy to store attributes in SimpleDB, along with pointers to where the media is stored in S3. SimpleDB creates an index for every attribute for quick searching. Different file types can have different attributes in the same SimpleDB domain. New file types or new attributes on existing file types can be added at any time without requiring existing records to be updated.

Empowering the Power Users

For a long time, databases have been just beyond the edge of what highly technical users can effectively reach. Many business analysts, managers, and information workers have technical aptitude but not the skills of a developer or DBA. These power users make use of tools like spreadsheet software and desktop databases to solve problems. Unfortunately, these tools work best on a single workstation, and attempts at sharing or concurrent use frequently cause difficulty and frustration; enterprise-capable database software requires a level of expertise and time commitment beyond what these users are willing to spend.

The flexibility and scalability of SimpleDB can be a great boon to a new class of applications designed for power users. SimpleDB itself still requires programming on the client and is not itself directly usable by power users. However, the ability to store data directly without a predefined schema and create queries is an enabling feature. For applications that seek to empower the power users, by creating simple, open-ended applications with dynamic capabilities, SimpleDB can make a great back end.

Existing AWS Customers

This chapter pointed out earlier the benefits of using EC2 for high-bandwidth applications. However, if you are already using one or more of the Amazon Web Services, SimpleDB can be a strong candidate for queryable data storage across a wide range of applications. Of course, running a relational database on an EC2 instance is also a viable and popular choice. Moreover, you would do well to consider both options. SimpleDB requires you to make certain trade-offs, but if the choices provide a net benefit to your application, you will have gained some great features from AWS that are difficult and time consuming to develop on your own.

Summary

Amazon SimpleDB is a web service that enables you to store semi-structured data within Amazon's data centers. The service provides automatic, geographically diverse data replication and internal routing around failed storage nodes. It offers high availability and enables horizontal scalability. The service allows you to offload hardware maintenance and database management tasks.

You can use SimpleDB as a distributed key-value store using the `GetAttributes`, `PutAttributes`, and `DeleteAttributes` API calls. You also have the option to query for your data along any of its attributes using the Select API call. SimpleDB is not a relational database, so there are no joins, foreign keys, schema definitions, or relational constraints that you can specify. SimpleDB also has limited support for transactions, and updates propagate between replicas in the background. SimpleDB supports strong consistency, where read operations immediately reflect the results of all completed and eventual consistency, where storage nodes are updated asynchronously in the background.

The normal window of time for all storage nodes to reach consistency in the background is typically small. During a server or network failure, consistency may not be reached for longer periods of time, but eventually all updates will propagate. SimpleDB is best used by applications able to deal with eventual consistency and benefit from the ability to remain available in the midst of a failure.

2

Getting Started with SimpleDB

The SimpleDB web service API exposes a small number of database request types. The myriad of configuration options that you find with other database products have intentionally been excluded. The SimpleDB API provides only nine operations, with the goal of enabling you to manage your data without requiring you to manage the database cluster. This chapter gets you up and running with these operations by developing several small applications. The chapter starts with some coverage of how to sign up for an account. The sign-up process is simple and straightforward. The expectation is that you have an account already or, if not, that you can easily make your way through the sign-up process without assistance. However, questions about the account sign-up process do arise on occasion, so for completeness, some basic information is included.

Gaining Access to SimpleDB

Like any Amazon Web Service, SimpleDB will only honor a request after it verifies that the request came from a valid account. With SimpleDB, this means using your AWS account credentials to place a digital signature on your request. As such, you will need to obtain the actual credentials first. This section briefly walks you through the process of signing up with Amazon and requesting access to SimpleDB. If you already have an existing AWS account with SimpleDB access, you can safely skip this section.

Creating an AWS Account

An Amazon Web Services account is just an Amazon.com account with web services turned on. The account serves as the top-level unit of billing for all of your AWS usage. You need to associate a credit card with your account before you can start using any of the web services. Amazon maintains detailed usage data for your account throughout the month that you can monitor at the AWS website. At the end of each month, Amazon generates the final billing for your actual usage of each Amazon Web Service and charges your credit card.

To create an Amazon Web Services account, go to the AWS website (http://aws.amazon.com) and click the link to create a new account. You can use your existing Amazon.com account if you have one, or you can create a new account.

Signing Up for SimpleDB

Once you successfully sign into your Amazon Web Services account, head over to the SimpleDB home page (http://aws.amazon.com/simpledb) and click the sign-up button to add the new service. If you do not yet have a credit card on file with Amazon, or if you have one but have not linked it to your web services account, you will be prompted for it now. Go ahead and enter your information. You cannot use any of the services without pre-authorizing a payment option. You should be aware, however, that at the time of this writing, Amazon has a free access tier for SimpleDB usage. The current free tier terms allow for 25 hours of SimpleDB box usage, 1GB of data transfer, and 1GB of data storage per month before charges begin to accrue. Also, be aware that all data transfer from EC2 to SimpleDB is always free.

Managing Account Keys

When you log into your Amazon Web Services account, you will be able to view your Account Access Identifiers. For SimpleDB, this will be an Access Key ID and a Secret Access Key. These will act as the username and signature generator for your SimpleDB requests. You will pass the Access Key ID with every request to identify your account. You prove the request is from you by computing a signature for each request using the Secret Access Key.

It is of the utmost importance that you keep your Secret Access Key a secret. Your keys provide full access to your Amazon Web Services accounts. Someone with your keys could corrupt or delete your data and rack up account usage charges to your credit card. Keep security in mind, and do not post your secret key on any Internet forum, hard code it into shared source code, or include it in an email message that is not secure. You can generate a new Secret Access Key at any time from your account at the AWS website.

Finding a Client for SimpleDB

Whether you write your own library or use someone else's, you need a SimpleDB client to code against. There is a directory of SimpleDB clients maintained at http://developer.amazonwebservices.com on the SimpleDB discussion forums. This list includes client libraries written and supported by AWS, as well as third-party libraries. AWS provides SimpleDB client libraries for Java, C#, PHP, Perl, and VB.Net.

This chapter uses the SimpleDB Reference Client developed in Chapter 10, "Writing a SimpleDB Client: A Language-Independent Guide." It is a Java client library specifically designed for the demonstration of SimpleDB concepts. In later chapters, it serves as a guide for how to write a SimpleDB client in any programming language, but it is used here because it makes example code easy to understand.

Building a SimpleDB Domain Administration Tool

One of the weaknesses of SimpleDB in its current form is the lack of robust and sophisticated tooling. The tooling for relational databases has become mature, and there are many tool options available. Amazon does provide a few basic tools and, in fact, continues to release new and better tools, but a lot of room still remains for innovation. Amazon's strategy of providing the infrastructure building blocks around which an ecosystem of tools and services can grow seems to be working well for its other web services. In time, client tooling could become a strong point for SimpleDB because one of the foundational principles is the small feature set on the service side. We begin the examples by developing a domain administration tool.

Administration Tool Features

Having a tool that can list all of your domains with the ability to create new domains is a pretty basic feature when using SimpleDB. Amazon has released an Eclipse plug-in that allows you to do that, but it is only available while eclipse is running. We are going to write this functionality in a command-line tool that will be available outside of an IDE. In this section, we develop a stand-alone administration tool that you can to use to manage your domains.

The tool will have the following features:

- A command-line interface
- Creation of new domains
- Deletion of existing domains
- Listing all the domains in your account
- Detailed listing for an existing domain

Key Storage

It is very important to treat your AWS credentials with care to prevent anyone from gaining unauthorized access to your account. Beyond the risk of loss or compromising of your data, an unauthorized user will be able to run up potentially large usage charges. I recommend that you never type your Access Key ID or Secret Access Key directly into source code files, even if it is only for sample code. All the code in this book will pull the AWS keys from a separate file. In the case of the admin tool in this section, the keys will be loaded from the file .awssecret in the user's home directory. You will need to create this file in order to allow the admin tool to authenticate. The format of the file is as follows:

```
AWS_ACCESS_KEY_ID=
AWS_SECRET_ACCESS_KEY=
```

When you create this file, add the appropriate values for your account after the equal signs.

Implementing the Base Application

The base application provides the code to parse the arguments and a framework to invoke the commands. Because this is a command-line tool, the base application, shown in Listing 2-1, is very simple.

Listing 2-1 **AdminTool.java Base Command-Line Application for the Admin Tool**

```
import java.io.*;
import java.util.*;

import com.simpledbbook.*;

public abstract class AdminTool {
   static String USAGE = "java AdminTool [-l] [-m] [-c] [-d] [domain]";
   protected SimpleDB simpleDb;
   protected String domain;

   public static void main(String[] argz) {
      AdminTool tool = createInstance(argz);
      tool.invoke();
   }

   private static AdminTool createInstance(String[] argz) {
      try {
         String cmd = argz[0];
         if (cmd.equals("-l")) {
            return new ListingTool();
         } else if (cmd.equals("-m")) {
            return new MetadataTool(argz[1]);
         } else if (cmd.equals("-c")) {
            return new CreateTool(argz[1]);
         } else if (cmd.equals("-d")) {
            return new DeleteTool(argz[1]);
         }
      } catch (Exception e) {}
      System.err.println(USAGE);
      System.exit(-1);
      return null;
   }

   abstract void doInvoke();

   private void invoke() {
      try {
         loadCredentials();
         doInvoke();
```

```
        } catch (Exception e) {
            System.out.println(e.getMessage());
        }
    }

    private void loadCredentials() {
        try {
            initSimpledbFromDisk();
        } catch (Exception e) {
            String errorMsg = "credentials not found in $HOME/.awssecret";
            throw new RuntimeException( errorMsg);
        }
    }

    private void initSimpledbFromDisk() throws Exception {
        Properties props = new Properties();
        String home = System.getProperty("user.home");
        props.load(new FileReader(new File(home, ".awssecret")));
        String accessKeyId = props.getProperty("AWS_ACCESS_KEY_ID");
        String secretAccessKey = props.getProperty("AWS_SECRET_ACCESS_KEY");
        simpleDb = new SimpleDB(accessKeyId, secretAccessKey);
    }

    protected AdminTool(String domainName) {
        this.domain = domainName;
    }
}
```

At the main method entry point, you can see that the `createInstance()` method returns an `AdminTool` reference. `AdminTool` is an abstract class that defines the common application features and delegates the specific implementation to a subclass. In `createInstance()`, the command-line arguments are parsed and an appropriate subclass of `AdminTool` is instantiated. Any exception at this point or the failure to find a matching argument will fall through to the usage message, and the application will exit.

The main method ends by calling `invoke()` on the tool instance. The `invoke()` method wraps the final two actions with exception handling. If an exception is thrown from this point on, it will be caught here, the exception message will be printed, and the application will terminate. The final two steps are loading the AWS credentials via the `loadCredentials()` method and calling the abstract `doInvoke()` method, which contains the tool-specific code in the subclass.

The `loadCredentials()` method acts as a pass-through to the `initSimpledbFromDisk()` method, re-throwing any exception as a generic exception with the appropriate message. Within `initSimpledbFromDisk()`, the file .awssecret in the user home directory is loaded into a Properties object. The Access Key ID and the Secret Access Key are retrieved and then used to initialize the SimpleDB client library.

The final member of the `AdminTool` class is the constructor that subclasses will use to store the target domain name.

Displaying a Domain List

Now that the base class has handled all the application setup, all that remains in each subclass is the specific tool operation. The `ListingTool` class shown in Listing 2-2 gives a first, but brief, look at coding with a SimpleDB client library.

Listing 2-2 **ListingTool.java Implementation of List Domains**

```
public class ListingTool extends AdminTool {

   ListingTool() {
      super(null);
   }

   @Override
   void doInvoke() {
      for (String domain : simpleDb.listDomains()) {
         System.out.println(domain);
      }
   }
}
```

The `ListDomains` operation in SimpleDB returns a listing of all the domains for the given account. Because no single domain name is required for this operation, the no-arg constructor passes null to the super class constructor in place of an actual domain name.

`ListingTool` overrides the `doInvoke()` method to loop through the results of the client library's `listDomain()` method, printing each name to the console.

Adding Domain Creation

The `CreateTool` class in Listing 2-3 is similar to the `ListingTool` class from Listing 2-2, with only a single constructor and an override of the `doInvoke()` method.

Listing 2-3 **CreateTool.java Implementation of Domain Creation**

```
public class CreateTool extends AdminTool {

   public CreateTool(String domainName) {
      super(domainName);
   }

   @Override
```

```
    void doInvoke() {
        simpleDb.createDomain(domain);
        System.out.println("Domain created: " + domain);
    }
}
```

In this case, a domain name is required, so the `CreateTool` constructor declares a single String parameter and passes through to the super class constructor where it is stored. The domain creation takes place with the call to the `createDomain()` method with the domain name as a parameter. If the call returns successfully, a message is printed to the console. Be aware that calls to the SimpleDB operation `CreateDomain` for domains that already exist have no effect, and an error is not raised.

Supporting Domain Deletion

Domain deletion is nearly identical to domain creation from a code perspective. Listing 2-4 shows domain deletion.

Listing 2-4 **DeleteTool.java Implementation of Domain Deletion**

```
public class DeleteTool extends AdminTool {

    public DeleteTool(String domainName) {
        super(domainName);
    }

    @Override
    void doInvoke() {
        simpleDb.deleteDomain(domain);
        System.out.println("Domain deleted: " + domain);
    }
}
```

The only difference between the `DeleteTool` class and the `CreateTool` class is the call to the SimpleDB library's `deleteDomain()` method and the text of the console message.

Listing Domain Metadata

The final tool in the `AdminTool` arsenal is the `MetadataTool`, found in Listing 2-5. This tool has a lot more code to it, but only the first line of the `doInvoke()` method pertains directly to SimpleDB. The remainder is code that gets and formats the values.

Listing 2-5 **MetadataTool.java Implementation of Domain Metadata**

```
import static java.lang.System.*;
import java.util.*;
```

```
public class MetadataTool extends AdminTool {

   public MetadataTool(String domainName) {
      super(domainName);
   }

   @Override
   void doInvoke() {
      Map<String, Long> info = simpleDb.domainMetadata(domain);
      long epochMillis = info.get("Timestamp") * 1000L;
      long deltaMillis = System.currentTimeMillis() - epochMillis;
      double deltaHours = deltaMillis / 3600000D;
      long items = info.get("ItemCount");
      long itemNameBytes = info.get("ItemNamesSizeBytes");
      long attrNames = info.get("AttributeNameCount");
      long attrNameBytes = info.get("AttributeNamesSizeBytes");
      long attrValues = info.get("AttributeValueCount");
      long attrValueBytes = info.get("AttributeValuesSizeBytes");
      long totalBytes = itemNameBytes + attrNameBytes + attrValueBytes;

      double totalGB = totalBytes/ONE_GB;

      String headerA = "'%s' using %.2f%% of 10GB capacity";
      String headerB = " (as of %.1f hours ago)\n";
      out.printf(headerA + headerB, domain, totalGB, deltaHours);

      String lineFmt = "%16s: %,10d (%,d bytes)\n";
      out.printf(lineFmt, "Item names", items, itemNameBytes);
      out.printf(lineFmt, "Attribute names", attrNames, attrNameBytes);
      out.printf(lineFmt, "Attribute values", attrValues, attrValueBytes);    }
}
```

The call to the client method `domainMetadata()` returns a map of metadata entry names to numeric values. Amazon serves the `DomainMetadata` operation values from a cache and not necessarily from a fresh computation at the time of the call. The data provides a recent picture of the domain's state typically from within the past 24 hours. The timestamp entry tells you the cache time for this domain's metadata values. `MetadataTool` uses the timestamp to calculate the metadata's age in hours.

There are three remaining dimensions of your domain described by the metadata: items, attribute names, and attribute values. For each of these is both a count that is given and storage size in bytes. `MetadataTool` pulls each of these values from the map, calculates the percentage of storage capacity in use, and then prints it all out to the console with some formatting.

Running the Tool

Before you can compile and run the tool, you'll need to have the Java Development Kit (JDK) 1.6 or later installed. The classpath also needs to be set so that it can find the SimpleDB client code imported by the tool. You can compile these five source files from the Chapter 2 source code directory and set the classpath with the following command:

```
javac -cp SimpleDBClient.jar *.java
```

After you compile these classes, you can run the domain-listing tool with the following command:

```
java AdminTool -l
```

If you are new to SimpleDB and have not yet created any domains, this tool prints no output for you yet. You can create a domain with the following command:

```
java AdminTool -c sample001
```

The length of domain names has to be between 3 and 255 characters, and there are rules covering which characters the `CreateDomain` operation will accept. The only characters you are allowed to use in domain names are a–z, A–Z, 0–9, '_', '-', and '.'

Packaging the Tool as a Jar File

This tool is useful for simple administration tasks, and it can be bundled into a Jar file for quick deployment on any platform that can run Java. Bundling the application in a jar file is done with the jar command-line tool that comes with the Java Development Kit (JDK). You will have to provide a manifest file that declares AdminTool as your Main-Class and provide that file as an argument to the jar tool. Once it is packaged, you can run the tool in a similar way using the command line:

```
java -jar AdminTool.jar -l
```

where "AdminTool.jar" is the name of your jar file. You can learn more about jar files from the Java website: http://java.sun.com/docs/books/tutorial/deployment/jar/.

Building a User Authentication Service

The requirement for user authentication is a common one: It is necessary in any publicly facing web application or web service. There are many ways to provide methods of user password collection, and there are just as many alternatives for storing that data. In many private intranet applications, there is a need to integrate with an existing authentication system, such as LDAP, Active Directory, or NTLM. On the public Internet, relational database tables are a more likely choice. In this section, you learn how to use SimpleDB as the data store for a user authentication service.

Integrating with the Spring Security Framework

User authentication is only one small part of the security picture. Overall security for an application is complex and difficult to get right. In the vast majority of cases, you integrate your code into a larger security framework rather than writing your own. One popular Java security framework is Spring Security. Spring Security is an open-source project and has been available for many years. One of the benefits of using the Spring Security framework is that it can be used in many different contexts, whether you run it as a web application or as a web service, or from within a desktop client.

Spring Security itself is large and somewhat complex. If you are not familiar with it already, getting it up and running is beyond the scope of this book. However, the data model is modular, and you can integrate the data storage portion in isolation and use it with a bit of sample code. The current list of supported back-end user data providers is quite extensive, but SimpleDB is not yet one of them. To create a SimpleDB user data provider for Spring Security, you need to create the following functionality:

- A user service that is able to load user data from SimpleDB
- A user class to hold the user data and user authorizations
- A feature to add and edit users

Representing User Data

The first thing you need is a way to represent the user data. The things you need to store for each user are as follows:

- The username
- The user's password
- A flag indicating if the user is currently enabled
- A list of authorizations or roles associated with that user

These elements can be stored together in a single class. Listing 2-6 shows this within the `User` class.

Listing 2-6 **User.java Implementation of a User Authorization Class**

```
package com.simpledbbook.user;

import java.io.*;
import java.util.*;

public class User implements Serializable {
   private String username;
   private String password;
   private boolean enabled;
   private List<String> authorities = new ArrayList<String>();
```

```
public User(String u, String p, boolean en, List<String> au) {
   username = u.intern();
   password = p.intern();
   enabled = en;
   au.get(0).charAt(0);
   for (String auth : new TreeSet<String>(au)) {
      authorities.add(auth.intern());
   }
}

String getUsername() {
   return username;
}

String getPassword() {
   return password;
}

boolean isEnabled() {
   return enabled;
}

List<String> getAuthorities() {
   return authorities;
}

@Override
public boolean equals(Object o) {
   if (o == null) return false;
   if (!(o instanceof User)) return false;
   User other = (User) o;
   if (other.username != username) return false;
   if (other.password != password) return false;
   if (other.enabled != enabled) return false;
   if (!other.authorities.equals(authorities)) return false;
   return true;
}

@Override
public int hashCode() {
   int prime = 37;
   int result = 23;

   result = result * prime + username.hashCode();
   result = result * prime + password.hashCode();
   result = result * prime + (enabled ? 1 : 0);
```

```
        for (String auth : authorities) {
            result = result * prime + auth.hashCode();
        }
        return result;
    }
}
```

The `User` class exposes an immutable view of a user where the class responsible for the instantiation passes all the data into the constructor, and it never changes. At the top of the class, you can see that the four fields storing the data are private, with the public getter methods below them.

One thing that is important to note about this class is how the constructor verifies all the data fields to be non-null. This ensures that all users of the class have completely valid and filled-out instances. Each `String` passed into the constructor is stored only after it is interned. This returns a canonical representation of the `String` that is easier to compare for equality. It also has the side effect of performing a check for null.

The list of `Strings` passed in with the name authorities is the set of roles the user has been granted. A `TreeSet` is used to remove duplicate entries and sort the remaining roles. The call to `intern()` for each element in the set serves the same purpose as it did for the single `String` fields.

The class finishes up by declaring the `equals()` and `hashcode()` methods. In order to uphold the general contract for `equals()` and `hashcode()`, equality and the hash code are computed using all four of the fields. In addition, any time the `equals` method returns true for two instances, they will also return the same hash code.

Fetching User Data with SimpleDBUserService

Now that the storage class is complete, a class is needed to retrieve the data from SimpleDB. This class will be passed a username, and it will need to look up the remainder of the data for that user and return a fully constructed user object. You can see the code for this user service in Listing 2-7.

Listing 2-7 **SimpleDBUserService.java Implementation of a SimpleDB Storage Class**

```
package com.simpledbbook.user;

import java.util.*;
import com.simpledbbook.*;

public class SimpleDBUserService {
    private static final String AUTH_NAMES = "authorities";
    private boolean enableGroups;
    private SimpleDB sdb;
    private String domainName = "users";
```

```
public User loadUserByUsername(String username) {
   Item item = sdb.getItem(domainName, username);
   List<String> auth = getAuthorities(item);
   String pass = item.getAttribute("password");
   String enabledString = item.getAttribute("enabled");
   boolean enabled = enabledString.equals("true");
   User user = new User(username, pass, enabled, auth);
   return user;
}

private List<String> getAuthorities(Item item) {
   if (!enableGroups) {
      return item.getAttributes(AUTH_NAMES);
   }
   List<String> groupNames = item.getAttributes("group");
   String query = buildGroupQuery(groupNames);

   return sdb.singleAttributeSelect(query, AUTH_NAMES);
}

private String buildGroupQuery(List<String> groupNames) {
   String f = "SELECT `%s` FROM `%s` WHERE itemName() IN(%s)";
   String groups = listToQueryString(groupNames);
   return String.format(f, AUTH_NAMES, domainName, groups);
}

private String listToQueryString(List<String> groupNames) {
   String result = "";
   for (String group : groupNames) {
      result = result + "," + group;
   }
   return result.substring(1);
}

public boolean isEnableGroups() {
   return enableGroups;
}

public void setEnableGroups(boolean groups) {
   enableGroups = groups;
}

public String getDomainName() {
   return domainName;
}
```

```
    public void setDomainName(String domainName) {
        this.domainName = domainName;
    }
}
```

At this point, you have to consider the name of the SimpleDB domain where you will store your user data. This class uses the "users" domain by default but allows a different name to be set via the `setDomainName()` method. Another consideration is whether you will store the user roles directly with the user or if you associate the user with a set of groups and assign roles to the groups at a higher level. This decision is dependent on your application domain, and this class supports both ways of storing the authorities. If the `enableGroups` flag is set, a different set of queries is used to look up the groups first and then the authorities. If `enableGroups` is not set, the roles are pulled directly from the user item.

The method `loadUserByUsername()` is the entry point for this class. It is called with the username that needs to be looked up. A SimpleDB `GetAttributes` call is done immediately to pull the user item. This item has, at a minimum, the encoded password and the enabled flag. Next, the item is passed to the `getAuthorities()` method, which determines how to obtain the roles based on the `enableGroups` flag. Finally, all the fields are passed to the `User` constructor, and the newly created `User` object is returned.

Salting and Encoding Passwords

So far, the user authentication service has only dealt with the raw storage features. However, for any legitimate authentication, you will need to salt and encode the passwords. Encoding normally involves some form of encryption so that the passwords do not sit in the database as plain text. Any form of encryption will protect you from an attacker who gains access to your database. But if the attacker also is able to gain access to your encryption key, he will be able to decrypt each password.

A good encoding method is to use a one-way cryptographic function. With one-way encryption, there is no way to decode an encrypted message to get the original text, even when you have the encryption key. This prevents decryption by an attacker with the key, but it is still vulnerable to a dictionary attack. In a dictionary attack, a large body of potential passwords is encrypted with the proper key. Each potential password is stored together with the encrypted version as a look-up key. The attacker can then look up encrypted passwords in the dictionary to find the original. Protection from the dictionary attack comes in the form of salting.

Salting is any process that applies a consistent change to the password value before encryption. This makes it much more difficult for an unauthorized user who gains access to the database to use a dictionary attack to find the original password values.

Therefore, the process for storing passwords involves first salting, followed by one-way encryption. When the time comes to verify the password of a user, there is no way to decrypt the password in the database and compare it. Instead, you just salt and encode the supplied password at verification time and compare it to the stored, salted, and encoded password. Within the Spring Security framework, these functions are implemented by existing framework classes. You have a variety of configuration options available to you for control of exactly how the passwords are salted and encoded. Whether you use the default configuration or make some configuration changes, Spring Security will already have salted and encoded the password before it calls SimpleDBUserService. Moreover, the passwords retrieved from SimpleDB need to already be encoded in order for the authorization check to succeed.

Creating a User Update Tool

Although the Spring Security framework has much of the functionality already, one thing it does not do is provide you with a way to add and update user data. This is something that you need to do for yourself. Because you cannot test out the data storage without users to test on, you will create your own user tool in this section. The requirements for this tool are straightforward, as follows:

- Add a user
- Toggle the enabled flag
- Add and remove roles for a user
- Add and remove the user from a group
- Add and remove roles for a user

The code for this tool can be found in Listing 2-8.

Listing 2-8 **SimpleDBUserTool.java Implementation of a Tool to Manage Users**

```
package com.simpledbbook.user;

import java.util.*;

import com.simpledbbook.*;

public class SimpleDBUserTool {
   private static final String AUTH_NAMES = "authorities";
   private static final String PASS_NAME = "password";
   private static final String ENAB_NAME = "enabled";
   private static final String GROUP_NAME = "group";
   private String domainName = "users";
   private boolean enableGroups;
   private SimpleDB sdb;

   public User storeUserByUsername(String username) {
      Item item = sdb.getItem(domainName, username);
      List<String> auth = null;
      setAuthorities(item);
```

```
        String pass = item.getAttribute(PASS_NAME);
        String enabledString = item.getAttribute(ENAB_NAME);
        boolean enabled = enabledString.equals("true");
        User user = new User(username, pass, enabled, auth);
        return user;
    }

    private void setAuthorities(Item item) {
        if (!enableGroups) {
            item.getAttributes(AUTH_NAMES);
        }
        List<String> groupNames = item.getAttributes(GROUP_NAME);
        String query = buildGroupQuery(groupNames);
        sdb.singleAttributeSelect(query, AUTH_NAMES);
    }

    private String buildGroupQuery(List<String> groupNames) {
        String f = "SELECT `%s` FROM `%s` WHERE itemName() IN(%s)";
        String groups = listToQueryString(groupNames);
        return String.format(f, AUTH_NAMES, domainName, groups);
    }

    private String listToQueryString(List<String> groupNames) {
        String result = "";
        for (String group : groupNames) {
            result = result + "," + group;
        }
        return result.substring(1);
    }

    public boolean isEnableGroups() {
        return enableGroups;
    }

    public void setEnableGroups(boolean groups) {
        enableGroups = groups;
    }

    public String getDomainName() {
        return domainName;
    }

    public void setDomainName(String domainName) {
        this.domainName = domainName;
    }
```

```
    public void setSimpleDBClient(SimpleDB simpleDb) {
        sdb = simpleDb;
    }
}
```

Summary

Invariably one of the things you notice when working with SimpleDB is that much of the code ends up revolving around the application logic and the business rules, with a somewhat small amount of SimpleDB code. That certainly holds true with the domain administration tool, where more than 60 lines of code end up devoted to application-level issues, with only a few lines of code calling SimpleDB. In this chapter, you have used a number of the SimpleDB operations and gotten a feel for how they work and what they do. The next chapter goes into much greater depth, covering each of the SimpleDB operations in turn.

3

A Code-Snippet Tour of the SimpleDB API

The AWS website hosts a comprehensive set of documentation on SimpleDB. The set of documents includes an officially maintained guide for developers, which provides thorough coverage of every API call. The problem with all this great documentation is that it covers SimpleDB as a raw HTTP web service, whereas most users are never going to program to the low-level guts of the service. Most users are going to use a SimpleDB client for which there is no direct coverage in the official docs. This is not the fault of AWS; after all, SimpleDB is a web service, and that is exactly what they have documented. Moreover, even though AWS has released SimpleDB clients for Java, PHP, C#, and VB.NET, those clients have essentially no documentation. The source code serves as documentation.

The purpose of this chapter is to fill the gap between the web service documentation and the clients that people actually use. To this end, each API call documented here comes with source code showing client usage. For the sample code, this chapter covers the three most popular SimpleDB clients, one in each of the three different programming languages. Each API call is documented to at least the same level as the official docs. In many cases, the chapter also includes additional information including details of how the API works in practice and pitfalls to avoid. For the API calls that have options, multiple source code listings are included so you can see how it works in different scenarios.

Selecting a SimpleDB Client

The selection of a client is normally dictated by the programming language you'll be using. There are SimpleDB clients for a wide variety of programming languages, which are free to use, usually with an open-source license. The limited feature set of SimpleDB makes a basic client straightforward to write. You can realistically throw together a barebones client over a weekend or two. If writing your own client, bare bones or otherwise, is something that interests you, Chapter 10, "Writing a SimpleDB Client: A Language-Independent Guide," provides thorough coverage of the topic. Perhaps owing to the simple

API, there are a number of clients available that have the minimal feature set, but do not appear to be actively maintained. You can find an updated list of currently available SimpleDB clients at SimpleDBBook.com.

At the time of this writing, some of the best-maintained SimpleDB clients are those featuring support for the full range of AWS APIs and not just SimpleDB. Here is a list of some popular client choices by programming language:

- **Java—** Typica is an open-source Java client for the Amazon Web Services: SimpleDB, EC2, SQS, and DevPay. Released under the Apache License 2.0, Typica may be the most popular of all the third-party SimpleDB clients. It is well maintained, keeping pace with new AWS features, and it sports additional SimpleDB utilities, such as a query tool and a command-line tool. Typica is one of the clients used for code samples in this chapter.
- **PHP—** Tarzan is a third-party PHP client with support for SimpleDB and half a dozen other Amazon Web Services. Tarzan has high-quality documentation and is released under the Simplified BSD License. This chapter's PHP code snippets use Tarzan.
- **C#—** The C# Library for Amazon SimpleDB is a SimpleDB client released by AWS under the Apache License 2.0. The other C# client that appears to be well maintained is the third-party product LightSpeed by Mindscape. LightSpeed is a fully featured object/relational mapping product with support for many databases. LightSpeed operates at a higher modeling level than the SimpleDB API and it is not open source. This chapter uses the C# Library for Amazon SimpleDB for the C# example code.
- **Python—** There are a few Python clients available. The open-source Boto project is actively maintained and is the most fully featured client, with support beyond SimpleDB for virtually every other AWS offering. This chapter does not include Python sample code.

The details of how you use each client in each respective language are different, but the underlying semantics of the SimpleDB operations remain the same. What happens on the back end as a result of your client calls is the focus of the following sections.

Typica Setup in Java

To compile and run the Java samples in this chapter, you will need to download the Typica client from the project website at http://code.google.com/p/typica/ and add the typica.jar file to your Java classpath. Typica has dependencies on other freely available libraries, and they are listed (with links) on the project website. At the time of this writing, the dependencies are commons-logging, JAXB, commons-httpclient, and commons-codec. The samples in this chapter are written against version 1.6 of Typica.

Once you have Typica and its dependencies in your classpath, there are several source code-level steps required for the snippets to run. You need the following three import statements:

```
import java.util.*;
import com.xerox.amazonws.common.*;
import com.xerox.amazonws.sdb.*;
```

You also will need to load your AWS credentials into the variables `accessKeyID` and `secretAccessKey`. The following code has been adapted from the examples in Chapter 2, "Getting Started with SimpleDB," and will load your credentials from a file named .awssecret in the current user's home directory. This is the same file used previously, so if you stored your credentials in the file for the Chapter 2 examples, you won't need to do it again:

```
private String accessKeyID;
private String secretAccessKey;

{
   try {
      loadCredentialsFromDisk();
   } catch (Exception e) {
      String errorMsg = "credentials not found in $HOME/.awssecret";
      throw new RuntimeException(errorMsg);
   }
}

private void loadCredentialsFromDisk() throws Exception {
   Properties props = new Properties();
   String home = System.getProperty("user.home");
   props.load(new FileReader(new File(home, ".awssecret")));
   accessKeyID = props.getProperty("AWS_ACCESS_KEY_ID");
   secretAccessKey = props.getProperty("AWS_SECRET_ACCESSS_KEY");
}
```

Adding these two member variables, the instance initializer, and the instance method to the top of your Java class file is an easy way to load your credentials without hard coding them into the source.

C# Library for Amazon SimpleDB Setup

The C# code samples require Visual Studio 2005 or later and .NET version 2.0+. You will need to download Amazon's C# from the AWS website (http://aws.amazon.com/resources/) under "SimpleDB" and "Sample Code & Libraries." Make sure your .NET project references `Amazon.SimpleDB`, and add these `using` statements to the top of your .cs file:

```
using System;
```

```
using System.IO;
using System.Collections.Generic;
using Amazon.SimpleDB;
using Amazon.SimpleDB.Model;
using Attr = Amazon.SimpleDB.Model.Attribute;
using RequestAttr = Amazon.SimpleDB.Model.ReplaceableAttribute;
```

For the purposes of avoiding name collisions and formatting code to fit on book pages, the length of Amazon's `Attribute` and `ReplaceableAttribute` class names were reduced.

As always, you should avoid hard coding your AWS credentials into source code files. There is no benefit to doing this, and you have the double drawbacks of needing to recompile on credential/environment change and the potential exposure of your credentials. The .NET platform has a number of easy ways to load program configuration data. For consistency with the Java samples, the following code will load AWS credentials from a file named .awssecret in the user home directory in the file format described previously:

```
private String id;
private String secret;

private void LoadCredentials()
{
    String home = (Environment.OSVersion.Platform == PlatformID.Unix ||
       Environment.OSVersion.Platform == PlatformID.MacOSX) ?
       Environment.GetEnvironmentVariable("HOME") :
       Environment.ExpandEnvironmentVariables("%HOMEDRIVE%%HOMEPATH%");
    Dictionary<String, String> data = new Dictionary<String, String>();
    String path = home + Path.DirectorySeparatorChar + ".awssecret";
    foreach (String row in File.ReadAllLines(path))
    {
        data.Add(row.Split('=')[0], row.Split('=')[1]);
    }
    id = data["AWS_ACCESS_KEY_ID"];
    secret = data["AWS_SECRET_ACCESSS_KEY"];
}
```

This will work under both Windows and Mono, and this is the same file used previously, so if you stored your credentials in this file for the Chapter 2 examples, you won't need to do it again. The C# snippet code uses the variables `id` and `secret` declared previously. To make these work, just be sure the declarations fall within your scope and that `LoadCredentials()` gets called before you first access them.

Tarzan Setup in PHP

The PHP sample code uses PHP 5+ and the Tarzan client Tarzan is available for download at http://tarzan-aws.com. Add the following required statements to the top of your PHP file:

```
require_once('tarzan.class.php');
require_once('config.inc.php');
```

The first line pulls in Tarzan, and the second line brings in your AWS credentials. Tarzan will automatically look for your credentials in the predefined constants: `AWS_KEY` and `AWS_SECRET_KEY`. You can set them in your config.inc.php file like this:

```
define('AWS_KEY', '<access-key-id>');
define('AWS_SECRET_KEY', '<secret-access-key>');
```

You must replace `<access-key-id>` and `<secret-access-key>` with the actual values of your AWS credentials.

Common Concepts

There are some commonalities among all the SimpleDB operations that you should be familiar with before you dive into the specifics.

The Language Gap

For each of the SimpleDB operations documented in this chapter, there are code samples demonstrating the operation with three different SimpleDB clients. Each of the clients is in a different programming language and each exposes a unique interface. This presents a challenge when deciding what vocabulary to use with the explanations because there is a split between the language of the web service and the language used in the multiple clients.

The approach of this chapter is to use the official SimpleDB web service lexicon when referring to the names of operations, parameters, error codes, and so on. These are the literal, case-sensitive terms that clients must use when communicating with SimpleDB, but those clients may not expose the exact same naming. For example, the nine SimpleDB operations are `CreateDomain`, `ListDomains`, `DeleteDomain`, `DomainMetadata`, `PutAttributes`, `GetAttributes`, `DeleteAttributes`, `BatchPutAttributes`, and `Select`. Even though the Tarzan function for domain creation is called `create_domain()`, this book will always refer to the name of the operation as `CreateDomain`. The details of how each client individually exposes each operation are covered alongside the code snippets.

SimpleDB Endpoints

The concept of a service endpoint is important for understanding the scope of all SimpleDB operations. Within the context of SimpleDB, an endpoint is a completely independent service cluster with its own domain name and internal servers distributed across data centers within a single geographical region.

Figure 3-1 illustrates how endpoints are geographically isolated and how a SimpleDB cluster at one of these endpoints spans more than one data center.

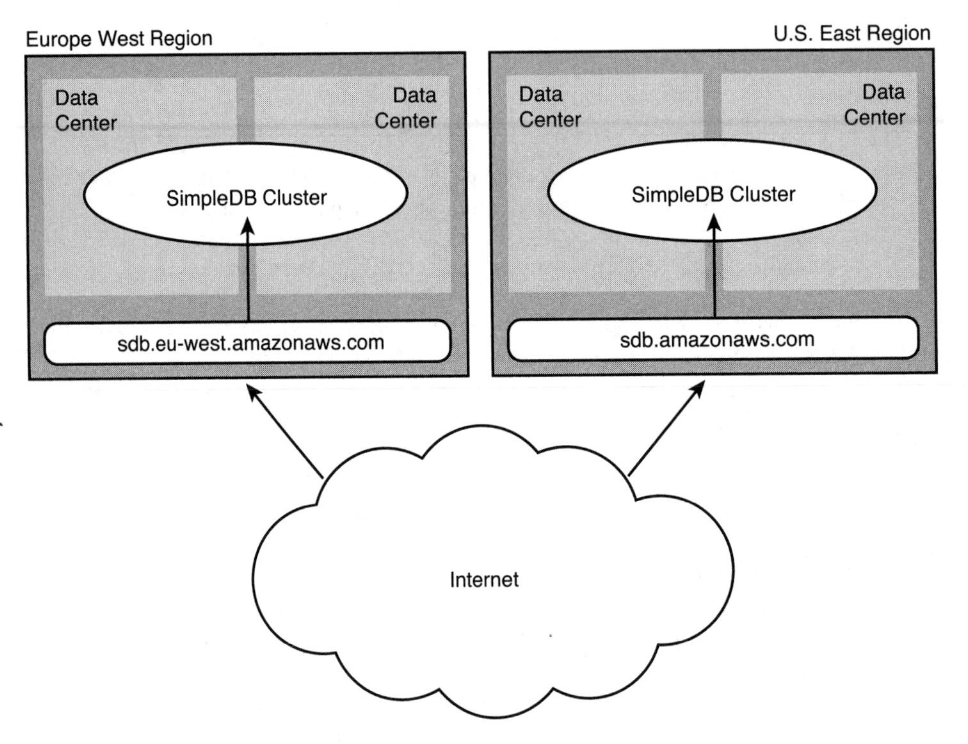

Figure 3-1 A SimpleDB endpoint is backed by a cluster of servers and hosted by the data centers in one region.

The current endpoints are as follows:

- **sdb.amazonaws.com**— Located in the eastern region of the United States (Northern Virginia).
- **sdb.ap-southeast-1.amazonaws.com**— Located in the Asia Pacific region (Singapore).
- **sdb.us-west-1.amazonaws.com**— Located in the western region of the United States (Northern California).
- **sdb.eu-west-1.amazonaws.com**— Located in the European region (Ireland).

When you successfully sign up for SimpleDB and supply your billing information, AWS grants you access to all endpoints. There is nothing special you need to do to gain access to a specific endpoint. All account charges across endpoints will accrue under the same billing to the same account. However, each endpoint is completely independent with respect to actual SimpleDB operations. Invoking an operation at one endpoint has no impact on the data stored at any other endpoint.

Most SimpleDB clients support the primary U.S. endpoint by default and support alternate endpoints via a constructor argument on the base client object. The code samples for the `ListDomains` operation demonstrate access to an alternate endpoint for all of the programming languages.

SimpleDB Service Versions

SimpleDB implements a web service versioning scheme. Every request must indicate which version of the API is being used. Service versioning allows a web service to introduce new features and phase out old ones, without breaking existing clients. The SimpleDB client normally handles the versioning of each request, and there is nothing specific for a user to do. However, as a user, you should understand the concept behind versioning as a means of understanding the capabilities of the clients you evaluate and compatibility with the code examples.

The code snippets in this chapter use version "2009-04-15" of the SimpleDB API. At the time of this writing, that is the most recent version. The code here is also fully compatible with the prior API version "2007-11-07." One notable change in the newer version is that it no longer supports two of the previously available operations. The newer functionality in `Select` has become the replacement for both `Query` and `QueryWithAttributes`. AWS deprecated both of them, and they are only available in the older version "2007-11-07" of the API. This book offers no coverage of `Query` and `QueryWithAttributes` but provides extensive coverage of `Select`.

Common Response Elements

Every SimpleDB operation has a specific set of parameters and responses. However, SimpleDB also returns two generic response values. Both `BoxUsage` and `RequestID` come back as part of every success response and also as part of certain error responses.

Box Usage

`BoxUsage` is a fractional approximation of how much CPU time is consumed servicing your request, in hours. Here is an example `BoxUsage` number from a `GetAttributes` request: 0.0000093382. For the purpose of clarity, this example value is a little more than 9.3 millionths of an hour, and it would take more than 100,000 requests with this usage to break the one-hour mark for billing purposes. That is an important purpose of this response value: to enable you to correlate requests and billing. At the end of the month, AWS bills you for the sum of all your `BoxUsage` numbers, in addition to the cost of storage and data transfer. Beyond the billing transparency, `BoxUsage` has a practical use in helping you tune your queries.

SimpleDB computes `BoxUsage` based on a number of different factors, depending on the operation. Some operations always return a constant `BoxUsage` and others compute a number based on some combination of request parameters, response data, and existing stored data. The important thing to understand is that the value is the result of a computation and not a measurement. It is not a record of actual CPU time; it is an estimate, which allows consistency from one request to another and uniformity across a heterogeneous network of machines. As a result, you are insulated from the variability in charges that might otherwise arise based solely on which machines happened to service your requests.

Request Identifier

The other universal response element is `RequestID`. `RequestID` is a unique identifier attached to each response, which AWS logs. It provides a mechanism for you to communicate with AWS support regarding issues with specific requests. For applications where this type of support is important, it is best to implement a mechanism to log the `RequestID`, timestamp, error code, and error message for errors.

With these common elements covered, let's move on to the actual SimpleDB operations.

CreateDomain

The `CreateDomain` operation allocates a new domain at the endpoint to which you are connected. The only parameter to `CreateDomain` is the domain name you want to create. Each domain name is unique only for the account making the request and the endpoint. Because each endpoint is completely independent, you can have domains with the same name at different endpoints. Also, domain names do not need to be unique across accounts, so you are not limited to only those names not yet taken by other SimpleDB users (as is the case with S3 buckets.)

> **Beware of Automated Domain Creation**
>
> `CreateDomain` and `DeleteDomain` are heavyweight operations. They each take a relatively long time to complete, on the order of a fraction of a minute as opposed to the fraction of a second typical of the other operations. And since your calls to them result in resource allocation on multiple servers, the box usage is even larger than the response time would suggest. As a result, you should treat `CreateDomain` and `DeleteDomain` as administrative functions and avoid calling them from automated code.
>
> One common scenario that can lead to problems is including domain creation as part of an automated unit test suite or an automated build process. This has the potential to rack up a lot of box usage charges unnecessarily. For example, if you create and delete three domains as part of unit test setup and tear-down, you will incur about two minutes of box usage cost, although issuing the calls concurrently may only take 20 seconds. This is roughly equivalent to 3,500 calls to `GetAttributes`. If the testing framework invokes the setup and tear-down functions before and after each test method, or if the tests are run by multiple users and an automated build each day, you can see how this could start to get expensive. You can view your current SimpleDB usage on the AWS website, but unless you specifically look at it, you may not even notice the usage until the bill is generated at the end of the month.

> You should use mock objects or a fake client for your testing. This is good general testing practice; your unit tests should be testing small sections of your own code and not large sections of Amazon's code. It also has the benefit of allowing your test code to run without the embedded credentials for an active AWS account.

CreateDomain Parameters

`CreateDomain` has only one parameter, as follows:

- **`DomainName`** **(required)**— The name of the domain to be created. The minimum length is three characters and the maximum length is 255 characters. The only valid characters for this parameter are letters, numbers, '_', '-', and '.'.

CreateDomain Response Data

`CreateDomain` does not return any operation-specific data. If the call returns an error message, the domain was not created. If there is no error message, the domain was created. Calling `CreateDomain` with the name of a domain that already exists does not result in an error. The call has no effect on the existing domain.

There are three operation-specific errors SimpleDB may return from a `CreateDomain`. The form of these errors depends on what client you use. Obvious errors may be prevented or checked by the client before a web service call is made. The following is a complete list of errors that can come back from a `CreateDomain` operation:

- **`MissingParameter`**— Returned when you fail to pass the `DomainName` parameter.
- **`InvalidParameterValue`**— Returned when the `DomainName` does not meet the length or valid character range requirements.
- **`NumberDomainsExceeded`**— Returned when your account already has the maximum number of domains. The default maximum is 100 domains. You can request a higher limit at the AWS website: http://aws.amazon.com/contact-us/simpledb-limit-request/.

The `MissingParameter` error is one that you are not likely to ever see. The SimpleDB client will require a value to be present.

CreateDomain Snippet in Java

Here is the Typica code to create a domain:

```
SimpleDB simpleDB = new SimpleDB(accessKeyID, secretAccessKey);
try {
   simpleDB.createDomain("users");
   System.out.println("create domain succeeded");
} catch (SDBException e) {
   AWSError error = e.getErrors().get(0);
   String code = error.getCode();
   String message = error.getMessage();
```

```
    System.err.printf("create domain failed: %s: %s", code, message);
}
```

If the call to `createDomain()` returns normally, the domain was created (or already existed). Any problem, including `InvalidParameterValue` and `NumberDomainsExceeded`, that results in a failure to create the domain throws an `SDBException`. Embedded in the `SDBException` is a list of `AWSError` objects. In the case of operation-specific SimpleDB error codes, there will only be one error, and that error will be holding the error code and message from the SimpleDB response.

CreateDomain Snippet in C#

In C #, this is how you create a SimpleDB domain:

```
AmazonSimpleDB simpleDB = new AmazonSimpleDBClient(id, secret);
CreateDomainRequest request = new CreateDomainRequest();
request.DomainName = "users";
try
{
    simpleDB.CreateDomain(request);
    Console.WriteLine("create domain successful");
}
catch (AmazonSimpleDBException ex)
{
    String code = ex.ErrorCode;
    String message = ex.Message;
    Console.WriteLine("create domain failed: {0}: {1}", code, message);
}
```

Request setup with the C# library for Amazon SimpleDB is a bit more verbose, but the error code and message are conveniently available as properties of the exception.

CreateDomain Snippet in PHP

The PHP code using Tarzan looks like this:

```
$sdb = new AmazonSDB();
$domain = $sdb->create_domain('users');
sleep(15);

if ($domain->isOK())
{
  echo 'create domain succeeded';
}
else
{
  echo 'create domain failed: ';
  $error = $domain->body->Errors->Error;
  echo $error->Code . ': ' . $error->Message;
}
```

The variable `$domain` holds the response in the form of a `SimpleXML` object. In the case of an error that prevents the domain from being created, you have to navigate through the XML response body to get to the error code and message.

ListDomains

The operation `ListDomains` returns a listing of all the domains associated with your account at that endpoint. If you have domains at different endpoints, you will need to issue this call to each to get a full list of your domains.

ListDomains Parameters

There are two optional parameters for the `ListDomains` operation. However, the most common usage is with no parameters at all. This is true because unless you have had your allotment of domains increased, you can get a full listing of all your domains using the no-parameter version:

- **`MaxNumberOfDomains`** **(optional)**— A number between 1 and 100 that specifies the limit of domains to be returned in response to this call. The default value of 100 is used if you do not provide a value.
- **`NextToken`** **(optional)**— A value obtained from a previous call to `ListDomains` that returned only partial results. Passing this value back enables you to pick up with the next page of results.

The `NextToken` allows you to page through results in the same way for `ListDomains` as it does with `Select`. The typical reason for getting only partial results is setting the `MaxNumberOfDomains` on the prior call to be smaller than the number of domains you have. You may never need to specify a limit via the `MaxNumberOfDomains` parameter, but you should be prepared to handle a `NextToken` returned to you with a partial result.

ListDomains Response Data

The response from a `ListDomains` request is terse. The following is a list of the response parameters returned from successful calls to this operation:

- **`DomainName`**— A list of the domain names.
- **`NextToken`**— A token indicating that a partial result has been provided. Passing this token to a subsequent `ListDomains` call will allow you to pick up where the last response left off.

A `NextToken` value does not have an explicit expiration, and there is nothing useful that you can really do with it, apart from passing it back. Despite the fact that it will not expire, you do not want to keep that value around for later use. You should use it for a follow-up request and then discard it. Domains that are created after a specific `NextToken` value is issued may not appear in response to requests with that old `NextToken` value.

The actual content of the NextToken value returned by SimpleDB is somewhat of a black box, in that you don't really know what is in there. It enables SimpleDB to resume processing your request mid-stream without having to route your follow-up requests to the same back-end server. It is an encoded value that SimpleDB expects you to pass back unmodified. If you are the curious type, however, you can work out what is inside it.

The full list of error responses that can come back from a ListDomains operation is equally brief:

- **InvalidParameterValue**— Returned when the MaxNumberOfDomains parameter is not between 1 and 100.
- **InvalidNextToken**— Returned when you pass a NextToken that is not valid.

ListDomains Snippet in Java

The Java code to perform a ListDomains operation for the European endpoint is here:

```
boolean secure = true;
String eu = "sdb.eu-west-1.amazonaws.com";
SimpleDB simpleDB = new SimpleDB(accessKeyID, secretAccessKey, secure, eu);
try {
   ListDomainsResult result = simpleDB.listDomains();
   for (Domain domain : result.getDomainList()) {
      System.out.println(domain.getName());
   }
} catch (SDBException e) {
   AWSError error = e.getErrors().get(0);
   String code = error.getCode();
   String message = error.getMessage();
   System.err.printf("list domain failed: %s: %s", code, message);
}
```

The endpoint for Europe is set by means of a four-argument alternate constructor. The extra two parameters beyond what we have seen already are a boolean indicating whether to use SSL and the endpoint domain. After the constructor, the code is the same regardless of endpoint. The result of the ListDomains() method is a List of Typica Domain objects wrapped in a ListDomainsResult object.

ListDomains Snippet in C#

In C#, you can produce a domain listing from the European endpoint, like this:

```
AmazonSimpleDBConfig config = new AmazonSimpleDBConfig();
config.ServiceURL = "http://sdb.eu-west-1.amazonaws.com/";
AmazonSimpleDB simpleDB = new AmazonSimpleDBClient(id, secret, config);
ListDomainsRequest request = new ListDomainsRequest();
try
{
    ListDomainsResponse response = simpleDB.ListDomains(request);
```

```
    ListDomainsResult listDomainsResult = response.ListDomainsResult;
    foreach (String domainName in listDomainsResult.DomainName)
    {
        Console.WriteLine(domainName);
    }
}
catch (AmazonSimpleDBException ex)
{
    String code = ex.ErrorCode;
    String message = ex.Message;
    Console.WriteLine("list domain failed: {0}: {1}", code, message);
}
```

The endpoint here is also set via a constructor; in this case, it takes an object of class `AmazonSimpleDBConfig`. There are numerous properties available to set on the configuration object, but the only one of concern here is the `ServiceURL`. The `ListDomainsResult` holds all of the domain names in `DomainName` property of type `List<String>`.

ListDomains Snippet in PHP

To list all the domains associated with an AWS account at the European endpoint with PHP, use the following code:

```
define('SDB_DEFAULT_URL', 'http://sdb.eu-west-1.amazonaws.com');
$sdb = new AmazonSDB();
$domain_list = $sdb->list_domains();
if ($domain_list->isOK())
{
  foreach($domain_list->body->ListDomainsResult->DomainName as $name)
  {
    echo $name . PHP_EOL;
  }
}
else
{
  echo 'list domain failed: ';
  $error = $domain_list->body->Errors->Error;
  echo $error->Code . ': ' . $error->Message;
}
```

Tarzan uses a constant to determine which endpoint to use. The first line of the preceding code snippet redefines that constant to be the URL of the endpoint in Europe. The list of names takes the form of an array of strings within the `ListDomainsResult`.

DeleteDomain

The `DeleteDomain` operation is the analog to `CreateDomain`. It permanently deletes all the data associated with the named domain. Like `CreateDomain`, calling `DeleteDomain` multiple times, with the same name as a previous call or one that does not exist will not result in an error. As with all operations, the scope of this operation is limited to the endpoint to which you issue the request. If you have domains with the same name at different endpoints, you will need to call `DeleteDomain` at each endpoint to delete them all.

`DeleteDomain` is a heavyweight operation as detailed in the `CreateDomain` warning section. Whether returning success in ten seconds or failure in one second, you will be charged for at least an order of magnitude greater box usage than with the lighter operations. Call `DeleteDomain` from automated processes (like tests) with great caution, or preferably not at all.

DeleteDomain Parameters

`DeleteDomain` accepts a single parameter. The parameter to this operation is as follows:

- **`DomainName` (required)**— The name of the domain to be deleted. The minimum length is 3 characters and the maximum length is 255 characters. The only valid characters are letters, numbers, '_', '-', and '.'.

Passing the name of an existing domain will ensure that you do not pass an invalid parameter here. Valid names that do not exist will be silently ignored.

DeleteDomain Response Data

No specific data comes back from a `DeleteDomain` operation with the exception of an error message. If an error message is returned, the domain was not deleted. A normal return from this operation indicates a successful deletion. Although the official documentation lists only a single error for this operation, there are actually two possible errors that could be returned as part of an abnormal response. Those two error codes are listed here:

- **`MissingParameter`**— Returned when the required domain name parameter is not present.
- **`InvalidParameterValue`**— Returned when the `DomainName` does not meet the length or valid character range requirements.

You will probably never see a `MissingParameter` error response since the function or method you call will require its presence. `InvalidParameterValue` is not listed as a `DeleteDomain`-specific error response in the official documentation, but you will get it if you call this operation with an invalid name.

The most likely scenario is that you pass the name of an existing domain to this operation. When an existing name is passed, you will never see either of these errors.

DeleteDomain Snippet in Java

Deleting a domain using Java is shown in this code snippet:

```
SimpleDB simpleDB = new SimpleDB(accessKeyID, secretAccessKey);
try {
   simpleDB.deleteDomain("users");
   System.out.println("delete domain succeeded");
} catch (SDBException e) {
   AWSError error = e.getErrors().get(0);
   String code = error.getCode();
   String message = error.getMessage();
   System.err.printf("delete domain failed: %s: %s", code, message);
}
```

The `deleteDomain()` method returns no value. If the method call returns without throwing an exception, the domain has been deleted.

DeleteDomain Snippet in C#

Here is the C# code to delete a domain:

```
AmazonSimpleDB simpleDB = new AmazonSimpleDBClient(id, secret);
DeleteDomainRequest request = new DeleteDomainRequest();
try
{
    request.DomainName = "users";
    simpleDB.DeleteDomain(request);
    Console.WriteLine("delete domain successful");
}
catch (AmazonSimpleDBException ex)
{
    String code = ex.ErrorCode;
    String message = ex.Message;
    Console.WriteLine("delete domain failed: {0}: {1}", code, message);
}
```

The `DeleteDomain()` method takes a `DeleteDomainRequest` as a parameter, and if it returns normally, the domain was deleted or did not exist. In the case of an error, an `AmazonSimpleDBException` is thrown, and the domain was not deleted.

DeleteDomain Snippet in PHP

This is how you implement domain deletion in PHP:

```
$sdb = new AmazonSDB();
$domain_delete = $sdb->delete_domain('users');
```

```
sleep(15);
if ($domain_delete->isOK())
{
    echo 'delete domain succeeded';
}
else
{
    echo 'delete domain failed: ';
    $error = $domain_delete->body->Errors->Error;
    echo $error->Code . ': ' . $error->Message;
}
```

As with Java and C#, nothing interesting is returned in the case of success. The normal return of the operation signals successful deletion, subject to eventual consistency.

DomainMetadata

The `DomainMetadata` operation returns detailed information about one domain. The information includes key size metrics across the dimensions of a domain, which have a billing component or enforced limits. This information, if saved periodically, is useful for tracking the growth of a domain over time. Tracking growth is important if you are concerned about reaching the domain size limits.

DomainMetadata Parameters

The full list of parameters that can be passed to this operation has a single entry:

- **`DomainName`** **(required)**— The name of the domain for which metadata is to be returned.

DomainMetadata Response Data

The response data contains numeric values for all the counts and sizes that pertain to your data storage within the specified domain. Here is the list of response values from this operation:

- **`ItemCount`**— A number representing the count of all items in the domain.
- **`ItemNameSizeBytes`**— The accumulated size, in bytes, of all the item names in the domain.
- **`AttributeNameCount`**— A number representing the count of all unique attribute names in the domain.
- **`AttributeNameSizeBytes`**— The total storage size of attribute names, in bytes. Each unique attribute name that you put into a domain counts once for storage purposes.

- **AttributeValueCount**— A number representing the count of all name/value pairs in the domain.
- **AttributeValueSizeBytes**— The total storage size of attribute values, in bytes.
- **Timestamp**— The time at which the metadata was computed, in Unix time.

In the case of a bad request, one of the following `DomainMetadata`-specific error responses comes back:

- **NoSuchDomain**— Returned if the specified domain name does not exist at that endpoint.
- **MissingParameter**— Returned if the request did not include a `DomainName`.

The two current domain size limitations are 1 billion attributes and 10GB of storage. You can see how close you are to the attribute limit by looking at the `AttributeValueCount` number. Adding up the three byte sizes in the metadata gives you the total user storage for the domain. This tells you how close you are to the 10GB limit. Plotting those two metrics over time in a report can inform decisions about using additional domains.

Another benefit to this metadata is the billing transparency it affords. AWS bills you for the storage you use in terms of GB per month. To arrive at the final storage number, the storage in each of your domains is sampled periodically. There are no assurances that the metadata is updated at the same frequency as the automated sampling. However, it does enable you to monitor the size of your own data storage at the finer grain level of the individual domain.

The metadata is not the result of a fresh computation for each call. The data is calculated and then cached. You can see how fresh the data is by looking at the Timestamp response value. Typically the metadata updates differently based on usage of the domain. Domains with normal everyday usage seem to update once a day between midnight and 1:00 a.m. Eastern time. New domains and rarely used domains do not show that same pattern. However, at various times, freshly computed metadata can come back from consecutive calls, so there are no hard and fast rules. Treat the domain metadata as if it were served from a day-old cache, even though it may sometimes be fresh. Feel free to use it in a graph that plots storage over time or in a chart that shows how evenly your data is distributed across domains. Just do not use it immediately after a call to `PutAttributes` or `DeleteAttributes` as a way to verify success. In the same way, it is not suitable for use in an automated verification step of a unit test or a data import tool.

DomainMetadata Snippet in Java

The metadata fetching code using Java looks like this:

```
SimpleDB simpleDB = new SimpleDB(accessKeyID, secretAccessKey);
try {
   Domain d = simpleDB.getDomain("users");
```

```
    DomainMetadataResult meta = d.getMetadata();
    System.out.printf("'%s': %d items", d.getName(), meta.getItemCount());
} catch (SDBException e) {
    AWSError error = e.getErrors().get(0);
    String code = error.getCode();
    String message = error.getMessage();
    System.err.printf("domain metadata failed: %s: %s", code, message);
}
```

The Typica class that holds the resulting metadata is `DomainMetadataResult`, and it defines seven properties for access to the seven data values in the response. This sample only accesses the `ItemCount` property.

DomainMetadata Snippet in C#

The code implementing a domain metadata request in Amazon's C# library is as follows:

```
AmazonSimpleDB simpleDB = new AmazonSimpleDBClient(id, secret);
DomainMetadataRequest request = new DomainMetadataRequest();
String domain = "products";
try
{
    request.DomainName = domain;
    DomainMetadataResponse resp = simpleDB.DomainMetadata(request);
    DomainMetadataResult meta = resp.DomainMetadataResult;
    Console.WriteLine("'{0}': {1} items", domain, meta.ItemCount);
}
catch (AmazonSimpleDBException ex)
{
    String code = ex.ErrorCode;
    String message = ex.Message;
    Console.WriteLine("...failed: {0}: {1}", code, message);
}
```

The `DomainMetadataResult` embedded in the response allows access to all of the metadata properties. Here, the sample code writes the `DomainName` and the `ItemCount` to the console.

DomainMetadata Snippet in PHP

In Tarzan for PHP, you pull the metadata for a domain like this:

```
$sdb = new AmazonSDB();
$meta = $sdb->domain_metadata('products');
if ($meta->isOK())
{
    $meta_values = $meta->body->DomainMetadataResult;
```

```
    echo 'products: ' . $meta_values->ItemCount;
}
else
{
    echo 'domain metadata failed: ';
    $error = $meta->body->Errors->Error;
    echo $error->Code . ': ' . $error->Message;
}
```

All of the resulting metadata values are accessible by name inside `DomainMetadataResult` via SimpleXML.

PutAttributes

`PutAttributes` is the operation that enables you to store data in SimpleDB. As the name suggests, each element of data you pass must be in the form of an attribute, which is simply a name/value pair. An example of a name/value pair that you can store is "song-title":"Everything". You can store more than one attribute at a time with this call, so the following is valid: "song-title":"Everything", "artist":"Michael Bublé", "album":"Call Me Irresponsible". Each attribute name can have multiple values as well. In the case of the previous example, you can add tags to the song data by storing additional attributes with the same name: "tags":"jazz", "tags":"alternative", "tags":"vocal".

All of the data stored by a single invocation of this operation is stored in the context of a single item. You specify that item by supplying an `ItemName` along with the attribute pairs. The concept of an item is roughly analogous to a database row. The `ItemName` is like a row's primary key; it needs to exist, and it needs to be unique.

In SimpleDB, you must always provide your own `ItemName`; there are no auto-increment fields. Because you do not define columns in SimpleDB, each item can have whichever attributes you chose. In this regard, `PutAttributes` fills the role of both SQL Insert and SQL Update, where none of the columns are predefined and all of them are nullable.

The only distinction between inserting and updating is an optional `Replace` flag. To continue with the prior example, if you want to add an additional tag to the song at a later time, you can issue another `PutAttributes` call with a single attribute: "tags":"contemporary". If you do that `PutAttributes` but set the `Replace` flag, instead of adding an additional attribute, the existing three "tags" attributes will be removed and only the new one will remain.

All of the changes in a single `PutAttributes` call are applied atomically so that subsequent read operations never return a partial update. In addition to the implicit atomicity, an explicit conditional check against one attribute can be included to add transactional semantics. You have the option of checking for the existence, non-existence, or specific value of any single-valued attribute in the item being updated. The write will succeed only when the condition is met and fails with a specific error code otherwise.

Do Items Even Exist?

Items are an interesting concept in SimpleDB. You'll notice from the API that there are no operations with "Item" in the name. There are no operations named `CreateItem`, `DeleteItem`, and so on. And, in fact, you cannot explicitly create or delete them. If you hold to the concept of an item, you would be forced to say that items are created the first time you issue a `PutAttributes` call with a given `ItemName` and that they are deleted when the last attribute with that `ItemName` is deleted.

The fact is that, in a way, items don't really exist in SimpleDB. What exists is the `ItemName`. Each `ItemName` is an immutable key that associates a group of attributes together. Nevertheless, the item is an important conceptual element. The limit of 256 attribute pairs that can be grouped together is most clearly expressed as an attribute limit on items. All calls to `PutAttributes`, `GetAttributes`, and `DeleteAttributes` require an `ItemName`, and thinking about these operations in terms of "performing actions on items" is natural. The entire basis of SimpleDB queries revolves around returning data matches at the item level. And the query limits, both the default and what you can specify yourself, are expressed in terms of item count. What is more, SimpleDB clients commonly use the item abstraction when creating classes and methods.

The idea of items is central to SimpleDB, and you will see it referred to at all levels, from official AWS documentation and code, to third-party SimpleDB clients, to anywhere people talk about it. This book uses the term often because the concept is important and easy to understand. But on a practical level, you should be aware that the `ItemName` is the tangible thing holding the concept together.

PutAttributes Parameters

As the primary write operation in SimpleDB, `PutAttributes` has a longer list of available parameters than the previously shown operations. The full list of possible request parameters is as follows:

- **`DomainName`** (required)— The name of the domain where the attribute(s) will be stored. This parameter must be the name of a domain that has already been created.
- **`ItemName`** (required)— The unique key with which the attributes will be associated. This can be a new `ItemName` for the purposes of an insert or an existing `ItemName` for the purposes of an update. The maximum length of this parameter is 1,024 bytes.
- **`AttributeName`** (required)— The name of the attribute, similar to a column name, passed as a list in combination with an `AttributeValue` and optionally a `Replace` flag. The minimum length is 1 and the maximum length of this parameter is 1,024 bytes.
- **`AttributeValue`** (required)— The value to be stored, passed as a list in combination with an `AttributeName` and optionally a `Replace` flag. This value must be present, but it can have zero length (the empty string). The maximum length of this parameter is 1,024 bytes.

- **`ExpectedName`** (optional)— The attribute name to check for a conditional write. This parameter is only valid when either an `ExpectedValue` or an `ExpectedExists` is also included. The maximum length of this parameter is 1,024 bytes.
- **`ExpectedValue`** (optional)— The value to check for a conditional write. This value must exist in SimpleDB in order for the conditional write to succeed. This parameter is only valid when an `ExpectedName` is also included. The maximum length of this parameter is 1,024 bytes.
- **`ExpectedExists`** (optional)— The flag to check for existence in a conditional write. When set to true, write only succeeds when the `ExpectedName` exists. When false, write only succeeds when the `ExpectedName` does not exist. This parameter is only valid when an `ExpectedName` is also included. The maximum length of this parameter is 1,024 bytes.
- **`Replace`** (optional)— The flag that specifies whether to replace the existing attribute value, passed as a list in combination with an `AttributeName` and an `AttributeValue`. If `Replace` is true, SimpleDB removes all of the existing attribute values. If `Replace` is false, SimpleDB adds the new value to any existing values. If this parameter is not given, a default value of false is used. If there is no existing attribute, the `Replace` flag has no effect.

The operation takes `DomainName`, `ItemName` and conditionals as individual parameters. `AttributeName`, `AttributeValue`, and `Replace`, on the other hand, are grouped together and specified once for each attribute you are sending in the `PutAttributes` call.

The maximum number of attributes that you can store in an item is 256. You can pass any number of them in a single call, up to the 256 limit, but it is wise to pass the fewest number of attributes possible for reasons of box usage charges. In cases where `PutAttributes` is used to update an existing item, this is easily accomplished by passing only the changed values. Even in cases where `PutAttributes` is used to insert new data, you may want to split the attributes into multiple calls to this operation if there are more than 52 attributes. Chapter 11, "Improving the SimpleDB Client," provides an in-depth analysis into the surprising pricing issues surrounding `PutAttributes`.

> **Tip**
>
> You can set the replace flag to true on any `PutAttributes` call, even if the item doesn't exist yet or the item doesn't have the attribute you are passing. It won't result in an error, but it also doesn't provide any benefit. A single `PutAttributes` call can accept hundreds of attributes. Because the replace flag is set at the individual attribute level, you can mix replace attributes with non-replace attributes in the same call. Of course, as always, all the attributes in a single call will apply to a single item.

The fact that `PutAttributes` accepts a variable amount of data presents a challenge to SimpleDB client developers. It is not a challenge because it is difficult to implement, the challenging part is trying to provide a high level of usability for many different use cases. Decisions have to be made about how attribute data is structured within the program.

Even if you never write a SimpleDB client yourself, these decisions affect you as the user of the client.

The typical solution for clients in statically typed languages like Java, is the use of an `Attribute` class to hold name, value, and the replace flag. As a user, you first create the object instances to hold the data and then pass those instances to the appropriate method of the SimpleDB client.

PutAttributes Response Data

`PutAttributes` does not return any operation-specific data. If the call returns an error message, none of the attributes were stored and none of the existing attributes requested to be replaced (if any) were removed. If the call returns normally with no error message, all of the attributes were stored and any existing attributes subject to replacement were removed. Attributes stored with this operation are subject to eventual consistency as they are automatically replicated in the background after this call returns. Any subsequent access with `GetAttributes` or `Select` may not reflect changes for a brief period during normal usage and longer periods during heavy load or a failure unless the `ConsistentRead` flag is set.

These are quite a few possible error codes. The full list of error codes that can come back in a `PutAttributes` response is as follows:

- **`InvalidParameterValue`**— Returned when the 1,024-byte size limit is exceeded by either the `ItemName`, the `AttributeName`, or the `AttributeValue`.
- **`MissingParameter`**— Returned when any of the four required parameters to this operation are omitted. However, your SimpleDB client will require you to pass these values, so this is an error code you are not likely to encounter in practice.
- **`NoSuchDomain`**— Returned when the domain name in the request did not exist at that endpoint.
- **`NumberDomainBytesExceeded`**— Returned when the 10GB per domain limit has been reached.
- **`NumberDomainAttributesExceeded`**— Returned when the 1 billion attributes per domain limit has been reached.
- **`NumberItemAttributesExceeded`**— Returned when the 256 attributes per item limit has been reached.
- **`AttributeDoesNotExist`**— Returned when the `ExpectedExists` parameter was set to true and the `ExpectedName` or `ExpectedValue` did not exist.
- **`ConditionalCheckFailed`**— Returned when the `ExpectedName` parameter unexpectedly exists or when `ExpectedValue` was different than the actual value.
- **`MultiValuedAttribute`**— Returned when the `conditional check was applied to a multi-valued attribute. Conditional checks can only be applied to single-valued attributes.`

If you fill up a domain to the limits with data, error responses from this operation is where you will find that out. Once a domain is full, you will no longer be able to perform any `PutAttributes` operations, even in cases where you are trying to submit replacements that would have a net result of less storage being used. The `PutAttributes` operation does not check to see what the result would be; it simply returns the error code as long as the domain is full. You are still free to use as many `GetAttributes` and `Select` operations as you wish. `DeleteAttributes` will work as well. Once you have deleted enough data to drop below the limit, `PutAttributes` calls will be accepted again.

> **Full Items**
>
> On the SimpleDB back-end, the code that rejects `PutAttributes` requests due to full items is separate from the code that actually applies the update. What this means is that the 256 attributes per item limit in SimpleDB is not as hard and fast as you might think it is. To ensure data integrity in an eventually consistent environment, the way the limit is implemented is this: If the item specified in the `PutAttributes` request has fewer than 256 attributes, the put is allowed. If the item has 256 attributes or more, the put is rejected. What this means is that if you have an item with 255 attributes and you submit a `PutAttributes` request with an additional 256 attributes, the call will succeed, giving you an item with 511 attributes.
>
> This can come as a surprise, as can the fact that an item with 256 attributes will cause the rejection of a `PutAttributes` that would replace attributes and leave the item below the limit.
>
> Whether you are considering the case of intentionally overstuffing your item or the case of filling to the exact limit, limit yourself to 255 attributes per item so you aren't stuck with items that can only be updated with `DeleteAttributes`.

PutAttributes Snippet in Java

Storing data with the `PutAttributes` operation in Java is shown with this code:

```
SimpleDB simpleDB = new SimpleDB(accessKeyID, secretAccessKey);
boolean replace = false;
ItemAttribute[] userData = new ItemAttribute[] {
   new ItemAttribute("userid", "Mocky", replace),
   new ItemAttribute("location", "Oswego", replace),
   new ItemAttribute("tags", "SimpleDB", replace),
   new ItemAttribute("tags", "Azure-Table", replace),
   new ItemAttribute("tags", "App-Engine", replace),
};

try {
   Domain domain = simpleDB.getDomain("users");
   Item newItem = domain.getItem("1234567");
   newItem.putAttributes(Arrays.asList(userData));
   System.out.println("put attributes succeeded");
} catch (SDBException e) {
```

```
    AWSError error = e.getErrors().get(0);
    String code = error.getCode();
    String message = error.getMessage();
    System.err.printf("put attributes failed: %s: %s", code, message);
}
```

Instances of the ItemAttribute class are used to the name/value pairs, each with a replace flag. In this example, the attributes are stored in an array and subsequently converted to a List for the putAttributes() call, where the actual web service call is made. Notice that the sample code stores the multi-valued attribute "tags" by creating a separate ItemAttribute for each value. Also notice that the putAttributes() method is in the Item class and not in the SimpleDB class.

PutAttributes Snippet in C#

To accomplish PutAttributes in C#, use this code:

```
AmazonSimpleDB simpleDB = new AmazonSimpleDBClient(id, secret);
RequestAttr[] userData = new RequestAttr[]
{
    new RequestAttr().WithName("userid").WithValue("Mocky"),
    new RequestAttr().WithName("location").WithValue("Oswego"),
    new RequestAttr().WithName("tags").WithValue("SimpleDB"),
    new RequestAttr().WithName("tags").WithValue("Azure-Table"),
    new RequestAttr().WithName("tags").WithValue("App-Engine")
};
PutAttributesRequest request = new PutAttributesRequest();
try
{
    request.DomainName = "users";
    request.ItemName = "1234567";
    request.WithAttribute(userData);

    simpleDB.PutAttributes(request);
    Console.WriteLine("put attributes successful");
}
catch (AmazonSimpleDBException ex)
{
    String code = ex.ErrorCode;
    String message = ex.Message;
    Console.WriteLine("put attributes failed: {0}: {1}", code, message);
}
```

This code sets up the PutAttributes call in the same way as the Java code sample. In the C# case, the client-specific attribute class used to gather the request data is ReplaceableAttribute, which has been remapped to the name RequestAttr. Notice that a separate attribute is used for each of the values in the multi-valued attribute "tags."

PutAttributes Snippet in PHP

This is how you store an item using PHP:

```
$sdb = new AmazonSDB();
$put = $sdb->put_attributes('users', '1234567', array(
    'userid' => 'Mocky',
    'location' => 'Oswego',
    'tags' => array('SimpleDB','Azure-Table','App-Engine')
));

if ($put->isOK())
{
    echo 'put attributes succeeded';
}
else
{
    echo 'put attributes failed: ';
    $error = $put->body->Errors->Error;
    echo $error->Code . ': ' . $error->Message;
}
```

The PHP code using Tarzan does not require any special classes for gathering up the request data. Associative arrays are used both for the mapping of attribute names to individual values and for the mapping of attribute names to arrays of values. The code snippet shows the latter type of mapping for the multi-valued attribute named "tags."

GetAttributes

`GetAttributes` is the operation that allows primary key access to the data you have stored in SimpleDB. You pass the `DomainName` and the `ItemName`, and you get back a listing of all the attributes associated with that item. If you don't need all the attributes, you have the option of also passing an `AttributeName` list with the exact attributes you want.

GetAttributes Parameters

There are two required and one optional parameter for `GetAttributes`. Here is the full list of those parameters:

- **`DomainName` (required)**— The name of the domain where the attributes are stored.
- **`ItemName` (required)**— The unique key identifying the attributes to return.
- **`AttributeName` (optional)**— The name of the attribute(s) to which the response should be restricted, passed as a list. If this parameter is omitted, all of the attributes associated with this item will be returned.

- **`ConsistentRead`** **(optional)**— The flag that specifies whether to perform a consistent read. When true, the most recent data is returned. Setting this flag to true may result in greater latency and lower throughput.

GetAttributes Response Data

The data that is returned by this operation is a list of name/value pairs that makes up the item you requested:

- **`AttributeName`**— The name of the attribute, similar to a column name.
- **`AttributeValue`**— The value associated with this `AttributeName` and this `ItemName` by a previous `PutAttributes` call. The maximum length of this value is 1,024 bytes. The data is returned in the form of plain string data.

The response data in its raw form as it comes back from SimpleDB is a list. The client you use may leave it as a list or convert it into a map, where the content of each `AttributeName` is a key and maps to one or more `AttributeValue` values. Be aware that the SimpleDB makes no guarantee with regard to the order of attributes in the response. Attributes in the response do not come back in the original order specified in `PutAttributes`, and they do not come back in the order of `AttributeName` request parameters. This undefined ordering can make map access a convenient way to access the data when compared to iterating over a list repeatedly in search of a specific attribute.

Attributes are allowed to have multiple values in SimpleDB. When these multi-valued attributes are returned via a `GetAttributes` response, there is a separate name/value pair on the list for each value. In the case where your client converts the list into a map, it will also convert multiple values into an array or a list for you.

There is not very much that can go wrong in the way of errors specific to a `GetAttributes` operation:

- **`NoSuchDomain`**— The error code returned if the `DomainName` parameter does not correspond to a domain created with your account at that endpoint.
- **`InvalidParameterValue`**— The error code returned if you pass an `ItemName` or an `AttributeName` longer than 1,024 bytes in length. Because you could not have stored any data with names that long, if you only pass existing `ItemName` and `AttributeName` parameters, you will never get this error code.
- **`MissingParameter`**— The error code returned if you fail to pass a `DomainName` or an `ItemName`. The API of your client will protect you from getting this error.

Note that it is not an error to pass an `ItemName` that does not exist. Instead, an empty list is returned. A request for an item that has not yet been fully replicated is not considered an exceptional case. As part of eventual consistency, it is possible that during a server or network failure, items that exist at one replica of your domain have not yet propagated to another.

> **Eventual Consistency for GetAttributes**
>
> Eventual consistency does not only apply to failure situations. It is built into the fabric of how SimpleDB works. All the data you store with `PutAttributes` is replicated on different back-end servers and across different Amazon data centers in the same region. This happens automatically behind the scenes. As a result, the updates you make with `PutAttributes` and `DeleteAttributes` will always take some time to propagate to all the replicas servicing a domain. Calls to `GetAttributes` immediately after an update will still return responses in accordance with the prior state of things.
>
> The `ConsistentRead` flag can be set on a `GetAttributes` request to eliminate the consistency window. Data returned from a consistent read reflects all of the prior writes. This allows you to immediately follow a write with a consistent read to verify what was written. If consistency cannot be established during a consistent read the call will return a ServiceUnavailable error. When that happens, the application can abort the task, however, it also has the option to turn off the flag and use the results of an eventually consistent read.
>
> Sub-second consistency times commonly occur during normal usage, but this is not guaranteed. Nor should you write an application that relies on a specific consistency time for correct function. If you need immediate read access to a value you just stored, consistent reads are the solution. Nevertheless, be aware that consistent reads may be more sensitive to hardware and network failures.

GetAttributes Snippet in Java

Getting back the data you previously stored via primary key is shown here in Java:

```
SimpleDB simpleDB = new SimpleDB(accessKeyID, secretAccessKey);
try {
    Domain domain = simpleDB.getDomain("users");
    Item item = domain.getItem("1234567");
    List<String> allAttributes = null;
    Map<String,List<String>> user = item.getAttributesMap(allAttributes);

    String name = user.get("userid").get(0);
    String location = user.get("location").get(0);
    List<String> tags = user.get("tags");
    System.out.printf("%s (%s) follows %s", name, location, tags);

} catch (SDBException e) {
    AWSError error = e.getErrors().get(0);
    String code = error.getCode();
    String message = error.getMessage();
    System.err.printf("get attributes failed: %s: %s", code, message);
}
```

With Typica, it is possible to retrieve the results of the `GetAttributes` operation as a `Map` or a `List`. In both cases, there is a single required parameter, which is the list of attribute names you are requesting. To get them all, pass `null` to the method. The preceding sample code passes `null` via the extraneous variable `allAttributes` to prevent a mysterious `null` parameter from causing reader confusion.

The data from this call comes back in the form of a `String` to `List<String>` mapping of attribute names to values. The map format is convenient when you know the names of the attributes you want to access. The values being inside a list provides the capability to handle both single-valued and multi-valued attributes in a consistent way. Note that this is different from the way the data is passed into Typica's `PutAttributes` call and that it requires the extra step of indexing into the list to access the value of single-valued attributes.

GetAttributes Snippet in C#

The same functionality discussed in the previous section looks like this in C#:

```
AmazonSimpleDB simpleDB = new AmazonSimpleDBClient(id, secret);
GetAttributesRequest request = new GetAttributesRequest();
try
{
    request.DomainName = "users";
    request.ItemName = "1234567";
    GetAttributesResponse resp = simpleDB.GetAttributes(request);
    GetAttributesResult user = resp.GetAttributesResult;
    List<Attr> attrs = user.Attribute;

    String name = attrs.Find(
        delegate(Attr a) { return a.Name == "userid"; }).Value;
    String location = attrs.Find(
        delegate(Attr a) { return a.Name == "location"; }).Value;
    List<Attr> tags = attrs.FindAll(
        delegate(Attr a) { return a.Name == "tags"; });

    Console.Write("{0} ({1}) follows: ", name, location);
    tags.ForEach(
        delegate(Attr a) { Console.Write("{0} ", a.Value); });
    Console.WriteLine();
}
catch (AmazonSimpleDBException ex)
{
    String code = ex.ErrorCode;
    String message = ex.Message;
    Console.WriteLine("get attributes failed: {0}: {1}", code, message);
}
```

The C# client only returns the data in the form of a list. Since access to attributes by name is a common need, this example shows one way to do it. Here, `List.Find()` and `List.FindAll()` are called, each with a delegate holding a specific attribute name. This offers compatibility with C# 2.0+. With .NET 3.0+, LINQ offers a more concise syntax to accomplish the same thing.

GetAttributes Snippet in PHP

Here is the PHP code to call the `GetAttributes` operation:

```
$sdb = new AmazonSDB();
$get = $sdb->get_attributes('users', '1234567');
if ($get->isOK())
{
  $xml = $get->body;
  $name = attribute_values($xml,'userid');
  $location =  attribute_values($xml,'location');
  $tags =  attribute_values($xml,'tags');
  echo $name[0] . '(' . $location[0] . ') follows: ';
  foreach ($tags as $tag)
  {
    echo $tag . ' ';
  }
}
else
{
  echo 'get attributes failed: ';
  $error = $get->body->Errors->Error;
  echo $error->Code . ': ' . $error->Message;
}

function attribute_values($xml, $name) {
  $xml->registerXPathNamespace("sdb","http://sdb.amazonaws.com/doc/2009-04-15/");
  $query = '//sdb:Value[../sdb:Name/text() = "' .$name. '"]/text()';
  return $xml->xpath($query);
}
```

The Tarzan response to the `GetAttributes` request is a SimpleXML object, which you are on your own to parse. To handle single-valued and multi-valued attributes consistently, XPath was used here for pulling the values out. The function `attribute_values()` was created to return an array of values given the SimpleXML and an attribute name. One peculiarity of SimpleXML is that any default namespace in the document needs to be registered with a prefix before the `xpath()` function will work properly. Additionally this registration sometimes needs to be called before each XPath evaluation, and the XPath expression must incorporate the prefix.

Those details are tucked away within the `attribute_values()` function. One side effect that remains is that an array is returned even in the case of single-valued attributes. Note the indexed access to both `$name` and `$location`.

DeleteAttributes

The `DeleteAttributes` operation enables you to remove data that has previously been stored in SimpleDB. When you call `DeleteAttributes`, you must always pass a `DomainName` and an `ItemName`. All the processing for a delete will take place within the scope of that single item. `DeleteAttributes` also accepts several optional parameters that allow you to control the granularity of the delete. You can delete attributes at three levels of granularity, as follows:

- **Delete the whole item.** If you pass only the required `DomainName` an `ItemName` to the operation, all the attributes associated with that `ItemName` will be deleted.
- **Delete any and all values of specific attributes.** If you pass a list of `AttributeName` parameters in addition to the required parameters, only the attributes you specify will be deleted from that item.
- **Delete only specific attribute values.** If you want to delete individual values from a multi-valued attribute, you can do that by specifying both the `AttributeName` and `AttributeValue` to be deleted.

When the `AttributeName` and `AttributeValue` are passed to this operation, it is done in the form of a list. If you want to delete several, but not all, values from a multi-valued attribute, pass each name/value pair as a separate entry in the list. When you pass a list of attributes for deletion, you are permitted to pass a list where some of the attributes include only a name while others include both a name and a value.

In addition to granularity, you can also specify one of three types of condition for the delete to succeed. You can condition the delete on an attribute having a specific value, on an attribute being present regardless of the value, or on the fact that an attribute must not exist.

DeleteAttributes Parameters

The full list of parameters for the `DeleteAttributes` operation follows:

- **`DomainName` (required)**— The name of the domain where the attributes are stored. This parameter must be the name of a domain that has already been created at that endpoint.
- **`ItemName` (required)**— The unique key of the item associated with the attributes to be deleted.
- **`AttributeName` (optional)**— The name of the attribute. Passed as a list, alone, or in combination with a matching `AttributeValue`. Only used when some, but not all, attributes in this item are to be deleted.
- **`ExpectedName` (optional)**— The attribute name to check for a conditional write. This parameter is only valid when either an `ExpectedValue` or an `ExpectedExists` is also included. The maximum length of this parameter is 1,024 bytes.

- **`ExpectedValue`** (optional)— The value to check for a conditional write. This value must exist in SimpleDB in order for the conditional write to succeed. This parameter is only valid when an `ExpectedName` is also included. The maximum length of this parameter is 1,024 bytes.
- **`ExpectedExists`** (optional)— The flag to check for existence in a conditional write. When set to true, write only succeeds when the `ExpectedName` exists. When false, write only succeeds when the `ExpectedName` does not exist. This parameter is only valid when an `ExpectedName` is also included. The maximum length of this parameter is 1,024 bytes.
- **`AttributeValue`** (optional)— The attribute value to be deleted. Passed as a list in combination with an `AttributeName`. This is only used when some values, but not all, of a multi-valued attribute are to be deleted.

If you omit the optional `AttributeName` and `AttributeValue`, the whole item will be deleted.

> **Note**
>
> All the attributes you pass for deletion will be deleted as a unit. However, the update will not be immediately visible from calls to `GetAttributes` or `Select`. The time it takes for updates to become visible is subject to eventual consistency. Don't do a delete and then immediately do a get to make sure it worked without also passing the `ConsistentRead` flag. If the delete has not been fully processed yet, you will get back old values.

DeleteAttributes Response Data

No operation-specific data values come back from a successful `DeleteAttributes` call. If the call returns normally, the delete was processed and the full contents of the request will be processed. If the operation returns an error code, nothing will be deleted:

- **`NoSuchDomain`**— The error code returned if the `DomainName` parameter does not correspond to a domain created with your account at that endpoint.
- **`InvalidParameterValue`**— The error code returned if you pass an `ItemName`, `AttributeName`, or `AttributeValue` longer than 1,024 bytes in length.
- **`MissingParameter`**— The error code returned if you fail to pass a `DomainName` or an `ItemName`. The API of your client will protect you from getting this error.
- **`AttributeDoesNotExist`**— Returned when the `ExpectedExists` parameter was set to true and the `ExpectedName` or `ExpectedValue` did not exist.
- **`ConditionalCheckFailed`**— Returned when the `ExpectedName` parameter unexpectedly exists or when `ExpectedValue` was different than the actual value.
- **`MultiValuedAttribute`**— Returned when the conditional check was applied to a multi-valued attribute. Conditional checks can only be applied to single-valued attributes.

It is not an error to pass an `ItemName` that does not exist; neither is it an error to pass an `AttributeName` or `AttributeValue` that does not exist. If there is no matching item, the call will return normally and nothing will happen. If there is no match for an `AttributeName` or `AttributeValue` parameter, it will be ignored while other valid attributes in the request are deleted. However, a single oversized parameter will trigger an `InvalidParameterValue` and no deletes in the request will be processed.

DeleteAttributes Snippet in Java

This Java code shows how to delete one specific attribute value from an existing item:

```
SimpleDB simpleDB = new SimpleDB(accessKeyID, secretAccessKey);
try {
   Item oldItem = simpleDB.getDomain("users").getItem("1234567");
   boolean replace = false;
   ItemAttribute delAttr = new ItemAttribute("tags", "App-Engine", replace);
   oldItem.deleteAttributes(Collections.singletonList(delAttr));
   System.out.println("delete attributes succeeded");
} catch (SDBException e) {
   AWSError error = e.getErrors().get(0);
   String code = error.getCode();
   String message = error.getMessage();
   System.err.printf("delete attributes failed: %s: %s", code, message);
}
```

As with the `putAttributes()` method in Typica, `deleteAttributes()` is called by passing a list of `ItemAttribute` objects to an instance of the `Item` class. This example shows the deletion of a single value from the multi-valued attribute created in the `PutAttributes` code snippet. For the purpose of this example, the Java Collections API is used to wrap a single attribute in a list. To delete more than one attribute, include a list with an `ItemAttribute` for each one you want to delete. To delete the entire item, pass null to the delete method. To delete the entire set of values for an attribute, omit the specific value ("App-Engine" in this sample) and only pass the attribute name inside an `ItemAttribute`.

DeleteAttributes Snippet in C#

Performing the delete in C# can be done using the following code:

```
AmazonSimpleDB simpleDB = new AmazonSimpleDBClient(id, secret);
DeleteAttributesRequest request = new DeleteAttributesRequest();
try
{
    request.DomainName = "users";
    request.ItemName = "1234567";
    request.WithAttribute(
        new Attr().WithName("tags").WithValue("App-Engine"));
    simpleDB.DeleteAttributes(request);
```

```
    Console.WriteLine("delete attributes successful");
}
catch (AmazonSimpleDBException ex)
{
    String code = ex.ErrorCode;
    String message = ex.Message;
    Console.WriteLine("delete attribues failed: {0}: {1}", code, message);
}
```

A `DeleteAttributesRequest` object must be configured with a `DomainName`, an `ItemName`, and a list of attributes to be deleted. To delete more than one attribute, add more attributes to the list. To delete the entire item, omit the attribute list from the request. To delete all the values of a single attribute, omit the specific value ("App-Engine" in this sample) and only pass the name to the `Attr`.

DeleteAttributes Snippet in PHP

Here is the PHP version of delete:

```
$sdb = new AmazonSDB();
$delete = $sdb->delete_attributes('users', '1234567', array(
    'tags' => 'App-Engine'
));

if ($delete->isOK())
{
  echo 'delete attributes succeeded';
}
else
{
  echo 'delete attributes failed: ';
  $error = $delete->body->Errors->Error;
  echo $error->Code . ': ' . $error->Message;
}
```

Tarzan's `delete_attributes()` method takes a `DomainName`, an `ItemName`, and an array. To delete an individual value from a multi-valued attribute, as shown here, pass an associative array of names to values. To delete all values of some attributes, pass just an array of names. Omit the third parameter to delete the whole item.

BatchPutAttributes

The `BatchPutAttributes` operation enables you to store the data for multiple items in a single call. All the data for a `PutAttributes` request is limited to a single item, whereas `BatchPutAttributes` allows you to store up to 25 items. `BatchPutAttributes` has the same capabilities and parameters as `PutAttributes`, but it has very different performance characteristics. There is more initial request overhead when using `BatchPutAttributes` as compared to `PutAttributes`. Although you can use this operation to store anywhere from 1 to 25 items at a time, it is really only worth it when the number is closer to 25 than to 1. If you only have a few items to store, individual `PutAttributes` calls are likely to be faster and more efficient.

There is no rule set in stone dictating the minimum number of items needed to make `BatchPutAttributes` worth the overhead. In fact, the important factors for deciding whether to batch up your puts have nothing to do with performance. One factor is the way SimpleDB handles errors. All of the items in a batch will be rejected or accepted as a unit. Items in the batch will never be partially applied. If your application needs to take individual actions based on the results of each item in the batch (for example, generating responses for application users), individual errors can be disruptive because just one of them causes the entire batch to fail. You can avoid most of the errors that can occur with `BatchPutAttributes` by sending a request that respects the operation limits. However, you may have no way of knowing ahead of time that one of the items in the batch is already at the 256-attributes limit and the whole operation will fail. This makes `BatchPutAttributes` potentially cumbersome for updating existing items.

If you only have a few items at a time to store, if you are updating existing items or if you need to minimize latency, my recommendation is to use `PutAttributes`. If you have a large quantity of new data to store and total throughput is more important than individual request latency, `BatchPutAttributes` is a better option.

BatchPutAttributes Parameters

The parameters for `BatchPutAttributes` are the same as `PutAttributes`. The difference is that instead of a single `ItemName` with a list of attributes, you have an `ItemName` list each with a corresponding list of attributes:

- **`DomainName` (required)**— The name of the domain where the attribute(s) will be stored. This parameter must be the name of a domain that has already been created.
- **`ItemName` (required)**— The unique key with which a list of attributes will be associated. This parameter is passed as a list, each with an associated sub-list of attributes. This can be a new `ItemName` for the purposes of an insert or an existing `ItemName` for the purposes of an update. The maximum length of this parameter is 1,024 bytes. The maximum number of `ItemName` parameters for a single request is 25.
- **`AttributeName` (required)**— The name of the attribute, similar to a column name, passed as a list in combination with an `AttributeValue` and optionally a `Replace` flag. The minimum length is 1 and the maximum length of this parameter is 1,024 bytes.
- **`AttributeValue` (required)**— The value to be stored, passed as a list in combination with an `AttributeName` and optionally a `Replace` flag. This value must be present but it can have zero length (the empty string). The maximum length of this parameter is 1,024 bytes.

- **`Replace`** **(optional)**— The flag that specifies whether to replace existing attribute values or merely add a new attribute value. This parameter is passed as a list in combination with an `AttributeName` and an `AttributeValue`. If this parameter is not given, a default value of false is used.

Your SimpleDB client will expose a specific interface for passing data in a batch. This usually involves either a collection of objects, each representing an item, or a map object, where each `ItemName` maps to a collection of attributes. In addition to the limits on specific parameters to this operation, there is a 1MB limit on the total request size.

> **Tip**
>
> To get the best performance from `BatchPutAttributes`, there are two criteria that must be met. The items must not yet exist and no replace flag should be passed. Items meeting these conditions appear to be processed by a faster algorithm than other items.

BatchPutAttributes Response Data

No operation-specific data comes back from `BatchPutAttributes` when the call is successful. However, there are quite a few potential errors:

- **`InvalidParameterValue`**— Returned when the 1,024-byte size limit is exceeded by either the `ItemName`, the `AttributeName`, or the AttributeValue.
- **`DuplicateItemName`**— Returned when two or more of the items have the same `ItemName`.
- **`MissingParameter`**— Returned when any of the four required parameters to this operation are omitted. However, your SimpleDB client will require you to pass these values, so this is an error code you are unlikely to encounter in practice.
- **`NoSuchDomain`**— Returned when the domain name in the request did not exist at that endpoint.
- **`NumberDomainBytesExceeded`**— Returned when the 10GB per domain limit has been reached.
- **`NumberDomainAttributesExceeded`**— Returned when the 1 billion attributes per domain limit has been reached.
- **`NumberSubmittedItemsExceeded`**— Returned when you try to pass more than 25 items in a single request.
- **`NumberSubmittedAttributesExceeded`**— Returned when you try to pass more than 256 attributes for an item in a single request.
- **`TooLargeRequest`**— Returned when the size of your request is greater than 1MB.
- **`NumberItemAttributesExceeded`**— Returned when any items in the batch already have 256 attributes stored in SimpleDB. This error can occur even if you are reducing the number of attributes in the item by means of the replace flag.

The error message that accompanies this error code includes the offending `ItemName(s)`.

Of all the possible errors, only the last one cannot be prevented on the client side before the request goes out. Any error that occurs will cause the whole batch to be rejected and none of the items will be stored.

> **Note**
>
> All the items that you include with a `BatchPutAttributes` request will be accepted or rejected as a unit. However, the updated items will not be immediately visible from calls to `GetAttributes` or `Select`. The time it takes for updates to become visible to normal reads is subject to eventual consistency, while consistent reads are capable of returning the new data immediately in most cases.
>
> Moreover, although the individual attributes in an item will be updated atomically, some items may be updated before others. Therefore, you cannot use `BatchPutAttributes` to guarantee transaction semantics, or consistency between items.

BatchPutAttributes Snippet in Java

Following is Java code to put multiple items at once:

```
SimpleDB simpleDB = new SimpleDB(accessKeyID, secretAccessKey);


// a collection to map item name to attributes
Map<String, List<ItemAttribute>> items;
items = new HashMap<String, List<ItemAttribute>>();

items.put("Cigar001", buildRomeoCigar("No. 2", "90"));
items.put("Cigar002", buildRomeoCigar("Toro", "89"));
items.put("Cigar003", buildRomeoCigar("Churchill", "94"));
items.put("Cigar004", buildRomeoCigar("Robusto", "81"));

try {
   Domain domain = simpleDB.getDomain("products");
   domain.batchPutAttributes(items);
   System.out.println("batch put succeeded");
} catch (SDBException e) {
   AWSError error = e.getErrors().get(0);
   String code = error.getCode();
   String message = error.getMessage();
   System.err.printf("batch put failed: %s: %s", code, message);
}

private List<ItemAttribute> buildRomeoCigar(String make,String rating) {
   boolean replace = false;
   ItemAttribute[] attributes = new ItemAttribute[] {
      new ItemAttribute("ProductType", "Cigar", replace),
```

```
      new ItemAttribute("Supplier", "Romeo y Julieta", replace),
      new ItemAttribute("Make", make, replace),
      new ItemAttribute("Rating", rating, replace)
   };
   return Arrays.asList(attributes);
}
```

In Typica, gathering up items in the batch takes some setting up. A `Map<String, List<ItemAttribute>>` must be assembled and passed to the `batchPutAttributes()` method. To demonstrate one possible way to do this, the `buildRomeoCigar()` method handles the repetitive portion of the setup. After each attribute list is placed into the map (keyed by `ItemName`), the operation is invoked on an instance of the `Domain` class.

BatchPutAttributes Snippet in C#

Sending a batch of puts in one request is shown here using C#:

```
AmazonSimpleDB simpleDB = new AmazonSimpleDBClient(id, secret);
BatchPutAttributesRequest request = new BatchPutAttributesRequest();
try
{
    request.DomainName = "products";
    request.WithItem(buildRomeoCigar("Cigar001", "No. 2", "90"));
    request.WithItem(buildRomeoCigar("Cigar002", "Toro", "89"));
    request.WithItem(buildRomeoCigar("Cigar003", "Churchill", "94"));
    request.WithItem(buildRomeoCigar("Cigar004", "Robusto", "81"));

    simpleDB.BatchPutAttributes(request);
    Console.WriteLine("batch put successful");
}
catch (AmazonSimpleDBException ex)
{
    String code = ex.ErrorCode;
    String message = ex.Message;
    Console.WriteLine("batch put failed: {0}: {1}", code, message);
}

private ReplaceableItem buildRomeoCigar(String id, String make,
   String rating)
{
   RequestAttr[] attributes = new RequestAttr[] {
      new RequestAttr().WithName("ProductType").WithValue("Cigar"),
      new RequestAttr().WithName("Supplier").WithValue("Romeo y Julieta"),
      new RequestAttr().WithName("Make").WithValue(make),
      new RequestAttr().WithName("Rating").WithValue(rating),
   };
   ReplaceableItem item = new ReplaceableItem();
   item.ItemName = id;
```

```
    return item.WithAttribute(attributes);
}
```

The C# code is similar to the Java code, except that a list of `ReplaceableItem` objects is used in place of a map. The `buildRomeoCigar()` method reflects these differences, taking an additional argument and returning a single instance that wraps the attribute list. No specific data comes back from a successful invocation of this operation. The items will be stored, subject to eventual consistency.

BatchPutAttributes Snippet in PHP

Here is the PHP code to make a `BatchPutAttributes` request:

```
$sdb = new AmazonSDB();
$batch = $sdb->batch_put_attributes('products', array(
    'Cigar001' => array(
        'ProductType' => 'Cigar',
        'Supplier' => 'Romeo y Julieta',
        'Make' => '"No. 2',
        'Rating' => '90',
    ),
    'Cigar002' => array(
        'ProductType' => 'Cigar',
        'Supplier' => 'Romeo y Julieta',
        'Make' => 'Toro',
        'Rating' => '89',
    ),
    'Cigar003' => array(
        'ProductType' => 'Cigar',
        'Supplier' => 'Romeo y Julieta',
        'Make' => 'Churchill',
        'Rating' => '94',
    ),
    'Cigar004' => array(
        'ProductType' => 'Cigar',
        'Supplier' => 'Romeo y Julieta',
        'Make' => 'Robusto',
        'Rating' => '81',
    ),
));

if ($batch->isOK())
{
        echo 'batch put succeeded';
}
else
{
```

```
        echo 'batch put failed: ';
        $error = $batch->body->Errors->Error;
        echo $error->Code . ': ' . $error->Message;
}
```

The `batch_put_attributes()` method takes a domain and an array. The array is constructed in much the same way as all of the arrays passed to Tarzan SimpleDB methods. It is an associative array with `ItemName` mapped to an array of name/value pairs. Each attribute value in turn, can be an array of values, allowing for multi-valued attributes.

Most of the example code is spent explicitly building up this array. The hard-coded values used for illustration make the code look verbose, but in fact, it is the most concise client when assembling batch put data in practice.

Select

The `Select` operation enables you to run queries against the data you have stored in SimpleDB. `Select` uses query syntax similar to SQL select statements with which you may already be familiar. There is a lot to know about the `Select` operation. This section covers how to call the operation, including the parameters, the response data, and the errors. The next chapter provides in-depth coverage of the syntax, options, and limitations of `Select`.

Select Parameters

There are only three parameters to `Select`, and one of them is required:

- **`SelectExpression`** **(required)**— The expression used to find matching items.
- **`NextToken`** **(optional)**— A value obtained from a previous call to `Select` that returned only partial results. Passing this value back (along with a `SelectExpression` with the same `WHERE` clause) enables you to pick up with the next page of results.
- **`ConsistentRead`** **(optional)**— The flag that specifies whether to perform a consistent read. When true, the most recent data is returned. Setting this flag to true may result in greater latency and lower throughput.

`SelectExpression` is the text of your query and is the only required parameter. There is no `DomainName` parameter; however, the query must apply to a single domain. The domain is passed within `SelectExpression` in the `FROM` clause. If you need to query multiple domains, you must submit a separate query for each domain. There is no way to search multiple domains with one `Select` operation. The details of `SelectExpression` are covered in Chapter 4, "A Closer Look at Select."

Select Response Data

The response data for the `Select` operation is as follows:

- **`ItemName`**— The name of the item matching your query, returned in the form of a list in combination with an optional list of `AttributeName` and `AttributeValue` pairs for each `ItemName`. `ItemName` is always present in successful `Select` responses, even if not specifically requested.
- **`AttributeName`**— The name of an attribute associated with an item matching your query, returned as a list, always in combination with exactly one corresponding `AttributeValue`.
- **`AttributeValue`**— The value of an attribute associated with an item matching your query, returned as a list, always in combination with exactly one corresponding `AttributeName`.The data is returned in the form of plain string data.
- **`NextToken`**— A token indicating that a partial result has been provided. Passing this token to a subsequent `Select` call (along with a `SelectExpression` with the same `WHERE` clause) will enable you to pick up where the last response left off.

The bulk of the response data is a list of items matching your query.The item forms the basis not only of `Select` responses but of query processing as well.All the results are matched at the item level. No comparisons are done between items, and there are no joins.

An `ItemName` value is always present in a successful response that contains data. It is possible for a response to contain no data if there are no matching results or if the time-out limit is reached before any matching items were found.You can request only `ItemName` without additional attributes, but if you do request attributes, they are returned as pairs with an `AttributeValue` for each `AttributeName`. In the case of multi-valued attributes, a name/value pair (with the same name) is returned for each value.The order of returned attributes is not guaranteed to match either the order you used in `PutAttributes` or the order in which you request them in your `SelectExpression`.

`NextToken` acts as a control valve.The SimpleDB service tailors the size of `Select` responses to keep request processing within service limits.There are two hard service limits on the `Select` operation.The maximum response size is 1MB; the limit on query processing time is 5 seconds.There is also a configurable limit on the number of items in the response, with a default of 100 and a maximum of 2,500. If SimpleDB reaches any of these limits while building your `Select` response, the partial results are returned with a `NextToken`.You can then repeatedly call `Select` again, passing the `NextToken` value with the same `SelectExpression`, and you will get the next page of results, either the full list of matches or until a limit is reached.A response without a `NextToken` signals the end of the matching items.

`NextToken` is useful for more than just restriction enforcement by SimpleDB.When used in conjunction with the `LIMIT` clause, it allows some of the functionality of a database cursor, but without maintaining continuous resource allocation on the server.You can fetch query results one at a time or in pages up to 2,500 at a time.You can seek ahead in the results to an absolute or relative position, and you can use concurrency to pull down many pages of results in parallel.

A specific `NextToken` value does not have an explicit expiration but it is not advisable to store it for later use. Added or deleted items matching your query, which appear earlier in your results than the `NextToken` value you may have saved, will not be reflected in subsequent calls that pass the old `NextToken` value. For example, if you scroll ahead 1,000 in a query result, the `NextToken` value will be pointing to item 1,001. If you store that token and use it later, `Select` will still resume at the same item and it will return fresh data. However, updates and deletes may have caused that item to now be at position 500 or 5,000 rather than the initial 1,001. It is best to use it for a follow-up request and then discard it, getting a new one when you need it.

What follows is the lengthy list of all possible error codes returned by `Select`:

- **`MissingParameter`**— Returned when you omit the `SelectExpression` parameter.
- **`InvalidParameterValue`**— Returned when your `SelectExpression` uses a `LIMIT` that is not between 1 and 2,500 or an attribute name longer than 1,024 bytes.
- **`InvalidNextToken`**— Returned when you pass a `NextToken` that is not valid.
- **`InvalidNumberPredicates`**— Returned when your `SelectExpression` contains more than 20 predicates.
- **`InvalidNumberValueTests`**— Returned when your `SelectExpression` contains a predicate with more than 20 comparisons.
- **`NoSuchDomain`**— Returned when `SelectExpression` contains a domain that does not exist at that endpoint.
- **`RequestTimeout`**— Returned sometimes when the query processing takes longer than 5 seconds.
- **`TooManyRequestedAttributes`**— Returned when `SelectExpression` requests more than 256 attributes.
- **`InvalidQueryExpression`**— Returned when your `SelectExpression` contains a syntax error.

The error you will most commonly see when learning to use the `Select` syntax is the last one, `InvalidQueryExpression`. It is triggered for all types of mistakes you can make using SQL syntax constructs, which are not valid in SimpleDB queries.

Select Snippet in Java

This code prints out a single page of select results in Java:

```
SimpleDB simpleDB = new SimpleDB(accessKeyID, secretAccessKey);
try {
   Domain domain = simpleDB.getDomain("users");
   printSelectResults(domain.selectItems("SELECT * FROM users", null));
} catch (SDBException e) {
```

```
    AWSError error = e.getErrors().get(0);
    String code = error.getCode();
    String message = error.getMessage();
    System.err.printf("select failed: %s: %s", code, message);
}

private void printSelectResults(QueryWithAttributesResult result) {
    for (String itemName : result.getItems().keySet()) {
        System.out.println(itemName);
        for (ItemAttribute attr : result.getItems().get(itemName)) {
            System.out.println("\t" + attr.getValue());
        }
    }
}
```

The sample code defines the `SelectExpression`, makes the call to `Select`, and prints the results all in the same line. The `null` parameter after `SelectExpression` in the call to `selectItems()` is the only other valid `Select` parameter: `NextToken`. It is `null` here since this is an initial query. The `printSelectResults()` method iterates through the map keys, which are returned by Typica. This map is in the same format that `batchPutAttributes()` required in the previous Java snippet. Each key is an `ItemName` and maps to an `ItemAttribute` list. The map could be empty if no items matched the `SelectExpression` query.

The prior example used a simple query. The following example shows how to fetch multiple pages of select results using `NextToken` and uses a much more specific query:

```
String select =
    "SELECT Rating, Make, Supplier" +
    "  FROM products" +
    " WHERE Rating > '85'" +
    "   AND ProductType = 'Cigar'" +
    " ORDER BY Rating DESC" +
    " LIMIT 2";

SimpleDB simpleDB = new SimpleDB(accessKeyID, secretAccessKey);
try {
    Domain domain = simpleDB.getDomain("products");
    String nextToken = null;
    QueryWithAttributesResult results = null;
    do {
        results = domain.selectItems(select, nextToken);
        printSelectResults(results);
        nextToken = results.getNextToken();
    } while (nextToken != null);

} catch (SDBException e) {
    AWSError error = e.getErrors().get(0);
```

```
    String code = error.getCode();
    String message = error.getMessage();
    System.err.printf("select failed: %s: %s", code, message);
}
```

In looking at the query, notice that there are only three specific attributes being requested. This query matches up with the data stored in the prior `BatchPutAttributes` code sample. Four items were stored in the "products" domain. This query only requests the items with a rating greater than 85 and only two at a time. Because three of the four items meet these criteria and the limit per page is two, the first `Select` will come back with two items and a `NextToken` allowing retrieval of the final match.

A loop is used when calling `selectItems()` to handle an unknown number of pages. The result is printed for each iteration, and the fresh `NextToken` is attached to the request. The existing request is reused with the same `SelectExpression` still attached. When no token comes back, the loop falls through.

Also, notice that the `query` calls for results to be sorted by rating, from high to low. When you run this sample code, look to see that all the ratings are greater than 85 and that they are sorted.

Select Snippet in C#

This is the C# version of the single-page query code:

```
AmazonSimpleDB simpleDB = new AmazonSimpleDBClient(id, secret);
SelectRequest request = new SelectRequest();
try
{
    request.SelectExpression = "SELECT * FROM users";
    printSelectResults(simpleDB.Select(request).SelectResult);
}
catch (AmazonSimpleDBException ex)
{
    String code = ex.ErrorCode;
    String message = ex.Message;
    Console.WriteLine("select failed: {0}: {1}", code, message);
}

private void printSelectResults(SelectResult result)
{
    foreach (Item item in result.Item)
    {
        Console.WriteLine(item.Name);
        foreach (Attr attr in item.Attribute)
        {
            Console.WriteLine("\t{0}", attr.Value);
        }
    }
```

```
}
```

Each item returned from a single request is printed out in turn. The code for handling multiple pages is shown here:

```
String select =
   "SELECT Rating, Make, Supplier" +
   "  FROM products" +
   " WHERE Rating > '85'" +
   "   AND ProductType = 'Cigar'" +
   " ORDER BY Rating DESC" +
   " LIMIT 2";

AmazonSimpleDB simpleDB = new AmazonSimpleDBClient(id, secret);
SelectRequest request = new SelectRequest();
try
{
    request.SelectExpression = select;
    SelectResult result = null;
    do
    {
        result = simpleDB.Select(request).SelectResult;
        printSelectResults(result);
        request.NextToken = result.NextToken;
    } while (result.IsSetNextToken());
}
catch (AmazonSimpleDBException ex)
{
    String code = ex.ErrorCode;
    String message = ex.Message;
    Console.WriteLine("select failed: {0}: {1}", code, message);
}
```

Notice that this query is only requesting three specific attributes. This query matches up with the data stored in the `BatchPutAttributes` code sample. With this query, only the items with a rating greater than 85 are requested and a limit of two items is specified. Because only three of the four items meet these criteria, the first select will contain two items, and a `NextToken` and a second call, which includes that token, will contain the final item.

A loop is used when calling `Select()` to handle an unknown number of pages. During each loop, results are printed, and the `NextToken` is attached to the existing request. The existing request is reused since it is still configured with the same `SelectExpression`. When no token is returned in the response, the loop falls through.

Also, notice that the `SelectExpression` value calls for results to be sorted by rating, from high to low. When you run this sample code, look to see that all the ratings are greater than 85 and that they are sorted.

Select Snippet in PHP

In PHP, you can fetch a single-page query like this:

```
$sdb = new AmazonSDB();
$select = $sdb->select('SELECT * FROM users');

if ($select->isOK())
{
  print_select($select);
}
else
{
  echo 'select failed: ';
  $error = $select->body->Errors->Error;
  echo $error->Code . ': ' . $error->Message;
}

function print_select($select)
{
  foreach ($select->body->SelectResult->Item as $item)
  {
   echo $item->Name . PHP_EOL;
   foreach ($item->Attribute as $attr)
   {
     echo "\t" . $attr->Value . PHP_EOL;
   }
  }
}
```

The code for multiple pages follows:

```
$select =
   "SELECT Rating, Make, Supplier" .
   "  FROM products" .
   " WHERE Rating > '85'" .
   "   AND ProductType = 'Cigar'" .
   " ORDER BY Rating DESC" .
   " LIMIT 2";

$sdb = new AmazonSDB();

$opt = null;
do
{
  $select_result = $sdb->select($select, $opt);
  if ($select_result->isOK())
  {
         $next_token = $select_result->body->SelectResult->NextToken;
```

```
        print_select($select_result);
    }
    else
    {
      echo 'select failed: ';
      $error = $select_result->body->Errors->Error;
      echo $error->Code . ': ' . $error->Message;
    }
    $opt = array('NextToken' => $next_token);
} while ($next_token != null);
```

The variable `$select` now contains a query that is only requesting three specific attributes. This query matches up with the data stored previously using the `BatchPutAttributes` code sample. The query criteria only allow items with a rating greater than 85 and limit two per response. Because only three of the four items meet these criteria, the first select will contain two items and a `NextToken`, and a second call, which includes that token, will contain the final item.

A loop is used when calling `select()` to handle an unknown number of pages. In the body of the loop, results are printed and the current `NextToken` value is attached to the existing request. The existing request is reused with the same `SelectExpression`. The loop falls through when a token fails to come back.

Also, notice that the `query string` calls for results to be sorted by rating, from high to low. When you run this sample code, look to see that all the ratings are greater than 85 and that they are sorted.

Summary

Each of the nine SimpleDB operations has been covered with multiple code samples. There are many ways to use and combine the basic operation building blocks, and this chapter has only scratched the surface of what is possible. One operation in particular is worthy of considerably more attention, and that is `Select`. The `Select` operation is important to just about any use of SimpleDB. Its syntax is similar enough to SQL users that it is easy to learn the basics. However, the next chapter will cover some subtleties in the `Select` API. All the details will be provided, along with a large serving of practical advice.

4

A Closer Look at Select

The last chapter concluded with the mechanics of how to call `Select`, how to handle the errors, and how to access the returned items. This chapter continues that discussion with a walkthrough of the query language used in `Select`.

The chapter starts by walking through the five clauses that make up the `Select` query language; some are required or conditionally required. Following that is the section on data formatting. Nowhere in SimpleDB is the storage format of your data more important than in the realm of queries. We then get into the nitty-gritty details of what SimpleDB allows when forming expressions and predicates. The comparisons and operators and how they interrelate is the real heart of `Select`. The chapter concludes with a look at query performance: how to measure it, how to improve it, and how to avoid the common query pitfalls.

No two people have the same level of technical background. To account for this, the chapter follows a logical progression and is filled with small query examples. Seasoned SQL veterans will be in familiar territory with this query language and may easily skim over the simpler bits by scanning the titles and examples. Be aware, however, that despite the similar syntax, there are differences.

Select Syntax

The SimpleDB `Select` API uses a query language that is similar to the SQL `Select` statement. This query language makes SimpleDB Selects very approachable with a gentle learning curve. Keep in mind, however, that SimpleDB applies the familiar SQL terminology to domains and attributes rather than tables and columns. These structures are analogous but not identical. Also, be aware that there are no relations, joins, or sub-selects.

Select But Not DELETE

The presence of an API roughly based on SQL Select statements might lead you to wonder if there are also other SQL statements available, such as `INSERT`, `UPDATE`, or `DELETE`. The answer is no; these other SQL statements do not exist in the SimpleDB API. All data, whether new or updated, is stored via calls to `PutAttributes`.

Notably, the bulk deletion capabilities of the SQL `DELETE` statement are absent. Data can be stored or retrieved in batches, but items must be deleted one at a time. AWS has a good record for responding to customer feedback, so if this becomes a highly requested feature, it could be the target of a future enhancement.

Required Clauses

The minimal Select statement consists of two required clauses—an output selection clause followed by a domain clause:

```
SELECT * FROM users
```

The output selection clause begins with `SELECT` and is followed by a specification of what output is requested. The domain clause begins with the keyword `FROM`, and because there are no joins in SimpleDB, ends with the case-sensitive name of a single domain to be queried. The domain name is subject to the Select quoting rule for names.

Select Keywords

Keywords in the SimpleDB Select query language will be uppercase in the examples in this book for clarity. However, they are not case sensitive. You can use lowercase in your own Select statements. A complete list of the Select keywords follow:

SELECT	IN	NULL
FROM	BETWEEN	ORDER
WHERE	AND	BY
LIKE	EVERY	DESC
INTERSECTION	IS	ASC
OR	NOT	LIMIT

In addition, lowercase is used for all of the example domain names and attribute names to easily distinguish between user-defined names and query language keywords.

Select Quoting Rule for Names

Domain names and attribute names can appear in various places within a Select expression. Depending on the characters used in a name, it may need to be quoted. The character used for quoting names is the backtick (`). Quoting is optional if the name contains only letters, numbers, dollar signs, and underscores and does not start with a number. In all other cases, the name must be quoted with backtick characters.

If the name itself contains the backtick character, it must be escaped when used in a Select expression. Substitute each backtick with two backtick characters. For example, the attribute name `cats`dogs` becomes ``cats``dogs`` when quoted and escaped according to this rule.

Note

SimpleDB imposes much stricter naming requirements on domain names than on attribute names. Because of the restricted set of characters, quoting is less frequently an issue for domain names. The only characters allowed in a domain name that trigger the name quoting rule are the dot (.), the hyphen (-), and a leading number.

Output Selection Clause

The initial clause of the `Select` expression lists the data to be returned for matching results. There are three ways to specify the output, all beginning with the `SELECT` keyword, as follows:

- Use an asterisk to request all attributes:

```
SELECT * FROM users
```

- Use a function to request the count:

```
SELECT count(*) FROM users
```

- List the attribute names specifically:

```
SELECT id, name FROM users
```

The size of an explicit attribute list can be from 1 to 256. A comma is used to separate attribute names when more than one is given. Each attribute name in this list is subject to the `Select` quoting rule for names (as discussed previously). You can also request the item name by including the function `itemName()` in the list:

```
SELECT itemName() FROM users
SELECT itemName(), `date-created` FROM users
```

Count Response Formatting

When you use `count(*)`, the format is special and perhaps a bit unexpected. The actual response is in the same structured XML data format as all `Select` responses with items and attributes. Here is an example:

```
<Item>
    <Name>Domain</Name>
    <Attribute>
        <Name>Count</Name>
        <Value>49</Value>
    </Attribute>
</Item>
```

> The thing to realize is that there is no real item named "Domain" with an attribute named "Count." This is just SimpleDB formatting the count data into the existing response format. Realize that to get the count data, depending on your SimpleDB client, you may need to make a call like the following in order to get the count value:
>
> ```
> result.getItems().get("Domain").getAttribute("Count")
> ```

WHERE Clause

Select expressions with only Domain and Output selection clauses will return all the items in the domain. The inclusion of a WHERE clause enables you to restrict query results to a smaller subset. This clause is not required in a Select expression, but if you do include it, it must immediately follow the Domain clause.

In a WHERE clause, you define a set of criteria, and only items that match all the criteria are returned. For example:

```
SELECT * FROM users WHERE `last-name` = 'Smith'
```

When using this Select expression, only those items having an attribute named "last-name" with a value of "Smith" are returned. Here, the equals operator is used in a single comparison. There are a dozen other operators that you can use, and you can combine multiple comparisons in a single query. The WHERE clause really forms the heart of the Select expression, determining the exact set of return items. A detailed discussion of the available operators and how they are used in the context of comparisons occurs later in this chapter.

Notice that both the attribute name and the attribute value are quoted in the preceding example. But also notice that they are quoted using a different character. Attribute names used in a WHERE clause are subject to the Select quoting rules for names. Attribute values, on the other hand, are subject to the Select quoting rules for values.

Select Quoting Rules for Values

Unlike names that require quoting only when they contain certain characters, attribute value constants must always be quoted within a Select. You can quote values using either the single-quote character (') or the double-quote character ("):

```
SELECT * FROM users WHERE lastname = "O'Reilly"
SELECT * FROM users WHERE displayname = 'Mikki "The Great" Larkin'
```

If the chosen quote character appears within the constant, it must be escaped. As with the backtick name quoting, escaping is accomplished by replacing each quote character with two of that same quote character. Rewriting the preceding examples using the alternate quote character for each demonstrates the escaping:

```
SELECT * FROM users WHERE lastname = 'O''Reilly'
SELECT * FROM users WHERE displayname = "Mikki ""The Great"" Larkin"
```

These two rewritten examples are functionally identical to the preceding two. The choice of quote character has no bearing on the outcome of the Select. It is merely a matter of preference or convenience.

Sort Clause

When you call `Select`, SimpleDB does not guarantee the order of the results by default. For example, when using the following Select expression, SimpleDB does not sort the results by `name` or `score`:

```
SELECT name, score FROM tests WHERE score < '75'
```

A common misconception is that results in this case are returned in the same order that you inserted them. However, this is untrue. The default ordering is undefined. If you want to guarantee the order of results, you must include a sort clause.

The beginning of the sort clause is signaled with the keywords `ORDER BY` immediately following the `WHERE` clause. You must specify a single attribute name to sort on, and may optionally include a sort direction. An example follows:

```
SELECT name, score FROM tests WHERE score < '75' ORDER BY score
```

This is the same as the prior `Select` example, but now the results will come back sorted on the value of the `score` attribute. The default sort direction is ascending if no direction is given.

```
SELECT name, score FROM tests WHERE score < '75' ORDER BY score ASC
```

This `Select` is the same as when no direction was given. To sort the results descending, use the following:

```
SELECT name, score FROM tests WHERE score < '75' ORDER BY score DESC
```

Guaranteeing the Existence of Sort Attributes

Because SimpleDB never enforces any form of required attributes, your sort attribute might not exist in all items that match your query. If this were to happen, SimpleDB would not really have a meaningful way to order your search results. You could argue that items without the sort attribute should just be included at the end of the results, following the properly sorted results. However, inclusion at the end does nothing to solve the ordering problem between those items at the end. Moreover, what is worse, if the sort attribute is not in the list of requested attributes, there would be no way of knowing which of the result items had the sort attribute and which did not.

SimpleDB prevents these issues by only accepting a sort when the accompanying `WHERE` clause guarantees the presence of the sort attribute. Constructing such a `WHERE` clause is not difficult. In fact, merely including the sort attribute in a comparison will usually be sufficient to meet this requirement. The preceding example does just this:

```
SELECT name, score FROM tests WHERE score < '75' ORDER BY score
```

Restricting matches to those items with `score` less than `'75'` implicitly requires the attribute to exist.

Here is a variation that fails this test and returns an `InvalidQueryExpression` response:

```
SELECT name, score FROM tests WHERE score < '75' ORDER BY name
```

In order to sort by `name`, the `WHERE` clause must guarantee the existence of that attribute. In this case, we do not want to add any specific restrictions to the `name`, so the inclusion of the `IS NOT NULL` comparison fits well:

```
SELECT name, score FROM tests
WHERE score < '75' and name IS NOT NULL ORDER BY name
```

The `IS NOT NULL` operator filters out any item from the results that does not have a value for that attribute.

Note

Even though SimpleDB does not perform any schema enforcement, you may still implement required attributes in your application logic. When this is the case, it means you must have gone to the trouble of ensuring that a certain attribute always has a value. It can then seem redundant and awkward that now, after having done all that, you must also add another comparison to your query that will always evaluate to true.

Consider, however, that the SimpleDB service has no way of knowing what your code is doing now, or what someone else might change it to do in the future. The sorting in SimpleDB was designed to return a meaningful response in all cases. Absent a schema, there needs to be some mechanism to achieve it.

LIMIT Clause

The final clause in a `Select` is the optional `LIMIT` clause. The function of this clause is to cap the number of results that will come back from a single call to `Select`. The syntax for this clause calls for the keyword `LIMIT` followed by a number from 1 to 2500. Here is an example of `LIMIT` used in a query:

```
SELECT name, score FROM tests WHERE score < '75' LIMIT 5
```

Every `Select` call is subject to limit processing; if you do not include a limit clause, SimpleDB uses the default `LIMIT` value of 100. As the search results list is built during query processing, if the size of the list reaches the limit value, processing stops and the results are returned. When this happens, SimpleDB returns a `NextToken` along with the search results. The `NextToken` is an encoded value that holds the state information necessary to allow processing to continue where it left off without the need for SimpleDB to maintain the state on the back-end. This allows SimpleDB, internally, to handle any query using any node that has a replica of the target domain. From the client side, query processing can be resumed by making the same Select call and passing the `NextToken`.

The `LIMIT` clause is most obviously useful in those cases where you truly care about only a certain number of results. For instance, when you want the name of the student with the highest test score:

```
SELECT name, score FROM tests
WHERE score IS NOT NULL ORDER BY score DESC LIMIT 1
```

Another common use of the `LIMIT` clause is to display search results one page at a time. Setting the `LIMIT` to the size of the page lets you fetch the exact number of results required for a single page. In this case, storing the `NextToken` will enable you to fetch the next page more conveniently in response to a future request.

It is true that a query `LIMIT` is always in effect, whether default or specified, but there are three cases where the `Select` call returns early without reaching the `LIMIT`. The first case is when the number of items matching the query is smaller than the `LIMIT` value. You will know this has occurred when the search response does not contain a `NextToken`. The lack of a `NextToken` always signals that the full set of matching items has been returned.

The other two cases where `Select` returns before the `LIMIT` is reached involve other service limits that take precedence. To maintain quality of service, SimpleDB enforces a per-request restriction on the size of the response it is willing to send, and on the length of time it is willing to spend. If the response size grows to 1MB or takes 5 seconds, the call will return immediately with the results thus far, if any, and a `NextToken`. Consequently, when you use a `LIMIT` clause to retrieve a specific number of items, you must check for the presence of a `NextToken` and the number of items in the response to determine if you need to issue another call to fetch the outstanding results.

Formatting Attribute Data for Select

All attribute values in SimpleDB are stored as raw character strings. This eliminates the work and deployment headaches of rolling out cluster-wide schema changes. However, the lack of a robust set of data types has serious implications for data formatting and queries.

The issue with string data, with regard to queries, is the way comparisons are performed, alphabetically from left to right. For instance, the following two names sort correctly, even though they are different lengths:

```
Samson
Samuels
```

Each character is compared in turn; this is a standard string comparison in all programming languages and databases. However, numbers and dates do not fare as well with lexicographical comparisons:

```
156
89
```

A left-to-right comparison wrongly places 156 as less than 89 after looking at only the first character because 1 comes before 8. The problem, of course, is that the decimal places need to be aligned, and left padding with zeros solves this problem:

```
156
089
```

This task is normally handled by a type system, which defines an exact length for each numeric type. Because SimpleDB has no type system, it remains an issue for the application developer to handle. Unfortunately, there is more to deal with than length and alignment.

Integer Formatting

The standard way to store integers is in a binary format using from 1 to 8 bytes depending on the maximum value that must be handled. Standard binary formats are not an option in SimpleDB where all data is stored as text. It is possible to define ad-hoc formats for individual attributes as you go, and this can be tempting especially when representing quantities like years where no additional formatting or padding is necessary. However, a more general approach is to use formats compatible with standard integer sizes.

The two most commonly used integer sizes in programming languages are 32-bit ints and 64-bit longs. When represented as text without thousands separators, these integers take 10 and 19 characters to represent. Using zeros to pad all integers to a length of either 10 or 19 characters allows SimpleDB querying to avoid decimal misalignment for all same length comparisons. Here is an example of a large and a small 32-bit integer padded to 10 characters:

```
2147483647
0000001010
```

Mere padding works perfectly well for positive integers, but it does not solve the sorting problem for negative numbers. With negative numbers, a higher number represents a lower value. The number -5 is numerically less than -1, which is exactly backward from lexicographical order. The solution is to add an offset value to every number before you zero-pad and store it. The offset must be large enough to push all possible values out of the negative. The lowest possible value for a 32-bit integer is -2147483648, so the smallest possible offset is 2147483648. The smallest 64-bit offset is 9223372036854775808. Using the minimum offset, the examples of large and small 32-bit integers become the following:

```
4294967295
2147484658
```

This minimum offset approach is now fully functional for integer queries when combined with padding. One unfortunate side effect of using this format is that the resulting numbers bear no resemblance to the original values. It could be argued that this is a storage format and that it, like a binary format, does not need to be readable. That argument carries weight, if you have the type information and the tools to automatically format all your numeric data and rewrite your application queries into this format. If you do not have the tools, manual offsetting becomes necessary in order to transform the base query you intend:

```
SELECT * FROM vendors WHERE `year-to-date-billing` > '25000'
```

into the offset and padded query that is required:

```
SELECT * FROM vendors WHERE `year-to-date-billing` > '2147508648'
```

No one reading that query without a calculator is going to know what the value is. If there is an arithmetic error, it is unlikely to be caught by someone reviewing the code. Although it is not possible to preserve readability for all values, we can tweak our offset value to make the positive numbers readable. If you take the minimum offset, with lengths of 10 and 19 characters, and round it up to the next digit, you get a much friendlier number. The 10-digit 2147483648 becomes the 11-digit 10000000000, and the same technique applies to 64-bit values. Here is the base query repeated from the previous example:

```
SELECT * FROM vendors WHERE `year-to-date-billing` > '25000'
```

The constant must now be converted into a new format and the result is almost as easy to understand:

```
SELECT * FROM vendors WHERE `year-to-date-billing` > '10000025000'
```

Ignoring the leading 1 does not require as much mental overhead. In addition, errors are detectable without a calculator. Negative numbers, however, retain the readability problem. A practical solution to that problem could come in the form of smart client-side tooling that can handle the formatting automatically.

Floating Point Formatting

Floating-point numbers pose an additional challenge. Not only can the numbers be positive and negative, but the exponents can be positive and negative as well. What is more, it is not possible to use an offset because of the limit on the number of significant digits that can be preserved. Adding a large offset to a tiny fractional number could potentially wipe out the data. There is no standard string representation for floating point numbers suitable for lexicographical sorting that preserves numerical order. But remember that special formatting is only necessary for numeric attributes that will be in query comparisons or sorts. If you do not need to compare the floating point numbers in a query, then you are free to represent them in any format.

If, however, you do need to compare them, a method exists to represent floating point numbers in a string format such that lexicographical text ordering rules result in proper numeric ordering. This format is not a standard, and it accommodates decimals only up to 64-bits in length. Doug Wood published the technique in a proposed Internet draft in 1999 entitled: "Directory string representation for floating point values." The draft appears to have received no additional work or approval beyond the initial proposal, which expired in 2000. Although the text of the proposal contains a few minor errors, the idea is suitable as a basis for query-friendly floating-point storage format in SimpleDB. However, the level of complexity puts its implementation beyond typical application development. This type of formatting is most appropriately found in a SimpleDB client.

Date and Time Formatting

As with all data stored in SimpleDB, there is no intrinsic type information associated with attributes that contain timestamps, and so there are no official requirements on how you must store them. Like other types of data, the only caveat is that if you want to use query comparisons and sorting with your date values, they must be formatted to sort chronologically.

The Internet standard timestamp format is defined by RFC 3339 and is widely used for the storage and transmission of dates over the Internet. Applying a string sorting to timestamps in RFC 3339 format results in a time-ordered sequence. This is the exact behavior required for query comparisons in SimpleDB. Because it is easy to create date strings in this format using built-in programming language facilities, this is the recommended format for all SimpleDB timestamp data.

RFC 3339 is a profile of the much more complex, international standard ISO 8601 and is based on the Gregorian calendar and the 24-hour clock. Timestamp rendering is in a format of increasing precision from left to right, for example:

```
2010-07-16T12:20:30Z
```

This example shows the four-digit year, two-digit month, and two-digit day separated with hyphens. The literal 'T' character marks the beginning of the time data. The hours minutes, and seconds each span two digits and are separated by a colon. All of these components are fixed length. The full four-digit year must always be used, and each of the remaining two-digit values must be zero padded when less than 10. The format ends with the time zone indicator—in this case, 'Z'.

Because of the convoluted and unpredictable nature of local time rules, the format is based on Coordinated Universal Time (UTC). If the timestamp directly represents a time in UTC, the literal 'Z' character appears immediately after the time to indicate no time zone offset. If the time is in a different time zone, the difference between that zone and UTC is represented as an offset in hours and minutes, as in the following example of a timestamp in the U.S. Eastern time zone:

```
2010-07-16T07:20:31-05:00
```

Notice that this example represents a point in time one second later in absolute time than the preceding one, but the difference in time zone causes it to appear earlier in a lexicographical sort. Converting all times to UTC is important for timestamps that represent absolute times—for instance, when used to track peak global request volume for a web service. If the timestamp is specifically representing a point in time in a certain time zone, retain the local time along with the appropriate offset. This would be the case, for example, if the data contains the time of day that subjects are awake during a sleep study. However, be aware that all timestamp data, whether local or absolute, can be meaningfully compared only to other timestamps in the same format. So, choose a single convention for each SimpleDB attribute name and stick with it.

This format also makes it possible to represent higher-precision timestamps using fractions of a second. To include this information, expand the seconds beyond two digits by placing a trailing dot (.) followed by the fractional digits:

```
2010-07-16T12:20:30.453Z
```

Case Sensitivity

All query comparisons in SimpleDB are case sensitive and based entirely on the byte value of each UTF-8 character. This means that the value 'Jones' is not equal to the value 'jones', because of capitalization. More than that, because all the uppercase letters have lower byte values than the set of all lowercase letters, inconsistent capitalization results in a sort order that appears wrong to case-insensitive eyes. The following example shows three names sorted alphabetically using UTF-8:

```
Richards
Stewart
jagger
```

In an ascending sort, all lowercase values will appear strictly after all uppercase values. This is the lexicographical order for UTF-8. If a case-insensitive query is needed, the solution is to store both the original value and a lowercase counterpart of the value, directing all query comparisons to the lowercase version. Here is an example:

```
SELECT name FROM members WHERE `name-lowercase` < 'watts' ORDER BY `name-lowercase`
```

Be sure that all string literals are also lowercase in these types of comparisons.

Expressions and Predicates

The earlier section on the `WHERE` clause briefly alluded to predicates and the comparisons within them. This section offers a more thorough dissection of this important area.

A predicate is the set of comparisons made for a given attribute within the `WHERE` clause. Here is an example of a single predicate with a single comparison:

```
WHERE date LIKE '200%'
```

Multiple comparisons for the same attribute are combined into the same predicate. For example:

```
WHERE date LIKE '200%' OR date > '1989'
```

This is still one predicate because all the comparisons are for a single attribute. You can use the operators `AND` and `OR` to separate comparisons. The order of comparison evaluation is from left to right within a predicate. Specify comparison grouping using parenthesis, as follows:

```
WHERE date LIKE '200%' OR (date > '1989' AND date <= '1993')
```

The SimpleDB query engine uses the full predicate to filter the target attribute values. Only items where the target attribute values match the full predicate are returned.

The `WHERE` clause can contain more than one predicate. Additional predicates are formed by including comparisons for different attributes, as follows:

```
WHERE date LIKE '200%' OR (date > '1988' AND date <= '1993')
AND `last-name` = 'Bush'
```

This is a two-predicate query. You are permitted to have as many as 20 predicates in a `Select` expression. Depending on how selective the predicates are, adding additional predicates can negatively influence query performance.

There is an index in SimpleDB for each attribute, and so an index is available for each predicate. SimpleDB attempts to choose the best index for each query as part of the execution plan. Indexes are discussed in greater depth later in this chapter.

Simple Comparison Operators

If you have even a passing familiarity with programming languages and with SQL, there will be a number of simple operators you will expect to have available when constructing query expressions. Most of these have been shown in example queries already. The discussion of comparison operators begins with this set of basic ones shown in Table 4-1. All of these operators take an attribute name or the function `itemName()` on the left side and a constant value on the right. You cannot put an attribute name or `itemName()` on the right side of the operator.

Table 4-1 **Simple Comparison Operators**

Operator	Meaning
=	Matches equality
!=	Matches inequality
>	Matches values strictly greater than
>=	Matches values greater than or equal to
<	Matches values strictly less than
<=	Matches values less than or equal to

Range Operators

When constructing a query using a simple operator, you can define an open-ended range with an expression like `length <= '10000001024'`. To define a more narrow range, you can add a second expression by using `AND`:

```
SELECT * FROM posts WHERE length <= '10000001024' AND length >= '10000000140'
```

The combination of a greater-than comparison and a less-than comparison gives you the flexibility to specify any range you may need. You can specify multiple ranges by enclosing each range in parenthesis and using the `OR` operator between them, as in a previous example.

If, however, you have the common case where you want to specify a range in terms of <= on one side and >= on the other, you can use the `BETWEEN` operator:

```
SELECT * FROM posts WHERE length BETWEEN '10000001024' AND '10000000140'
```

This will return the same results as the prior example. The `BETWEEN` operator takes the standard attribute name or `itemName()` on the left and two constant values separated by `AND` on the right. The comparisons matches are inclusive: Values are returned when they are equal to or between the constants.

IN() Queries

In addition to queries that match all values in a range, there is a function that lets you match a set of discreet values. The `IN()` function has the same capabilities as a long set of equals operators. Instead of writing this:

```
WHERE id = '1' OR id = '2' OR id = '3' OR id = '4' OR id = '5' OR id = '6'
```

The `IN()` function lets you abbreviate it like this:

```
WHERE id IN('1','2','3','4','5','6')
```

The `IN()` function takes an attribute name or `itemName()` on the left and a list of comma-separated constants between the parenthesis. You can include a maximum of 20 values as arguments to the function. When using the `itemName()` function with the `IN()` function, it serves as a form of batch get.

> **Tip**
>
> It is an error to attempt more than 20 comparisons in a single predicate within the `WHERE` clause of a `Select`, and each parameter to the `IN()` function counts as a comparison. If you use all 20 available `IN()` parameter slots, you will not be able to use any other comparisons in that predicate. However, comparisons with different attribute names are in different predicates. A maximum of 20 predicates are allowed. This means that you can make up to 20 separate calls to `IN()` each with 20 constants within a single Select, provided that no single attribute exceeds the comparison limit. Nevertheless, just because it is possible does not mean it is advisable. Examine the performance implications carefully before relying on such a technique.

Prefix Queries with LIKE and NOT LIKE

The `LIKE` operator enables you to perform substring text matching as part of a query. When using `LIKE`, the percent sign (%) is the wildcard character. To do a prefix search, put the prefix constant followed by the percent sign within single quotes:

```
WHERE name LIKE 'Wil%'
```

You can also place the wildcard character at the beginning:

```
WHERE name LIKE '%Smith'
```

Finally, it can be placed at both the beginning and the end:

```
WHERE name LIKE '%son%'
```

Placing the wildcard at the beginning will circumvent the index and potentially require a table scan. This is an expensive operation, so combining it with other selective comparisons is advised.

You can use the NOT LIKE operator to match values that do not contain the specified constant. The usage is the same as LIKE:

```
WHERE name NOT LIKE 'Wil%'
WHERE name NOT LIKE '%Smith'
WHERE name NOT LIKE '%son%'
```

IS NULL and IS NOT NULL

Testing for the existence of an attribute within an item can be an important condition, and the IS NOT NULL operator enables you to do it. This operator takes a single attribute name on the left side:

```
SELECT * FROM users WHERE `email-confirmation` IS NOT NULL
```

The IS NULL operator matches items where no value exists for the named attribute:

```
SELECT * FROM users WHERE `email-confirmation` IS NULL
```

A common use for IS NOT NULL, beyond the need to find values that exist, is to meet the requirement of the WHERE clause to ensure that the sort attribute exists in all matching rows:

```
SELECT * FROM users ORDER BY `date-created`
```

This Select returns an InvalidQueryExpression error because you cannot sort on an attribute that might not exist in the result set. The easiest way to ensure existence is add an IS NOT NULL test, as follows:

```
SELECT * FROM users WHERE `date-created` IS NOT NULL ORDER BY `date-created`
```

Multi-Valued Attribute Queries

An important consideration overlooked thus far is what is going to happen with these comparisons for attributes with multiple values. The answer to this question is that each attribute value is considered individually. Given the function of the operators as discussed so far, considering each attribute individually might seem to be problematic. It is very possible to construct queries where every item with a multi-valued attribute is returned. For example:

```
SELECT * FROM products WHERE count != '100'
```

Every item with more than one value for the "count" attribute will end up matching this comparison because each value is required to be unique, therefore at least one value must be something other than "100." It is just as easy to construct a query that is guaranteed to match none of the items with multiple values. For example, consider that the "products" domain has multi-valued attribute named "size" containing the available sizes for the product. A query to find products that come in both medium and small might look like this:

```
SELECT * FROM products WHERE size = 'S' AND size = 'M'
```

The preceding query can never return any values because both comparisons are evaluated together as a single predicate against each value.

Beyond the mere avoidance of these problems, it is necessary to have a way to isolate the individual values of a multi-valued attribute for comparison purposes. The SimpleDB query language defines two constructs to fill this role: the `INTERSECTION` operator and the `EVERY()` function.

Multiple Predicate Queries with the INTERSECTION Operator

To illustrate the difference between the single predicate queries demonstrated so far and multiple predicate queries, here is an example scenario. Consider a data set where each item in the domain is the bookmark of a user. One of the attributes stored with a bookmark is tag. Tag can hold multiple values as defined by the user. This is the query to get bookmarks with a specific tag—for instance, "css":

```
SELECT * FROM bookmarks WHERE tag = 'css'
```

This works as expected for both items with a single tag attribute set to "css," as well as items with many tag values, one of which is "css". You can run into problems when selecting for bookmarks tagged with two specific tags, though:

```
SELECT * FROM bookmarks WHERE tag = 'css' AND tag = 'html'
```

This does not work, and is actually guaranteed to always return no results. The reason has to do with the way SimpleDB executes queries. This query, as well as each of the queries shown so far, is a single predicate query. The behavior of the single predicate is as if all of the conditions are combined into exactly one matching expression for each attribute in the query. These expressions are then compared against each value individually. In the case of the preceding tag query, the two conditions `= 'css'` and `= 'html'` are applied together to each value of the tag attribute. Because no value can equal both "css" and "html," the query always returns empty.

To solve this problem and apply criteria separately to multiple attribute values, the `INTERSECTION` operator enables the definition of multiple predicates. To adjust the previous example:

```
SELECT * FROM bookmarks WHERE tag = 'css' INTERSECTION tag = 'html'
```

Now, instead of two comparisons combined into a single predicate, two separate predicates are created. The behavior of `INTERSECTION` is as if each predicate is run as a separate query in isolation and then only those items appearing in the results of both predicates are returned. The limit on the number of predicates is 20.

Dividing a query into predicates with the `INTERSECTION` operator is mainly useful for selecting attributes with multiple values. Although `INTERSECTION` can also be used with single value attributes, it does not produce different results than using AND, but usually results in slower performance.

Selection with EVERY()

SimpleDB enables you to query for multi-valued attributes based on matching a comparison against every existing value, rather than just a single value, which is the normal case. To match a comparison for every attribute value, you use the `EVERY()` function. The function is applied to the attribute name or the `itemName()` on the left side of the comparison operator. For example:

```
SELECT itemName() FROM bookmarks WHERE every(tag) LIKE '%.net'
```

The preceding query will not return items that have a tag value ending in ".net" if other tag values with other endings are present. The `EVERY()` function can be applied to any of the operators, but it does not make sense to use it with `IS NULL` or `IS NOT NULL`:

```
SELECT * FROM students WHERE EVERY(`test-score`) BETWEEN '060' AND '075'
SELECT * FROM students WHERE EVERY(`project-status`) IN('Completed','Excused')
```

When `every()` is combined with the equals operator, it enables you to select items with exactly one value and no more:

```
SELECT itemName() FROM bookmarks WHERE EVERY(tag) = '.net'
```

Query Results with the Same Item Multiple Times

One of the things to consider when constructing a query for multi-valued attributes is whether it is possible for more than one value to match the criteria. Consider, again, the fictitious domain that contains tagged bookmarks. A query to find all bookmarks with a tag that ends with ".net" might look like this:

```
SELECT itemName() FROM bookmarks WHERE tag LIKE '%.net'
```

Table 4-2 shows the sample data set for these examples.

Table 4-2 **Sample Data: Items with Multiple Tag Values**

ItemName	Tag
Bookmark0	ajax.net vb.net
Bookmark1	asp.net aspx
Bookmark2	jscript.net json.net
Bookmark3	system.net c#

First, you can see that all four of these bookmarks have at least one tag ending in ".net". The second thing to notice is that Bookmark0 and Bookmark2 each have two different tags that match the criteria. When SimpleDB processes this `Select`, it will return each of these items exactly once without duplicates:

```
Bookmark0
Bookmark1
Bookmark2
Bookmark3
```

The issue arises, however, if the `Select` contains a sort directive on the attribute with multiple matches. Suppose the query is changed to read as follows:

```
SELECT itemName() FROM bookmarks WHERE tag LIKE '%.net' ORDER BY tag
```

Now you can see that returning each matching bookmark exactly once is going to be a problem. Looking at the sorted list of tag values, Bookmark0 has a match at the beginning with "ajax.net" and the end with "vb.net". And this is exactly how SimpleDB responds to this query: with Bookmark0 at both the beginning and the end of the list:

```
Bookmark0
Bookmark1
Bookmark2
Bookmark3
Bookmark0
```

An additional point to notice is that Bookmark2 also has two tags that match the criteria but it is not returned twice in the results. The reason for this is that the two tags ("jscript.net" and "json.net") appear sequentially in the sorted list. SimpleDB returns the same item as many times as necessary to satisfy the `ORDER BY` directive. However, separate entries for the same item are never generated for sequential `ORDER BY` matches.

Improving Query Performance

The SimpleDB Select query language does not have nearly the same capabilities as SQL and so is less powerful, but by the same token avoids a great deal of the complexity. However, there is still quite a bit that you can do with it, and the opportunity certainly exists to create complex and inefficient queries. Achieving good query performance is important no matter what database or query language you use.

Attribute Indexes

An index is a database structure that occupies extra storage space for each record in exchange for faster data retrieval. In a typical relational database, you must create and manage each index. This includes deciding which and how many columns to index for each table, as well as when to rebuild the indexes. Performing the analysis on each index to determine if it is providing more benefit than cost can be time consuming.

SimpleDB, on the other hand, handles all the indexing automatically. An index is created for each unique attribute name in a domain, and every attribute value is added to the index at the time you store it. There is no maintenance work of any kind for you to do with SimpleDB indexes. Although you do not have any direct control over the indexing, having an understanding of it can help you get the best performance from your queries.

Composite Attributes

Although SimpleDB indexes every value, at the time of this writing, each index is single column only. AWS has suggested that they may implement multi-column indexes in the future, but not the immediate future.

In the meantime, AWS suggests a way to simulate a multi-column index with an additional synthetic attribute. This technique is specifically applicable to queries where the main two attributes being searched are in the following configuration: one of them is being tested for equality, the other one is a being tested for a range. These types of queries are actually quite common, depending on the type of data you are storing. An example is searching for items with the following:

```
userid='001' and  viewcount > '00025'
```

If this query becomes too slow, you can simulate an index that spans both the `userid` and `viewcount` columns by creating a synthetic attribute. The synthetic attribute is just a new attribute created programmatically that is a duplication of the two field values concatenated together. This value must be set for all items, and it must be kept up to date any time one of the values gets a `PutAttributes` call.

In this example, the new attribute might be called `` `userid-viewcount` `` and the Select statement to take advantage of it would have this comparison in it:

```
`userid-viewcount` LIKE '001%' and  `userid-viewcount` > '00100025'
```

Now both comparisons are using the same index. The actual `userid` has to be concatenated at the beginning of the constant `viewcount` value. This works with the strictly greater-than operator because the first comparison has already restricted the output to only those items with `userid` beginning with "001".

Performance with Composite Attributes

Generating an extra attribute for each item that must be kept in sync is an advanced technique. It has the drawbacks of added complexity, added storage, and added bandwidth. You definitely want to be sure it is warranted before you implement it. If you do implement it, keep the following in mind:

- You probably will only need to span two columns with this technique. It is possible to do more, if there is more than one equality test in your Select, but using two may well be sufficient.
- Although you are using the synthetic field for comparison and maybe even for sorting, you do not need to return that field and then parse it; just return the regular fields as you need them.

- The performance gain from this technique will depend on the correlation between the two values. If there are only a few items for each `userid` or only a few items meeting the `viewcount` criteria, this technique will not be very helpful. If there are many matches to both criteria but very few in common, this method should give a sizeable performance boost.
- In the case where the composite criteria is highly selective, many more comparisons can safely be added to the query without hurting performance, since only a few items remain to be filtered.
- You must be careful to maintain the proper field length and padding when composing a composite attribute from formatted numbers or dates.

Judicious Use of LIKE

When using the `LIKE` operator in a query to do wildcard matching, placement of the wildcard character can have a large impact on performance. Placing the wildcard at the end, as in this example comparison, allows the index to be used when fetching results:

```
`name` LIKE 'Will%'
```

This yields excellent performance. However, placing a wildcard character at the beginning like the following prevents the index from being used and results in a full table scan that, depending on your data, is likely to be much slower:

```
`email` LIKE '%@yk.com'
```

This is true with the character data indexed in any type of database, since characters are indexed from left to right. In a relational database, you have the option to create an index with the characters reversed and use a reverse function in the SQL query. You create a similar solution in SimpleDB. You cannot create the reversed index directly and there is no built-in reverse function, but if you include an extra attribute in your data with values that you have reversed yourself, the reversed index will be created for you automatically. This leaves you with the task of reversing the literal value in the query yourself, as in the following:

```
`email-reversed` LIKE 'moc.ky@%'
```

Now the wildcard is back on the right where the index can be used.

Of course, you don't want to be in a situation where you have constant string values typed into a hard-coded query in reverse. In reality, you don't want to be in a situation where any of the query literals are hard coded; they should be passed in as parameters. Publicly available SimpleDB clients today do not have support for a programming model where prepared statement type constructs are used. Hopefully, in the near future, such functionality will be available. It is conceivable that client-side functions like `reverse()` could also be implemented in such a layer.

Performance with LIKE

When you need to improve the performance of queries that contain `LIKE`, following are some good recommendations, in order of importance:

1. First, use the wildcard character at the end.
2. If you have to use it at the front, measure the performance and do not automatically assume it will be too slow.
3. Try to find ways to add additional comparisons to the predicate to allow the index to be used and reduce the breadth of the scan.
4. If it is still too slow, also consider the request volume of that query before you start adding new synthetic fields.
5. If you need to, add an additional field that is the reversal of an actual field.

Like composite attributes, be aware that you will need to keep this extra field updated with the real value at all times. However, do not feel bad about it as if it were strictly a hack. It is no more overhead than adding an extra index; it is just more work because you have to manage it yourself. In an ideal world, some form of data mapping layer would handle this for you on the client, and you would not have to deal with it yourself.

Running on EC2

Deploying your application into the Amazon cloud is going to result in less network latency for all of your requests when compared to accessing SimpleDB via the public Internet. That doesn't mean that latency will necessarily be bad from the outside. It certainly doesn't mean it is ill-advised to store and retrieve your data from the outside. Nevertheless, it does mean that for the absolute best performance, if EC2 deployment is an option, you would be wise to test the differences and consider it.

This is especially true for high levels of small, concurrent requests, for which SimpleDB is optimized. Small and quick requests actually incur a much higher Internet latency penalty when viewed as a percentage. For example, if you make a Select call that takes 50ms to process but then incur an additional 100ms round-trip Internet latency, the overall call time increased by 200%. However, if you issue a `Select` that takes 3000ms, adding on 100ms latency only results in a 3.3% increase.

Skipping Pages with count() and LIMIT

When you need to access data that is many pages deep into a result set, the round-trip costs can really kill performance. A shortcut to quickly accessing these pages relies on the way `NextToken` works. A `NextToken` combines the SimpleDB internal search state with the `WHERE` and sort clauses. Each `NextToken` can be used to resume the query by passing it back along with the original query string. However, as long as the `WHERE` clause and the sort attribute do not change (and obviously the domain), you are free to change the return attributes and the `LIMIT`.

The technique for skipping ahead involves setting the `LIMIT` to the number immediately preceding the first value you need. If you want to start at result number 1000, you initially set the LIMIT to 999. Instead of including the actual attributes you want, you set the output listing to count(*). This has the effect of reducing both the query time and the response size. Once the query returns with the desired count, you resubmit it with the actual attribute list and the desired LIMIT value.

Even though count(*) is faster, there is no guarantee that it will reach your target LIMIT on the first request. In this situation, the response will contain both a count value and a NextToken. The count value is the actual number of items counted in the current NextToken. To make this tactic work, you will need to call your query in a loop and maintain a total count so far until you reach the desired LIMIT. Although you very well may reach the correct LIMIT on the first try, you have to be prepared for the cases where you do not. At each page along the way, reevaluate the temporary LIMIT and adjust as necessary. To expand on the last example, if you need the actual query to start at result number 1000, your temporary LIMIT is 999. If the first response with count(*) comes back with a count value of 501, you will need to submit another request with count(*) and an updated LIMIT of 498.

> **Tip**
>
> The maximum LIMIT you can specify within a normal Select expression is 2,500, but this limit does not apply when you use count(*). You can specify a LIMIT value as high as you need but the actual count value returned will depend on the complexity of the query and the data in your domain. Even with simple queries on a large domain it is unusual to get back a count greater than 200,000, but sometimes you may get back zero. Remember to use a loop and update the total count so far and compute a new LIMIT value during each iteration.

Measuring Select Performance

When there is an issue with query speed, you need to be able to measure the performance accurately. The measuring itself is unusually not difficult, but there can be subtle issues that prevent you from getting accurate numbers. You really do need accurate numbers in order to make the best optimization decisions, so here is a checklist of performance measurement items to consider. It is likely that many of these points will seem obvious:

- Isolate the Select call from any code interference. There are a number of different ways that unwanted code interference could be occurring. The SimpleDB client you are using could be having issues with connection management, running out of available threads or available connections. Memory leaks in your code or in the SimpleDB client may eventually influence performance. Excessive object creation or parsing inefficiencies while handling large result sets can make queries appear artificially slower in proportion to the size of the XML response. Monitoring memory usage and trying queries in a different client or tool can help rule out these issues.
- Isolate the SimpleDB response time from the network latency. Accessing SimpleDB from an EC2 instance in the same region as your domain will always provide the

lowest latency. Even in the cases where your application is not deployed to Amazon's cloud, it can still be beneficial to do some performance testing there. The benefit is that latency is eliminated as a variable from the equation. By using EC2 Spot Instances, it might be possible to do the testing for less than three cents an hour.

- Be aware of service-level spikes. There are rare delays that occur when making SimpleDB requests that result in response times being much longer than normal. They might not happen for days at a time, and when they do happen, they seem to occur for 1 in 10,000 to 1 in 5,000 requests. This is not Internet latency, since it happens on EC2, but it could be network related. Make sure that you can reproduce any slow query times you see and that it was not just an outlier.
- When using test data, make sure it is as close as possible to the size and composition of the production data. This problem could bite you in either direction. `Select` performance decreases as the size of the domain increases. If your test data set is smaller than the production data set, testing could give you a false sense of query performance. Alternately, some queries will take much longer based on the composition of your data. For example, if your test data has a disproportionately large number of users with the email address "example@example.com," then multi-predicate `Select` statements using the email address attribute could end up with a workload that is much higher in test than in production.
- Be aware of SimpleDB caching that may be occurring behind the scenes. Although the implementation details of the service are not known, based on observation, it seems clear that there are different levels of performance based on how frequently or how recently certain domains or queries are used. These differences appear consistent with caching. Ensure a period of "warming up" while testing queries by issuing the Select calls for several minutes at a level consistent with how actual usage might occur prior to taking measurements. This is especially true with test data that sits idle much of the time.
- Eliminate any unnecessary `NextToken` paging. When a query returns partial results along with a `NextToken`, subsequent calls may not be passing the correct `LIMIT` value. When this happens, it is an issue with the SimpleDB client or with how you use it. The problem is when the results come back with a number just shy of the `LIMIT`, whether default or explicit. For example, if you omit the `LIMIT`, SimpleDB uses the default of 100. If the response contains only 95 items, because of a large response size or a long processing time, the SimpleDB client may be configured to automatically send a follow-up call with the next token. Alternatively, you may make the follow-up call yourself. This is a perfectly valid action, but if the `LIMIT` on the subsequent call is not being set to 5 and remains as the default 100, this could result in net doubling of the response time. If the first 100 is all that is needed, the query time will be artificially high.
- Compare both box usage and actual execution time. The box usage number returned from each `Select` call is an estimation derived from both the complexity of

the query and the data in the domain. Although it is not an actual measurement, it is still useful for comparison between different queries called against the same domain.

Given that query times tend to increase as domain size increases, keeping historical performance data can yield key insights when combined in a report along with historical domain metadata. If you are able to log automated performance measurements, these reports can become trivially easy to produce.

Automating Performance Measurements

Logging query performance measurements automatically is a powerful solution that delivers great insight with very little effort. You could do this yourself by adding a layer on top of any SimpleDB client, but it is best done as a built-in part of the client. It is convenient when the client logs details of each request and response in a way very similar to the way a web server logs requests.

Web server logs have long been used to analyze data about web sites and about website users. At a high level, web server logs are stored as text files with relevant information listed about each HTTP request, with one line per request. It is an easy-to-parse format, and tools exist to read these log files using a user-specified configuration of fields and to generate reports. Having a large set of historical data is useful for capacity planning and tracking performance metrics over time. It also provides you with specific information for your own troubleshooting efforts and when dealing with AWS support.

Following is a list of useful fields you might want to log:

- **Timestamp**— Logging each request time with a precision down to the millisecond enables you to establish a definitive request order. If you do not need a high level of detail, consider using a less-granular timestamp.
- **Application**— If you have multiple applications aggregated into a single report, or if your SimpleDB access is from a web service with more than one client application, this field is useful.
- **Action**— The SimpleDB API call being made is important information. It gives you the ability to pick out the Select calls for analysis.
- **Domain**— If request levels to or response times from a certain domain are higher, you want to know about it.
- **Select query**— This is only included for Select calls. Knowing the exact query turns out to be very useful for performance analysis. Including the entire raw query is a good first step. However, an even better format for the Select statement is in a prepared statement format with the parameters at the end. This lets you see overall numbers for queries that differ only on parameter value, while preserving the ability to drill down into detail.
- **Bytes transmitted**— This is useful for self-monitoring bandwidth usage, as well as identifying `BatchPutAttributes` calls near the size limit.

- **Bytes received—** This field allows for correlation between response size and response time. It also lets you self-monitor bandwidth and identify Select responses being paged at the 1MB limit.
- **HTTP response code—** The magnitude of the HTTP response code indicates the general class of response. The 200s mean success, the 400s indicate a client error, and the 500s indicate a server error. Of particular interest are the HTTP 503 throttling response rates.
- **Box usage—** This is good for query performance analysis and for self-monitoring account charges.
- **Request id—** This lets you correlate errors on your end with the SimpleDB logging that AWS support people are able to view.
- **Actual response time—** This is the time in milliseconds between when the last request byte is written to when the last response byte is read. The more accurately you can collect this number, the better.

You may want to log more fields or fewer. But having these logs can provide a great deal of insight when dealing with a black box service like SimpleDB that offers very little configuration and very little insight as to what is going on.

Summary

In this chapter, the SimpleDB `Select` query language has been explained with a level of detail that should empower you to construct your own queries, measure their performance, and take the necessary action to improve them. One thing you may have noticed is the discussion on performance largely ignored issues of application design, data sharding, and caching. This was not an error of omission, but an intentional focus on the base performance of queries. There are many actions that can be taken at a higher level to improve performance, but after those things have been done, performance still needs to be addressed at the basic level. Addressing that need was part of this chapter. Higher-level performance enhancements, for `Select` and other calls, is the subject of Chapter 9, "Increasing Performance." The next chapter deals with the details of bulk data operations.

5

Bulk Data Operations

This is a short chapter about the various ways to get large quantities of data into and out of SimpleDB. Actually, this really should not be a short chapter. There should be a data import and export facility built into SimpleDB, but there is not. As a result, migrating data in and out of SimpleDB on a large scale is more cumbersome than it ought to be. There is no easy or automated way to do this. Unlike S3, where you can upload the data directly or have physical storage media delivered to an AWS data center and imported for you, with SimpleDB, it is more likely that you may have to write your own tool to do this. The two available approaches to accomplish these tasks are manually with Select and `BatchPutAttributes` calls, or with a third-party product handling it for you.

At the time of this writing, there are two SimpleDB tools boasting backup and restore/import features. They turn up easily in a web search. At this point in time, however, neither of them is mature or feature rich. You may have to deal with tool issues, such as not being able to select the domain name for a data restore, or a requirement to back up all of your domains, rather than selected domains.

Third-party tool developers who might consider filling this gap are in a bit of an awkward position. One of the problems is that SimpleDB is still in beta, and AWS has been tight-lipped with the SimpleDB roadmap. It was expected that a bulk-load facility would be released, and after a time, `BatchPutAttributes` was subsequently added to the API. It is not known if that is the final word on import or if the API will be enhanced with another solution that is yet to be released. This makes it risky to invest the engineering costs to build a robust and general-purpose import/export tool as a product because a new SimpleDB feature could make it obsolete.

Because of this environment, the current crop of third-party tools has evolved out of homegrown solutions designed for the needs of internal projects that have later been polished and released into the market. Before looking at these tools, let's consider the type of issues involved in writing your own import tool.

Importing Data with BatchPutAttributes

Getting your data into SimpleDB is such a common issue for new SimpleDB users that it is surprising that it has not yet been adequately addressed with an official tool. It is in the best interest of AWS to allow easy data import. They shouldn't be merely allowing it, however; they should be "enabling" it, with a robust and fully featured solution. In the meantime, you don't have those solutions, and you may need to create your own.

In the absence of an official data import tool or API operation, the most effective remaining option is `BatchPutAttributes`. `BatchPutAttributes` is much faster for adding a large number of items than individual `PutAttributes` calls. However, there is some baseline overhead associated with the call that typically makes it a bit too sluggish for time-sensitive tasks like building a web page.

The following sections cover the things that you should think about while designing your import tool, even though you probably will not need to implement all of them. Depending on your data, each feature may be required or optional. If you are building a tool for one specific data import run, you have the freedom to meet the specific needs of the project. Alternately, a more general solution could be useful across different projects. The more of these features that you implement, the more general purpose your import tool will be.

Calling BatchPutAttributes

The simplest import solution is to loop through your data rows and call `BatchPutAttributes` with bundles of 25 items. This solution is simple to write, but making the calls sequentially in a single thread is not going to be the fastest solution. Nevertheless, don't be fooled by the myriad of considerations presented here; the simple solution could still be your best option.

Consider the development time for some of the advanced options and weigh that against the time that a simpler solution could be chugging away at the import. Unless you have reuse in mind, spending two development days to achieve an eight-hour import time savings may be a bad trade. It might be difficult to know how long it will take to work the multi-threaded kinks out of your tool, but you can figure out pretty quickly the rate at which the simple solution can insert items.

Mapping the Import File to SimpleDB Attributes

If you are writing an import tool, you likely have a file that you want to import. You need a way to specify which fields in the import file should be included or excluded. You also need a way to designate which field to use as the item name, or that one should be generated.

The last chapter established the need to apply formatting to certain types of attributes that will be in queries. Consistency is required in the application of that formatting, and this begins with the initial import. Having a way to specify which format to apply to each field is part of the mapping. For instance, integers may need padding or offsetting, and floats may need only formatting for parts of searches. Multiple columns or single columns with delimited values may need to be placed into multi-valued attributes.

At its simplest, mapping data can be just a list of field names and types and even then only for fields that need special handling. It might be easy to put this type of project-specific mapping information directly into your tool's source code, but this is the type of thing that frequently needs tweaking, and allowing the mapping to change separately from the source code will go a long way toward making the tool reusable.

Supporting Multiple File Formats

Many different data export file formats are in common use. The list of popular file formats includes delimited flat files, JSON, and XML. Although you may only have one that you need to support right now, separating the code that processes that format can leave a nice space to hook in other formats later.

A key concern is the backup format you will use for your production domains. If the formats are compatible, your import tool can become your restore tool. One way to handle this is to use a base format for imports that is very SimpleDB-centric with formatting and multi-valued attribute support already in place, without the need for mapping. Support for other file formats can then be added later by creating a single new conversion utility for the target format.

This approach has the benefit of allowing you to support only the file formats that you actually need and enabling you to verify the full result of the mapping and formatting before you begin to upload data. This verification would be additional code to write, but if you opt to write it, it would be useful as part of a backup file verification process in the future.

Storing the Mapping Data

You have a few options when it comes to how to store the mapping between the import file and SimpleDB attributes. It could just be parameters to the import tool stored in a script or you could make a separate file format for it. In more complex cases, having a separate file capable of representing relationships (like XML or JSON) can be valuable.

These complex cases include times where data is bound for different domains, different regions, and even different accounts. In this scenario, you may need a way to store a hierarchy of parameters in your mapping configuration. This might include cases where separate accounts are used to support various deployment scenarios like development, testing, staging, and production.

Reporting Import Progress

For small deployments, the time requirement to process the import might not be a concern. For larger data sets that will take hours to import, the percentage of import completion is valuable information. As you design and implement your tool, consider ways to display the import progress or status.

It is always possible to run queries on the domain to count the number of records. Eventual consistency normally gives you a count that is only a few seconds old. This can be sufficient provided you know the total number of records to be imported or even when you just need to verify that the import tool is still adding records.

Creating Right-Sized Batches

When creating an import tool using `BatchPutAttributes`, the 25-item limit on a single batch is immediately obvious. However, the second limit on batch size is one that you might not be aware of, and, depending on your data, you might not run into it during testing. You might not even encounter it immediately during actual use. If you are going to reach this limit, you don't want it to happen while in the middle of importing a large data set.

The maximum request size of a `BatchPutAttributes` call is 1MB. It is uncommon to reach this limit. Part of the reason is that, although 256 attributes are allowed per item, actual data commonly has many fewer than that, typically less than a few dozen. However, be aware that the SimpleDB request-formatting characters are included in the 1MB limit, and that the length of those character strings are longer for `BatchPutAttributes` than for other operations. For example, a small name/value pair might look like this:

```
CreationDate=2010-08-01T13:3A37:3A59.723
```

It shows up within a `BatchPutAttributes` request in a much more verbose and URL-encoded form like this, taking up more than double the size of the raw data:

```
&Item.17.Attribute.14.Name=CreationDate
&Item.17.Attribute.14.Value=2010-08-01T13%3A37%3A59.723
```

The typical ways to reach the 1MB limit are by filling up many attributes to the 1,024 limit or by using all 256 attributes in an item. Doing either of those things does not guarantee that you will reach this limit, just that your chances are increased. The only step you need to take is to check the request size before you send it and move items that overflow the limit into the next batch.

Managing Concurrency

Even in the case of inserting large numbers of items with `BatchPutAttributes`, there is still an obstacle to maximizing throughput. The difficulty is in the fact that the call is not blazingly fast, but it can be called concurrently. This is both a benefit and a drawback. The drawback is the difficulty in the implementation of your own multithreaded import tool. The threads need to be coordinated, and some state will need to be shared across threads.

Multithreaded code is error prone to write even for concurrency experts. This is the type of task that, for typical application developers, is distinctly non-simple. Application developers who are unfamiliar with writing multi-threaded code will find it to be difficult to write a custom multi-threaded import tool. Although it may be difficult depending on your background, it is certainly not impossible. If you take on this task and need some guidance, here are some suggestions for getting it done.

Storing data in SimpleDB using the `BatchPutAttributes` call can yield higher data throughput versus plain `PutAttributes` calls by a factor of six or seven. In addition, the box usage charges for batches are in the neighborhood of 30% to 40% less. Even so, you are going to want to issue these calls concurrently to get the best data transfer rate.

Concurrency is going to involve either multiple threads or non-blocking I/O. The choice is going to depend on which SimpleDB client you use, unless you write your own. The number of simultaneous connections required to maximize throughput depends, in large part, on the size of the items. There is no single optimal number for all situations. The best way to manage this is to track throughput dynamically as you increase the concurrency and be prepared to back off when you encounter either throttling with 503 ServiceUnavailable errors, or HTTP timeouts.

Resuming a Stopped Import

If all goes well, each import will complete successfully without any problems. However, a persistent network outage, a corrupt record, or a software defect could cause your import to fail. With large imports, the cost of restarting from the beginning after a problem is high. Consider keeping track of the import progress and saving it to disk regularly for use as a resume point. This could be simple in the case of data that comes with predefined row IDs, or more complex if you have to insert auto-numbering as part of the import.

Either auto-numbering will need to be deterministic to support resumption, or some sophisticated query logic will need to be added to ensure that items are not added multiple times with different item names. If you use the technique of pre-converting the import file into a SimpleDB-friendly format, as mentioned earlier, the automatically generated item name situation will be much easier to handle.

Verifying Progress and Completion

When the import is complete, you will naturally want to check SimpleDB to verify that all the records were added. Even when the import tool includes a status message that verifies success, direct confirmation from the database is desirable. When performing this verification, use calls to `Select` and not calls to `DomainMetadata`.

The `DomainMetadata` call has the exact information you would want for verifying an import, including the number of items and unique attribute names in the domain. However, the metadata is not guaranteed fresh. It is subject to caching much longer than eventual consistency delays. The correct way to an up-to-the-minute count of items in a domain is to issue a query using the count function. For example:

```
SELECT count(*) FROM `product-details`
```

This query returns the number of items in the domain, subject to paging with a returned `NextToken`. The proper handling of paging with the count function is documented in the previous chapter. Minimally, you need to resubmit the query with the returned `NextToken` until the query returns without a `NextToken`. The total count is the sum of counts returned with each page. Using `ConsistentRead` with these Select statements will yield verification that is not subject to errors arising from eventual consistency delays.

Properly Handling Character Encodings

All of your data in SimpleDB is stored as UTF-8 character strings. Be careful with the handling of character data to be sure you don't encode it to a platform-default encoding when the proper encoding is UTF-8. Character encoding involves the conversion of characters to bytes. A common place this issue comes up is in the code that converts text back and forth between String objects and byte arrays. This process always involves a character encoding, and if one is not specified explicitly, a default encoding is being used, and it may not be what you think it is.

Different programming languages and libraries have different ways of setting the default encoding, but the safest way to handle it is to make an explicit call with the proper encoding name whenever converting between strings and bytes. It is also a good idea to perform testing of the import tool with a variety of Unicode characters to ensure that they are stored in the way that you expect.

Backup and Data Export

Maintaining a backup copy of all your data is an important part of any data storage solution. SimpleDB's automatic domain replication across data centers should reduce the number of circumstances where a backup is required. Less risk, however, does not eliminate the need for backups. A mistakenly deleted domain does not benefit from replication. It can only be restored from a backup.

Beyond maintaining a backup copy in case of disaster, you may also discover someday that you need to take your data and leave SimpleDB. This is more of a concern with database services than with database products; you are more at the mercy of the service provider. For example, if you are not satisfied with MySQL, you can choose a different product, but you never have to worry about your version of MySQL becoming unavailable to you. Although AWS is not known for account bannings and large price increases, these things are beyond your control; they are unlikely yet still involve risk. Having a backup of all your data under your control removes the risk that your data could be made completely unavailable to you.

The ideal backup solution would be for SimpleDB to have an export function built in that you could call and then collect your backup file at completion. As with the bulk load facility, however, such a feature has not been made available. This leaves you with the same two options: Use a third-party backup tool or write your own.

Using Third-Party Backup Services

There are backup solutions that not only back up data, but also re-import the data for you. Some of these currently will, or promise future versions that will, also import data for you. Each has some peculiarities, but the support is very responsive. The two currently available services that do SimpleDB backups are SimpleBackr and BackupSDB.

SimpleBackr is a free SimpleDB backup service hosted at SimpleBackr.com. SimpleBackr examines your domains and enables you to start a backup process that saves all the data from all of your domains. The backup files are saved in JSON format to a bucket in your S3 account. The bucket structure matches the calendar date on which the backup was taken, and each domain gets its own JSON backup file. Figure 5-1 shows a screenshot of SimpleBackr.com.

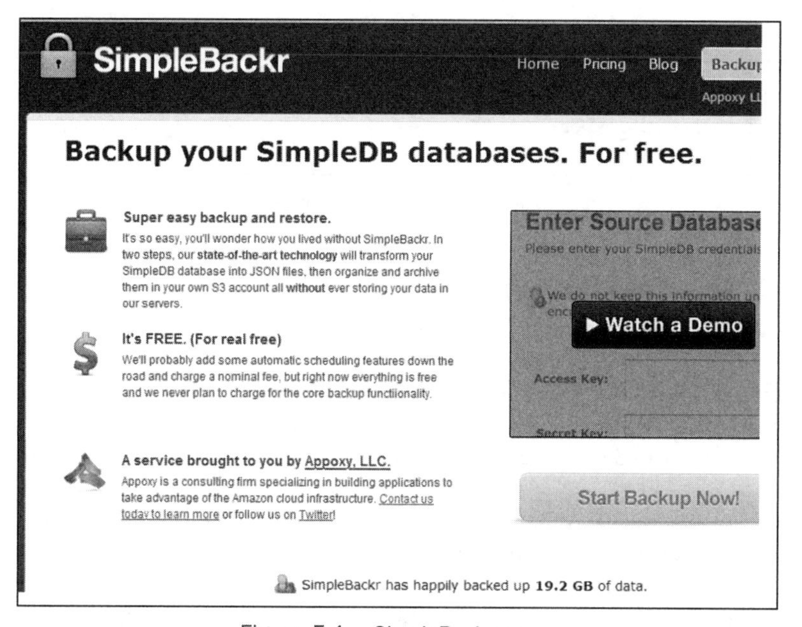

Figure 5-1 SimpleBackr.com

BackupSDB.com is another website that offers a backup service for SimpleDB domains. BackupSDB enables you to select individual domains for backup and individual backups for restore. It maintains a detailed backup and restore history log of all your activity on the site. When backing up a domain, the data is saved to a set of XML files with 1,000 records per file. These files are then zipped up into a master backup file. BackupSDB is a paid service that also has a free service tier that limits the number of items backed up. Figure 5-2 shows a screenshot of the BackupSDB website.

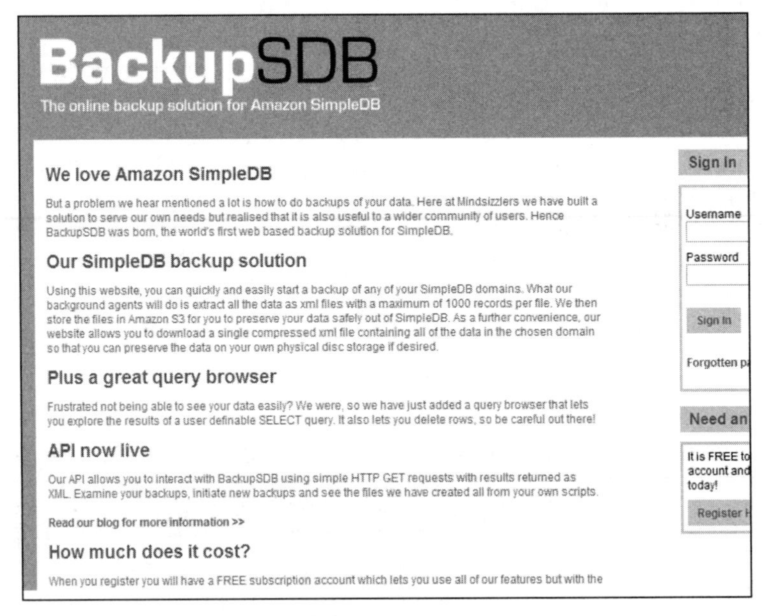

Figure 5-2 BackupSDB.com

Writing Your Own Backup Tool

If you decide to write your own backup tool, there are a few things to consider. First, and this is true of all SimpleDB backups, there is no way to lock the domain. A backup is not going to be a snapshot of the entire domain at one instance in time if changes to your data occur during the backup. The only way around this is if you are able to stop all writes to the domain during the backup. However, SimpleDB is designed around data consistency at the item level, and this is maintained in any backup you take. SimpleDB is not relational, but you can still have one item reference another. However, if you have a relationship between two items that will break if they are not updated atomically, not only do you have a backup problem, but you also have a consistency problem.

One feature that can be beneficial is a backup verification routine that checks for orphaned items or bad references. This function would need access to some minimal knowledge of your data layout, but in return, you would be able to confirm the consistency of your backup or resolve any issues.

As a mechanism to download your data, use a `Select` call requesting all attributes and page through the entire domain. Setting a sort criterion may be helpful if your SimpleDB usage supports it. As the backup process pages through the data, updates to items you have already fetched will not make it into the backup, whereas updates to items appearing in upcoming pages may make it in. If you arrange the sort criteria such that the data most likely to be updated appears in the final pages, you will end up with a backup that is closer to a snapshot in time. If most of your updates involve new items with item name values that are strictly increasing, use a sort on `itemName()`. If each of your items has a time stamp indicating that last modification time, use that as a sort criterion.

Be aware that it may take some time for a backup of a large domain to complete. To mitigate this, run the backup from an EC2 instance in the same region to minimize round-trip request latencies. An obvious step is to run the backup during an off-peak time, and if possible, suspend writes to that domain. That is not always practical, but if it is, it will improve both the speed of the backup and the consistency of the data within the backup file.

Choose a backup file format that is convenient for restoring. Because you are writing your own backup code, and you have to choose a file format of some kind, you might as well make it as easy as possible. Keep in mind how you want to be able to restore the data. If you want the ability to insert the data into SimpleDB as well as other databases, that will lead you to a different file format than data meant only for SimpleDB. If your restore procedure involves multiple simultaneous upload processes, consider saving your data into multiple files.

Restoring from Backup

Your backup efforts are meaningless if you do not have the ability to restore a backup. If you have a restore procedure but don't test your backup files with it, any confidence you have in the system is misplaced. Restoring backup data to separate AWS account can enable you to test the backup and restore without affecting your production domains. This can be especially useful if you already have a separate account for use in development and testing. If the sensitivity of the data allows, a regularly scheduled backup from production can be restored to development. This allows development efforts to benefit from near-live data while also testing the integrity of the restore operation.

Summary

If you have a large quantity of import data, you cannot live without a SimpleDB import tool. This is true even if you only want to evaluate SimpleDB. Then, once you have production data in SimpleDB, you should not live without a backup tool. Through some combination of third-party tools and future SimpleDB enhancements, the tooling landscape should begin to look much better. Until that time, writing your own tool may be the best option. You may be able to get a lot of mileage out of a simple tool that you write yourself or that is already available as a service today.

If you do anything out of the ordinary with your SimpleDB data, chances are that third-party backup and restore services will not be able to handle it, and you will have to provide your own tooling support. The next chapter details some out-of-the-ordinary things you might want to do to work around the built-in SimpleDB limitations.

6

Working Beyond the Boundaries

Once you start working with SimpleDB and start trying to find ways to make it fit with your application, you may run into one of the downsides of a compact and relatively new API: the lack of support for all the data access patterns you'd like to use (for example, reliance on transactions). Moreover, many of the operations that are present have limitations in place that may not be suitable for the way you want to use the service.

It comes as no surprise that the most common SimpleDB questions from developers revolve around how to lift or work around the AWS-imposed limitations. SimpleDB does not make a suitable data store for every application. For some situations, there is just no practical way to make SimpleDB do what you can do with a relational database. However, some creative workarounds exist for those situations where only a few issues are standing in the way. This type of information is important for the practical user of SimpleDB but can be hard to find, if it is available at all. This chapter details a number of practical strategies for working around the SimpleDB service limitations.

The approach of this chapter is to suggest specific strategies but not specific implementation. Examples are given that include queries and pseudocode, but not in a cookbook style. The spartan set of API calls in SimpleDB serve as primitive building blocks. Each suggestion needs to be applied differently depending on the application, the programming language, and the deployment environment. Consider these suggestions as a springboard for your own application design.

However, before you consider implementing a workaround for something in SimpleDB, you should have a good understanding of why things are the way they are. There is a difference between working around the system and subverting the system. Examine the reasoning behind the SimpleDB qualities and claims so that you can avoid unnecessary frustration.

Availability: The Final Frontier

Perhaps the biggest claim made about SimpleDB is that it provides high availability. Availability is an important reason to use SimpleDB, and some consistency and speed is traded off to get it.

However, speed and consistency are easier to measure than availability. With a service like SimpleDB, it is hard to know from the outside what will happen during various failure scenarios. There may be internal failures that occur that we do not even know about. Those hidden failures, handled swiftly or automatically, are a credit to AWS, but can make it difficult for users to understand the difference between a system that hasn't had a failure yet and one that handles failures gracefully.

Consider the July 2009 Google AppEngine outage that lasted for six hours. Google AppEngine provides a data store that has some similarities to SimpleDB in that it is entirely hosted and managed by Google in its data centers, as SimpleDB is hosted and managed by AWS in Amazon data centers. One week after the outage, Chris Beckmann (Google AppEngine PM) provided a very detailed explanation for the outage, including a timeline of events throughout the failure. One sentence highlights the difference between the AppEngine data store and SimpleDB, as follows:

> "Since needed application data was completely unreachable for a longer than expected time period, we could not follow the usual procedure of serving of App Engine applications from an alternate data center, because doing so would have resulted in inconsistent or unavailable data for applications."

This is a key insight into the different levels of availability. The root cause of the problem was a software bug, but that's not the whole story. The interesting part is that there was a choice to be made. Google engineers had a 30-minute-old copy of all the data for the thousands of AppEngine apps. They could have just switched it on at a different data center. However, the choice was essentially made for them because they had a consistency guarantee to uphold. Some data would be missing, some would be stale, and in the end, they would have no way to reconcile the divergent updates to stale data.

With SimpleDB, that same choice has already been made, but the difference is that availability is chosen over consistency. It has already been decided, and the mechanism is already in place to synchronize up the stale or temporarily missing data.

The important thing to realize is that outages inevitably occur, even at Google and Amazon, and this leaves a choice for the developers who use these services. If an outage causes the temporary loss of 30 minutes worth of data, is it better for your app to continue running without that data and have it synced up later or is it better for the app to wait out a six-hour outage unavailable to all users, even those unaffected by the data issue?

SimpleDB is a solution for those applications that would benefit from continuing to offer users access to the system even if the data is stale for a while. If all the data in the application belongs to the user—for example, in an email application—the user is probably going to argue for the ability to keep working even if the data entered between 6:00 a.m. and 6:30 a.m. is absent for a while. When the application provides quantifiable business value, the decision can be far easier to make. When you weigh the cost of your entire online shopping cart application going down for all users for six hours in the middle of the day, against the cost of serving 30-minute-old stale shopping cart data to only those users who were active between 6:00 a.m. and 6:30 a.m., there might be a dollar value difference you can compare.

A big part of the value of an eventually consistent system like SimpleDB lies in the ability to maintain availability during an outage. It also lies in being able to reason about the qualities that you want your application to have, and in the ability to choose a database that supports those qualities.

Boundaries of Eventual Consistency

One of the things that people commonly wonder about when first getting into SimpleDB is how eventual consistency affects an application. How far do you have to go to avoid data corruption, and is it a practical choice for building applications?

Item-Level Atomicity

The first thing to understand is that even though the SimpleDB consistency guarantee is relaxed compared to relational databases, there is still atomicity and durability. The unit of atomicity is the item. When you update the attributes of an item via a single `PutAttributes` request, the entire update is applied atomically. It may take some time before the update is fully visible to clients attempting to retrieve that item via a call to `GetAttributes` or `Select`. This is the same type of delay you might see with a master-slave relational database cluster, where the slave database services queries, even though it is always slightly out of sync with the master that accepts all the writes. The time it takes to replicate in SimpleDB is called the consistency window. Regardless of the consistency window, SimpleDB always presents an internally consistent view of the item. The item will have the prior state of the attributes or the new state of the attributes; it will never have a mixed state, where some of the new attribute values have been applied and some have not. This is atomicity at the item level.

At a higher level of granularity, this does not hold. If you issue a batch put and update two items at once, subsequent reads of that data could result in one of the items being updated but not the other. But, again, within each item, partial updates will never be shown. Given how lean the SimpleDB API is, `BatchPutAttributes` is the only higher level of granularity. There are no transactions and so no opportunity for dirty reads or any isolation levels. It could be said that if an application requires transactions, SimpleDB will not be the right choice of database, and this might be true. But if the real application requirement is for atomicity rather than strictly transactions, placing all the necessary data inside one item can accomplish that. This can serve as a workaround for the lack of transactions: Place the data that must change atomically within a single item and update it using a single call to `PutAttributes` using a conditional write. In SimpleDB, `PutAttributes` can be used for all three of initial inserts, updates, and deleting or clearing of values.

Looking into the Eventual Consistency Window

So then, understanding that eventual consistency does not equate to the absence of consistency, the question becomes: How long is the eventual consistency window? The time required for consistency is never a constant number. All data is replicated across multiple data centers. It happens over a fast network, and those data centers are in the same region, but it is still an operation across data centers. As with any distributed database, network and hardware failures can occur. During normal operations, even under peak usage, eventual consistency times are usually under a second, but this is not guaranteed. A faster alternative to waiting is using consistent reads, which are on average just as fast as normal reads but are slower or unavailable during outages.

The difficulty is that it is probably a mistake to design your application such that it works when consistency is reached in one second but fails otherwise. The reason it may be a mistake is because this is the primary benefit of SimpleDB. This is the benefit achieved by the tradeoffs, and so this is the reason to use it: because it remains available to accept your writes in the midst of failure when consistency is not, for the moment, possible. When everything is going wrong and serious failures have not yet been rectified, you, and your users, still have access to your data; even if the writes are not immediately visible, they will not be lost and consistency will eventually be reached. To write an app that fails when the consistency window grows past some arbitrary number of milliseconds, is to snatch defeat from the jaws of victory. It is to trade down your consistency guarantee to achieve higher availability and then throw away the availability.

There is nothing wrong with making extensive use of consistent reads throughout an application. If you produce an application that uses SimpleDB but is unable to maintain a, possibly degraded, level of service during a partial failure that causes consistent reads to fail, you may be missing one of SimpleDB's big benefits. It is not necessarily easy to take advantage of this benefit, but it does not need to be hard either. The central question is what you will do when calls to `GetAttributes` and `Select` return stale values. Alternatively, in the case of newly added data, what do you do when they don't return the items that you expect them to?

One thing that people commonly want to do is to check if the value is consistent. In fact, sometimes there is a tendency to want to check every single value and make sure it is consistent before proceeding. Although this is possible to do, it is highly impractical. If your app can only maintain correctness when every value become consistent before proceeding, building it atop SimpleDB could be considered the creation of a software monument to wasted time. There's nothing wrong with consistency, the issue is that SimpleDB alerts you when a consistent read cannot be guaranteed and enables you to proceed with eventual consistency instead. If you are building an application that permanently requires strong consistency that is unable to tolerate eventual consistency, it might be better to save yourself the trouble and just use a relational database with strong consistency. There are better ways to deal with the eventual consistency; there are ways to work with it rather than try to eliminate it.

Read-Your-Writes

For many applications, particularly applications where each of the data items is owned by exactly one user, consistency becomes a more narrow concern. For example, consider an application that maintains a set of to-do lists for users. If all of the lists are private, consistency involves how each user sees his or her own data, and it makes no difference to Jill whether Jack's data is consistent.

This narrowing holds even in cases where the data is made public. Pretend that these are now wish lists and not to-do lists. If Jack adds a new pail to his wish list, it is important that the publicly visible list be updated, but if that update is delayed by a full second, the delay is probably not even noticeable. However, it is quite important for Jack to see a consistent view of his own list. If he adds an item and then finds it immediately absent from the list, it will look like the update failed. This level of consistency, where each read reflects the results of every prior write by the same client, is called read-your-writes.

Allowing a client to see an always-consistent view of the data he is changing is a level of consistency that is useful in many situations. A relational database will give you this level of consistency automatically by virtue of the strong consistency guarantee. A relational database cluster, on the other hand, may not be able to guarantee read-your-writes when a slave database services client reads. SimpleDB does not have the notion of a connected client, however, and does not guarantee read-your-writes consistency. Each request is independent, and there is neither a persistent connection nor a session layer. This is not really a concern for batch-processing situations like indexing or data import; this is the concern when handling requests for connected users who are submitting updates. This applies equally to application users for a website, a desktop app, or a mobile app.

It is important to realize that it is easy to build a system with guaranteed read-your-writes consistency (or stronger) on top of SimpleDB by using consistent reads but that it comes by giving back some of the availability. Having said that, it is possible to build a system that provides read-your-writes most of the time. There is a situation that you need to be aware of when using SimpleDB—during an outage, you may be unable to achieve read-your-writes for some users until the problem is resolved. Knowing that, the remaining issue is the implementation of a system that can give you that consistency most of the time while still offering (potentially degraded) service during an outage.

Implementing a Consistent View

When it comes down to the practical matter of how to deliver a consistent view to your users when consistent reads are failing, there are two types of strategy you can use: data access patterns and caching. These techniques are independent and can be used together to achieve the best outcome.

Optimizing Data Access Patterns

Many of the data access needs of an application are dictated by the application's requirements. However, the database access patterns are frequently a consequence of application design. Modern technologies, particularly web technologies, make it possible to sculpt the application's data access to achieve a quicker and more responsive user experience. These same technologies can also help you work within the SimpleDB eventual consistency window.

There is one primary data access pattern that causes eventual consistency issues: a write immediately followed by a read. In most cases, this means a call to `PutAttributes` for a specific item and then a query whose results should reflect the changes to that item. It could also be a `GetAttributes` request for the same item that follows the `PutAttributes`.

As an example of the query scenario, consider the way forums typically work on the Internet. You view a thread of comments and you decide to post your own comment, so you click on the reply link. After typing in your comment, you click on the submit button; the server saves your comment to the database (subject to any rules) and then redirects your browser to the thread page, where your new comment is posted at the end. In a hypothetical forum application based on SimpleDB, the place where things could go wrong is in the redirect after the new comment is saved. If the part of the application that saves the post is completely separate from the part that subsequently displays the post, some trade-offs are being made. This pattern is not inherently bad, but with an eventually consistent database, the new comment could fail to turn up in the subsequent query because it is performed so quickly after saving the data. Using a consistent read solves this problem much of the time but if one of the replicas storing your domain data fails, it can cause consistent reads to return an error while normal reads continue to work with eventual consistency.

The real problem with this situation is that the necessary data is available in memory but is being dumped. The solutions to this problem all involve holding on to that data rather than dumping it. One option is to use a dispatch mechanism rather than a redirect for populating the follow-up query. Rather than round tripping to the user's web browser, a dispatch hands off the request to a different handler on the server. The unnecessary Internet latency is avoided, and because dispatch allows data passing, the important data is not discarded. In this scenario, the handler that saves the comment to the database passes that comment to the handler responsible for displaying a thread. The thread display handler needs one extra capability: merging the passed data into the normal query results.

This technique, and others like it, works well with SimpleDB because consistency is normally reached before the user can make another request. When looking at the data access patterns in an application, whenever you see a write immediately followed by a read, it is OK to use a consistent read but it is also wise to add error handling that either handle it in the same request if the immediacy is required, or place a user action between them if it can wait. This allows you to benefit from the high availability built into SimpleDB.

Another example of this principle is the display of user profile information. Consider a web application where the user has a profile page and can change some aspects of how it appears. In the use case where the user saves a profile change and automatically receives a redirect to the profile page, the same data access pattern emerges as with posting forum comments. In this case, the follow-up action is a lookup rather than a query, but the immediate redirect is what causes the problem. In addition, the question that needs to be asked is the same: Does the user need to see this data immediately? If the answer is yes, then handling it in the same request can eliminate the need for consistent reads. Depending on the application, this user profile issue may be solved using the same dispatch technique discussed previously.

There are also other solutions to consider. Asynchronous JavaScript and XML (AJAX) can be used to update pages in-place, without triggering a new page load. This type of functionality becomes easier to implement each year as more supporting tools and frameworks are created. AJAX has both user experience benefits and server resource benefits. It is a powerful tool when designing user interactions with SimpleDB-based web applications.

The principle to remember when examining data access patterns is that discarding data between a back-to-back—that is, without user interaction—write-and-read will cause problems. The normal flow of user actions is not too quick for eventual consistency to catch up in the vast majority of cases. This forms a sweet spot where responses to user actions usually have a naturally consistent appearance, provided you avoid artificially quick data access.

Session Scope Caching

Although the normal delay between a user's clicks can make eventual consistency look like read-your-writes consistency most of the time, in some situations it is not enough. Sometimes a user clicks quickly; other times, high-traffic loads or large request sizes lengthen the eventual consistency window. These conditions, which can happen during normal operation, should be handled appropriately.

One useful technique is a cache at the user level for holding updates that have not yet become consistent. A typical way to implement caching at this level is within the session object on the web server. This is appropriate when there is only a single web server or within a web server cluster using sticky sessions. This cache should be small and only store updates the user has made in the last few seconds, which most of the time will only be a single item. This special-purpose caching can smooth out the bumps commonly encountered with the normal operation of eventual consistency, fast clicks, and users with multiple browser windows.

Caching for Fast Data Access

The aggressive use of caching at various levels yields great benefits for applications based on SimpleDB. This is true when working to scale up applications that use any type of database, but even more so with SimpleDB because it is intended to be fast enough, rather than blazing fast.

At the time of this writing, there is no standardized or widely acknowledged "best" caching technology to recommend. There are many options, and you should consider using what is easily available. Consider caching the results of calls to `GetAttributes` and `Select`. Caching query results is especially important for queries that are large or time consuming and return a `NextToken`. Also, consider making sure query strings appear in canonical form so the results can be cached effectively. For example, if you use a `Select` to fetch five items at once, your query may look like this:

```
SELECT * FROM media WHERE itemName() IN('01', '02', '03', '04', '05')
```

Be sure that the item name constants that you pass to the query always appear in the same order; otherwise, they will be cached as different queries.

Handling Text Larger Than 1K

The limit of 1,024 bytes per attribute value is one of the SimpleDB limitation most complained about by users. It is large enough for any small data type but not nearly large enough to store the text of comments, descriptions, articles, or reviews. Taking this limit alone at face value rules out a vast swath of potential applications. Fortunately, there are ways to work around this limit.

Getting around this limit can allow you to store large blocks of text using SimpleDB, but do not make the mistake of thinking you will end up with a text-searching engine as a result. SimpleDB provides basic query capabilities, but it isn't a good solution for full text search. The `Select` operator `LIKE` lets you search for attributes that contain the text you specify, but it's not particularly fast, it is case sensitive, and it doesn't provide relevance nor does it match different word forms. If you need to index documents for search, consider something like Apache Lucene. The purpose of these large text workaround suggestions is to enable you to store the text for later retrieval in cases where the need to search it is minimal or nonexistent.

Storing Text in S3

A very simple option is to store the actual text in Amazon's Simple Storage Service and use a SimpleDB item attribute to point to the location of the text file. If the application using this data is on EC2 in the same region, it will have fast free data transfer to both S3 and SimpleDB. It can be made available using the same AWS credentials used with SimpleDB. Additionally, S3 supports versioning, so you can easily maintain older versions of files. Depending on the application, it may be useful to store the previous S3 text file version-identifiers as attribute values in SimpleDB for quick access or querying. Even though the actual text data in this case in not available to SimpleDB queries, you may want to store keywords, topics, or tags in SimpleDB for this purpose.

When storing the large text in S3, consider storing the full bucket location and path of the text file. This can work in the same way as when you store any type of file in S3, and you may want to implement a common mechanism for referencing data in S3. It may be helpful to use a naming convention to match domains to buckets if the data is not going to be used externally.

Storing Overflow in Different Attributes

When you know the maximum size of the text that you need to store, and if it is larger than the 1k attribute limit, you may be able to reserve a few attributes for storing that text. For instance, if the maximum text length is 100k, you can break it into 100 1k chunks and have 100 attributes like 'BodyText', 'BodyText01', 'BodyText02', and so on. This can work even if you don't know what the maximum size of the text will be, so long as you don't overflow the number of attributes allowed within an item.

A situation where this technique is useful is storing user-entered data where the text could be large in theory, but where a very low percentage of entries ever exceed 1,024 bytes. In these cases, an attribute like 'BodyText' will hold the full text in almost all cases, with extra overflow attributes for those few items that actually need it.

Examples of applications where this can be useful include user comments on blogs, product review websites, and social news and bookmarking sites. Assuming that users will generally type in 1,024 bytes or fewer is reasonable in many situations, even though it may not be intuitive.

Consider an extreme example of this principle: the website stackoverflow.com. Stack-overflow is a large question-and-answer site for programming questions, where the users are specifically encouraged to post detailed questions and responses. Not only is markup permitted within the user-submitted text, but it is also stored in the database with the full HTML markup.

With these forces pushing the size of user posts upward, it is interesting to note that more than 72% of questions and answers on the site are smaller than 1,024 bytes. Stack-overflow does not use SimpleDB, but they do publish data dumps that can be analyzed, and they are an excellent example of how difficult it can be to get users to type in large blocks of text, even for a fraction of the time.

The trade-off from using this approach is that you lose a few of the conveniences you would normally have with a query. You cannot easily do a query for text matches across the variable number of attributes. Also, it makes it difficult to use that attribute specifically as part of the output selection clause; you end up needing to use `SELECT *` anytime you need that attribute in a query. However, the benefit is that it is easy to split up and re-assemble the text because it doesn't require any special processing. It is most applicable when the majority of read operations are in the form of `GetAttributes` rather than `Select`. In these cases, you don't suffer the query inconvenience.

It is more difficult to update the text stored in these types of items, however, because there are more steps involved. Anytime the text needs to be updated, you must be sure to delete any attributes no longer used. The procedure for processing an update of text would be something like this:

1. Read the item using `GetAttributes` or `Select`.
2. Reassemble the original text using the attribute naming conventions.
3. Present this text to the user.
4. Accept the user's new text and break it into chunks.

5. If the new text has fewer chunks, create blank values to overwrite the old chunks that need to be cleared.
6. Call `PutAttributes` with the new attribute values, setting the replace flag to true for each.

6a. If you are willing to make the comparisons, you can exclude unchanged attributes.

7. Optionally, call `DeleteAttributes` for the now-blank chunks.

The extra step specific to storing extra text is to count the chunks and pass the empty string as a new value for each of the abandoned overflow attributes. You might be tempted to just delete the empty attributes and not overwrite them first with an empty value. However, performing the update in one step is the only way to get atomicity. If you do not do it in one step, you will have an item with bad data until consistency is reached. During a failure, you could have bad data for an extended period. By performing it in one step, the item will always have good data: either the old text or the new text.

Storing Overflow as a Multi-Valued Attribute

Another option is to use a multi-valued attribute to store all the text. For example, if you have 100k of text, you might have an attribute named 'Body' with 100 separate values. The benefit of this approach is that you retain the ability to write queries that target the attribute, such as the following:

```
SELECT * FROM posts WHERE Body LIKE '%turbine%'
```

One of the drawbacks of this approach, however, comes from the fact that there is no guaranteed ordering of multi-valued attributes. Therefore, you have to insert some sort of modifier into each text chunk to indicate order.

Although you would not split text this short, it illustrates the issue. If you have the text "I went to the market last Thursday" and split it into three parts of a multi-valued attribute named Body, SimpleDB might respond to your `GetAttributes`, or you `Select` with the following:

```
Body: ["the market", "I went to ", " last Thursday"]
```

Unless you insert some ordering, you will not be able to reconstruct the original text:

```
Body: ["02:the market", "01:I went to ", "03: last Thursday"]
```

Inserting attribute-ordering information into the text value takes up some extra space, but it opens up the possibility of doing text searches on the attribute, which is not there when overflowing text to different attributes.

Entities with More than 256 Attributes

Another of the common limits that users try to work around is the 256-attributes-per-item limit. In reality, this limit is not as strict as the other limits. There is some subtlety to the way it is implemented; it was designed with flexibility and speed as higher priorities than enforcement.

The complicating issue is that `PutAttributes` serves the role of both inserting and updating data. Calls to `PutAttributes` that include the replace flag could actually result in an item with fewer values rather than more. A naïve enforcement of this limit would reject calls to `PutAttributes` based only on the existing attribute count and the number of attributes in the request. However, that implementation would reject many valid requests that merely replace existing values.

This could be handled in two other ways. One way would be for SimpleDB to fully apply the updates in each `PutAttributes` request to the item and then examine the results before deciding if the call should be rejected. A much less computationally intensive technique would be to relax the limit by only enforcing it on items already past the limit. The latter approach is the way SimpleDB is implemented. `PutAttributes` calls are rejected when the item already has 256 or more attribute values. This allows the successful replacement of all 255 attributes that may exist in an item by calling `PutAttributes` with 255 new values and the replace flags set to true.

One negative side effect of this enforcement mechanism is that for all practical purposes, the limit is 255 and not 256. As soon as you have 256 attributes in an item, additional calls to `PutAttributes` are blocked, even though you have not exceeded the limit and even if you are trying to replace a value. You must first delete at least one attribute value before you can make the replacement. Therefore, 255 is the limit of attribute values you can store and still update the item with put calls.

Alternately, a different consequence of this implementation assists those seeking to exceed this limit. Because you can only get the resulting NumberItemAttributesExceeded error when the item is already full, you can easily exceed the limit by inserting the initial 255 attributes and then adding an additional 256 attributes. Thus, you easily can store 511 attributes in any item.

You must be aware, however, that these overstuffed items have limited usefulness, since you can never update the values without first deleting most of them. Also, although SimpleDB has worked this way since it entered public beta, there is no guarantee that it will always work this way; use it at your own risk. Even if you do overstuff your items, this type of hack is only applicable for data that will be primarily read only.

Paging to Arbitrary Query Depth

A frequent requirement, when displaying the results of a query, is to enable the user to navigate through the results in pages. The basic function of fetching another page of results is built into SimpleDB with the `NextToken`. Unfortunately, there are many things you might want to do with search results pages that SimpleDB does not directly support.

One of the common ways to display search results in pages is to begin by showing the results for the current page, and also showing links to each of the other pages. This has the benefit of quickly allowing the user to see how many pages there are and going to one specific page quickly. However, as a practical matter, when there are many pages, there is seldom a good reason for the user to navigate to an arbitrary middle page. Usually, either the next page or the last page is the next navigation target. As such, it has become common, on the web, to see search results that do not include full pagination but only the more common first, last, next, and previous links. This can serve to reduce visual clutter, and it is well suited to SimpleDB, where getting the full query result count can be time consuming for a large domain. When going to the next page, you may be able to simplify the use case by only allowing a "next page" and not arbitrary paging. You can do this in SimpleDB by using the `LIMIT` clause:

```
SELECT title, summary, votecount FROM posts WHERE userid = '000022656' LIMIT 25
```

You already know how to handle the `NextToken`, but if you use this tactic, you can support "previous page" by storing the breadcrumb trail of next tokens (for example, in the web session) and re-issuing the query with a previous `NextToken` rather than a subsequent one.

However, the general case for handling arbitrary pagination in SimpleDB is the same for previous and next. In the general case, the user may click on an arbitrary page number, like five, without ever having visited page four or six.

You handle this in SimpleDB by using the fact that NextToken only requires the `WHERE` clause and `ORDER BY` clause to be the same to work properly. So, rather than querying through every page in sequence and pulling down all the intervening items, you can usually do it in two steps, as follows:

1. Issue your query with a limit value of where the desired page should start, and SELECT `count(*)` instead of the actual attributes you want.

2. Use the NextToken from step one to fetch the actual page data using the desired attributes and the page size as the LIMIT.

Listing 6-1 shows a first pass at the pseudocode to implement this.

Listing 6-1 **First-Pass Pseudocode for Jumping to an Arbitrary Search Page**

```
int targetPage, pageSize;
...
int jumpLimit = pageSize * (targetPage - 1);
String query = "SELECT %1 FROM posts WHERE userid = '000022656' LIMIT %2";
String output = "title, summary, votecount";
Result temp = sdb.select(query, "count(*)", jumpLimit);
Result data = sdb.select(query, output, pageSize, temp.getToken());
```

In this code, `%1` and `%2` are String substitutions and `sdb.select()` is a fictitious method that includes the String substitution code along with the SimpleDB call.

Whether or not you can accomplish this in two calls to SimpleDB (as shown in the code) will depend on the complexity of your `WHERE` clause and the size of your data set. The preceding code is simplified in that the temporary result may have returned a partial count if the query took more than five seconds to run. You would really want to put that line in a loop until the proper count is reached. To make the code a little more realistic, I have added the loop, placed it within methods, and abandoned the String substitutions. The updated code is shown in Listing 6-2.

Listing 6-2 **Updated Pseudocode for Jumping to an Arbitrary Search Page**

```
private Result fetchPage(String query, int targetPage) {
    int pageSize = extractLimitValue(query);
    int skipLimit = pageSize * (targetPage - 1);
    String token = skipAhead(query, skipLimit);
    return sdb.select(query, token);
}

private String skipAhead(String query, int skipLimit) {
    String tempQuery = replaceClause(query, "SELECT", "count(*)");
    int accumulatedCount = 0;
    String token = "";
    do {
        int tempLimit = skipLimit - accumulatedCount;
        tempQuery = replaceClause(tempQuery , "LIMIT", tempLimit + "");
        Result tempResult = sdb.select(query, token);
        token = tempResult.getToken();
        accumulatedCount += tempResult.getCount();
    } while (accumulatedCount < skipLimit);
    return token;
}

private int extractLimitValue(String query) {...}
private String replaceClause(String query, String clause, String value){...}
```

This is the general idea without error handling, and works for any arbitrary page, excluding page 1.

Exact Counting Without Locks or Transactions

When using SimpleDB, you may find that you need to store a count of something. It may be how many times something has been viewed, placed in a shopping cart, ordered, and so on. With SimpleDB, this involves the normal read, increment, and then write process, and it works fine if there is only one process executing that cycle. However, if there is contention for any given item or attribute involved in the count, eventual consistency can result in missed counts.

With the advent of conditional writes and consistent reads exact counting has become easy for the general case. A normal read is followed by an incremented write conditioned on the prior value. If the write fails, use a consistent read to pull the new value, increment, and do another conditional write. This is the recommended way to perform counting in SimpleDB, however during high contention or outages this technique can break down. When you want to get the highest levels of availability from a SimpleDB based counter, you need a way to deal with those rare times when eventual consistency is the only consistency available.

Eventual consistency does not lend itself naturally to the implementation of a distributed counter because there is no way to lock a row or perform a transaction. Although not straightforward, it is certainly possible to do. Two potential approaches to make it work are using one item per count and storing the count in a multi-valued attribute. The first is the easier way that uses a new item for each count but requires periodic maintenance to clean up the old items. The second technique maintains the count as an attribute within the item being counted. This protocol can be much more convenient to use and requires no ongoing cleanup, but the implementation complexity is significantly higher.

Using One Item Per Count

The easiest way to accumulate a count is to make a different item for each increment of the counter. This approach is very focused on the individual count values, since they account for a whole item each. As such, it is possible to store additional audit data along with each count, like a timestamp, a user ID, or an IP address.

When storing counts this way, you will probably want a domain that only holds these counts. The domain can store the counts for many different things, and you can indicate which thing is being counted with another attribute. The domain can be the focus of a large volume of quick puts from many unrelated processes and requires no coordination between them. For uniqueness and decentralization, the item names should be UUID values. When you need to fetch the count, presumably much less frequently, you issue a query. For example:

```
SELECT count(*) FROM `shopping-cart-adds` WHERE `product-id` = '5869926'
```

Over time, this domain continues to grow and, as a result, the queries will incrementally take longer to execute. A simple way to keep the query time low when you are counting many things in the same domain is to `Select` based on the attribute name instead of the attribute value. You would need to store the data slightly differently, but the query would be very similar:

```
SELECT count(*) FROM `shopping-cart-adds` WHERE `5869926` = 'product-id'
```

As you can see, the attribute name and the attribute value are swapped for the attribute that identifies the thing being counted. This makes the queries more efficient based on the fact that a separate index is created for each attribute name. Instead of searching through a large index, the query uses a smaller index where all the items match your criteria.

Faster Counts with NextToken Caching

Over time, the count query may begin to take so long to execute, you get back a `NextToken` requiring a second query to get the full count. If the multi-page query takes too long for your needs, one option is to cache the `NextToken` at a well-known value and query only for updates that are more recent. To accomplish this, you will need to store a timestamp with each count and that attribute will need to be added to the query as a sort criteria. To update the shopping cart example:

```
SELECT count(*) FROM `shopping-cart-adds`
WHERE `5869926` = 'product-id' AND timestamp IS NOT NULL
ORDER BY timestamp
```

If the query begins returning a `NextToken` once there are 120,000 matching count items, you can manipulate the limit value to get a token at the 100,000 mark and pass that token to subsequent queries for the remainder of the cache period. You do not need to use a round number like 100,000; you might want to regenerate the token each day to a recent value for each of the things being counted to keep the queries fast.

Cleaning Up Old Counts with Summary Records

Specific `NextToken` caching is useful in general when you want to keep all the historical items, but if older counts have little value and the count volume is very high, you may want a way to clean out the old items. One solution to that problem is a summary record, where you roll up all the counts collected so far for each thing being counted and then delete the original items. The summary record is just an item with a timestamp, count, and a way to identify the thing being counted. The timestamp granularity should be down to the millisecond. This also requires that the normal count items contain a timestamp. The summary records don't need to be in the same domain; the choice of where to store them is up to you.

Using a summary record involves two things: pulling it along with each count query and updating it periodically. Computing the count is now a three-step process. You have to first pull the summary record and then perform the original query, adding the additional criteria of a timestamp strictly greater than what was in the summary record. Finally, add the two counts together. Here is what the updated query might look like:

```
SELECT count(*) FROM `shopping-cart-adds`
WHERE `5869926` = 'product-id' AND timestamp > '2010-01-10T22:50:21.453Z'
```

You will also need a way to update each summary record periodically. This can be done on a schedule (every hour, for instance), or dynamically based on some other criteria, like whenever the query returns more than one page. Just make sure that when you update your summary record, you base it on a time that is far enough in the past that you are past the eventual consistency window. A delay of one minute is safe when there is no outage.

This solution works well in the face of concurrent updates, even if many summary records are written at the same time. As long as each one contains a total that is consistent with the timestamp, it doesn't matter which one wins the last-write-wins contest, because they are all correct. It also works well when you expand your count items across multiple domains. You can pull the summary records from all the domains simultaneously and then issue the queries to all domains in parallel. The reason to do this is when you need higher throughput for a certain thing being counted than what you can get from one domain. In addition, it also works well with caching. If your cache fails, you have an authoritative backup.

The time will come when someone needs to go back and edit, remove, or add a record that has an old timestamp value. The code that performs that change needs to also update the summary record for that domain or the count will be off until the summary record is recomputed.

As with any SimpleDB-based solution, this will give you a count that is coordinated with the data currently viewable within the consistency window. In practice, it is likely to be several seconds behind.

Storing the Count in a Multi-Valued Attribute

Sometimes the count is not a first-class concept. The data model has been decided, and the count is one of many values of some other entity. In a traditional database, it would be an integer field like any other. It doesn't merit its own database table, or in SimpleDB, its own domain. You can accomplish this, in spite of eventual consistency, but not with a simple integer.

Because it is not possible to do an atomic read-increment-write during the outages that cause conditional writes to fail, the new data must be added without destroying the old. A multi-valued attribute is used for this reason. In addition to the count, a version number needs to be included as part of the value. A single authoritative version of the count is not possible, so there needs to be a way to specify which version is being updated. One possible format includes the previous version, the current version, and the value—for example, using `System.currentTimeMillis()` in Java to generate version numbers, as follows:

```
1263163821453:1263163821531:89
```

Here you retrieve a count of 89 that was stored as version 1263163821531, and it is based on version 1263163821453. If this is the value you find when you read this attribute and you want to add one to the count, you would write the following value without setting the replace flag:

```
1263163821531:1263176339225:90
```

The previous value is not removed, and you end up with an audit trail of updates that are reminiscent of a version control revision-history. This requires you to do a few extra things, as follows:

- You need to be able to parse the revision tree, identify divergent versions, and merge them whenever the item is read, to get an accurate count.
- A simple version number isn't going to work, so you may want to make it a timestamp, as shown in this code, or include a timestamp in addition to a version number. A process ID could be added as well, to prevent collisions.
- You can't keep an infinite audit trail in one item, so you'll need to issue deletes for older values as you go.

What you get with this technique is like a tree of divergent updates, as depicted in Figure 6-1. There will be one value, and then all of a sudden, multiple updates will occur—you will have a bunch of updated counts based off the same old value, none of which knows about each other because of eventual consistency.

```
1263163821531:1263176339225:90
1263176339225:1263176340021:91
1263163821453:1263163821531:89
1263163821531:1263176340183:90
1263163821531:1263176339941:90
```

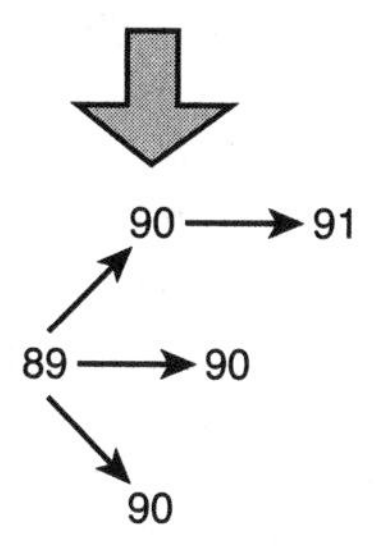

Figure 6-1 Multi-valued attribute representing a count and the corresponding revision tree of count values

Parsing the revision tree means taking the set of values and finding all the values that are not part of the most recent branch. Looking at the example shown in Figure 6-1, the most recent branch ends with the count at 91. Also notice that the version numbers ending in 183 and 941 are not counted as part of the most recent branch. Merging the count values involves combining all the divergent branches to get the total count. The code reading this attribute value needs to be able to figure out that the correct count for this example is 93.

Figuring this out can be done if you include for each new value the version of the value(s) you are updating. There are ways to make this more robust and more complex. If you have to implement this yourself, it may seem like rocket science and is probably overkill. This is why SimpleDB may not be the best choice for making simple counters.

> **Note**
>
> These counters may seem complex, but if all these implementation details were hidden from you, and you just had to call `increment(key)`, it would not be complex at all. With SimpleDB, the client library is the key to making the complex things simple. The problem is the lack of publicly available libraries that implement robust degraded-mode compatible routines like this.

Testing Strategies

Unit testing a SimpleDB-based application is not really a boundary, but it can be an obstacle. If you don't get it right, the tests can be both ineffective and time consuming, which can be a source of frustration. Furthermore, the eventual consistency inherent in SimpleDB provides its own set of testing challenges. You will benefit from keeping testing in mind from the beginning of your SimpleDB development.

Designing for Testability

Your SimpleDB applications will always use a SimpleDB client, whether from a third party or of your own creation. A big part of testability in this situation involves writing to an interface and not an implementation. The difficulty in this will depend on the language and client you use. The basic approach is to create a wrapper class around the client and write your application against the wrapper instead of the client.

Writing to an interface in this manner has three primary benefits. First, it prevents you from being locked into the details of a particular version of a particular client. When a new version comes out or when you decide to try a different client, all of the changes you need to make are conveniently located in one location.

Second, it gives you an appropriate place to put convenience methods and work around the idiosyncrasies of a SimpleDB client. A wrapper is a good place, for example, to put a `GetAttributes` function that returns the values in the form of a map instead of a list. Another example is a `Select` function that automatically issues the follow-up queries based on how many results you want back. This frees your application code from ever seeing the `NextToken`.

The third benefit of writing to the interface is that testing becomes easier. When you run unit tests on your application code, you don't want to test the SimpleDB client, HTTP client, and the SimpleDB service all at the same time. The unit tests should test only the code being written. This enables the tests to run quickly while maintaining a narrow focus. Writing to the interface allows your tests to swap in a substitute test fixture in place of the SimpleDB client. The test client can respond to calls quickly without waiting for responses over the network. It can also support your testing scenarios by storing values in memory between test method calls.

Alternatives to Live Service Calls

Avoiding live services calls in your tests is important. Not only will they slow down your tests, which should execute quickly, they also incur expense and make it more difficult to test eventual consistency. You might think that using live service calls to SimpleDB is a good way to test eventual consistency because your tests are forced to deal with the genuine article. However, the fact is that the duration of real-life eventual consistency is beyond your control, and this is not the same from one test run to the next.

Creating your own tests that use configurable response times and eventual consistencies will enable you to test your application in a wide variety of situations and do it on every test run. This is something that cannot be achieved when your test code is dealing directly with SimpleDB and gives your test a high level of repeatability.

Summary

SimpleDB can be very convenient for simple applications. It can also be a great benefit for applications that are not simple. Whether simple or complex, all types of application design may require some creative thinking to handle the boundaries and limitations enforced by the SimpleDB service. Although you can implement these creative extensions as an application designer, they are probably best handled as part of the implementation of SimpleDB clients. If you use an open-source SimpleDB client and find that you need to add additional functionality, consider contributing it back to the project.

7

Planning for the Application Lifecycle

Over time, long-running applications need more storage space in SimpleDB and may need to support a higher traffic load. Planning for this situation ahead of time and tracking historical usage will serve as an aid to decision making. This chapter covers practical considerations when planning for the future of a SimpleDB application.

Capacity Planning

Planning for the level of storage and bandwidth an application will need is important. Often, the default level of storage and bandwidth available from a database is more than enough to cover the expected usage of an application. This is commonly true of web applications based on a relational database that you manage yourself using reasonably fast hardware. However, with SimpleDB, the limit of 10GB domains can cause an application to run out of space eventually, or even be insufficient from the beginning.

Additionally, there are costs associated with your every use of the database service. Part of the planning you do may need to deal with what the costs will be in the beginning and how they will grow over time. When considering SimpleDB costs, there are both storage costs and box usage costs to factor into your calculations.

Estimating Initial Costs

When you first move to a pay-as-you-go model, it is difficult to know what the actual costs will be. The more basic the service, the easier it is to compute. Storage on S3 is a very simple example—if you know the size of the data you need to store, calculating storage and transfer costs is a straightforward computation. EC2 is not necessarily as simple if you use a framework that automatically spins up new instances as needed. Although you may not know whether the peak will require, for example, 5 or 10 servers, it is possible to calculate the cost of each scenario individually to get an approximation.

Estimating costs in SimpleDB is different from S3 and EC2, though. The storage and transfer costs are just as easy to calculate, but for most applications, the box usage costs are likely to be both the largest percent of the costs and, initially, the largest unknown. The actual box usage numbers returned with SimpleDB responses are not true measurements, but estimates based on a wide variety of factors. You can analyze the numbers, but that doesn't provide a direct indication of what the actual box usage numbers will be in total for a production deployment. A good approach, and maybe the best you can do, is to store a quantity of data similar in size and composition to what you expect to use in production and do some testing to find out how much the various operations are going to cost you.

Some of the costs are fixed, like the cost of a `GetAttributes` call. Other costs are variable based only on what you pass. An example of this type is the `PutAttributes` call, which generates a box usage charge as a factor of how many attributes you store, plus a fixed overhead charge. Calls to `Select` generate a box usage that is much more difficult to predict. Despite the difficulty in estimating ahead of time, all the calls are easy to measure after the fact, and so this is an effective method for gathering that data. However, perform the testing on a domain with as much data as you expect in production, because the costs can vary considerably. If one of the main queries you execute comes back with low box usage numbers with a small domain size, this does not mean that it will always come back with low numbers. In fact, the numbers could both become much larger and then multiply if you need to fetch additional pages because of long query times.

This brings up another important point. Not only do the box usage numbers for `Select` calls grow as the domain grows, but the execution time grows as well. This is entirely expected—the more data you have, the more time it takes to query it. Just be aware that because you are dealing with an external service, you should run performance tests that are as realistic as possible.

Keeping Tabs on SimpleDB Usage with AWS Usage Reports

There are several ways to track your SimpleDB usage over time, and you should definitely use one of them. You don't want to be surprised by extremely high costs, and the best way to avoid the surprise is to track the usage. One way to track SimpleDB usage costs is to use the Amazon-provided reporting.

AWS makes detailed reporting available on the website under the account options. You can select from among all the services for which AWS bills the account. After selecting SimpleDB from the list, you get options for the type of billing. Figure 7-1 shows the AWS usage report page and the usage type options. Types include data transfer in, data transfer out, storage costs, number of requests made, and box usage.

There are separate selections available for the preceding report types in the different regions, so one entry is for "BoxUsage" and another entry is for "EU-BoxUsage." Additionally, you can select to have all the types of usage included in the report. After selecting the type of usage, you can also choose if you want to restrict the report to one particular operation. The choices are the nine SimpleDB operations, plus an option for just storage followed by an option to include them all. Once the set of operations to report on has been made, you can also choose the time period to report on. The choices are the current

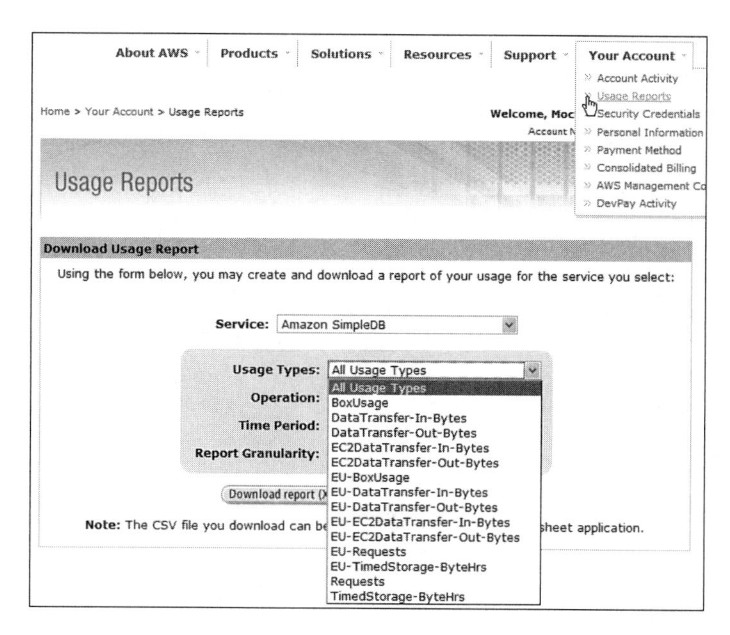

Figure 7-1 AWS usage report page: available usage types

billing period, previous billing period, last week, last month, and custom date range. This enables you to view and compare historical data in addition to data for the billing period currently in progress.

The final option on the AWS report screen lets you select the granularity of the report data. The choices are hours, days, or months. There will be an entry in the report for each time period within the billing period you selected earlier. Selecting hours in combination with a large custom date range can lead to a very large report file. For example, if you chose all operations, report by the hour, and report on a full month's worth of usage, you will get an entry in the report for each hour of each day of the month for each of the operations—for a total of more than 7,000 entries, if you have round-the-clock usage.

Once you have made all the selections, you can choose to download the report as an XML document or as a CSV file. The report you get is just a long list of raw data, so you will need some means to analyze it. If you have a spreadsheet program and prefer to use that for your reporting, that can be a viable option. A sample CSV report download is shown in Figure 7-2, as displayed in a spreadsheet program. To be practical, in the long term, this would either require some sort of automation within the spreadsheet to convert the data into the final report, or else the time commitment (or staff) to do it manually.

If you do not like the idea of generating the report within the spreadsheet or if you want a higher level of automation, the XML document format can be parsed by a program of your own or by a reporting tool. There are a wide variety of reporting tools that accept XML. The XML usage report format is much more verbose than the CSV report, as is typical of XML. Figure 7-3 shows a sample XML report as viewed in an XML editor.

	A	B	C	D	E	F
1	Service	Operation	UsageType	StartTime	EndTime	UsageValue
2	AmazonSimpleDB	StandardStorage	EU-TimedStorage-ByteHrs	1/1/2010 0:00	1/1/2010 1:00	0
3	AmazonSimpleDB	StandardStorage	TimedStorage-ByteHrs	1/1/2010 5:00	1/1/2010 6:00	53294501328
4	AmazonSimpleDB	Select	Requests	1/1/2010 14:00	1/1/2010 15:00	60
5	AmazonSimpleDB	Select	DataTransfer-Out-Bytes	1/1/2010 14:00	1/1/2010 15:00	426379
6	AmazonSimpleDB	Select	DataTransfer-In-Bytes	1/1/2010 14:00	1/1/2010 15:00	41700
7	AmazonSimpleDB	Select	BoxUsage	1/1/2010 14:00	1/1/2010 15:00	0.064873075
8	AmazonSimpleDB	Select	Requests	1/1/2010 18:00	1/1/2010 19:00	56
9	AmazonSimpleDB	Select	DataTransfer-Out-Bytes	1/1/2010 18:00	1/1/2010 19:00	231099
10	AmazonSimpleDB	Select	DataTransfer-In-Bytes	1/1/2010 18:00	1/1/2010 19:00	39889
11	AmazonSimpleDB	Select	BoxUsage	1/1/2010 18:00	1/1/2010 19:00	0.087981657
12	AmazonSimpleDB	Select	BoxUsage	1/1/2010 19:00	1/1/2010 20:00	0.035006029
13	AmazonSimpleDB	Select	Requests	1/1/2010 19:00	1/1/2010 20:00	26
14	AmazonSimpleDB	Select	DataTransfer-Out-Bytes	1/1/2010 19:00	1/1/2010 20:00	100469
15	AmazonSimpleDB	Select	DataTransfer-In-Bytes	1/1/2010 19:00	1/1/2010 20:00	18533
16	AmazonSimpleDB	Select	DataTransfer-Out-Bytes	1/1/2010 20:00	1/1/2010 21:00	64285
17	AmazonSimpleDB	Select	DataTransfer-In-Bytes	1/1/2010 20:00	1/1/2010 21:00	11458
18	AmazonSimpleDB	Select	BoxUsage	1/1/2010 20:00	1/1/2010 21:00	0.02105391
19	AmazonSimpleDB	Select	Requests	1/1/2010 20:00	1/1/2010 21:00	16
20	AmazonSimpleDB	DomainMetadata	DataTransfer-In-Bytes	1/1/2010 21:00	1/1/2010 22:00	497
21	AmazonSimpleDB	Select	DataTransfer-Out-Bytes	1/1/2010 21:00	1/1/2010 22:00	139654
22	AmazonSimpleDB	Select	BoxUsage	1/1/2010 21:00	1/1/2010 22:00	0.135222549
23	AmazonSimpleDB	ListDomains	DataTransfer-Out-Bytes	1/1/2010 21:00	1/1/2010 22:00	449
24	AmazonSimpleDB	ListDomains	BoxUsage	1/1/2010 21:00	1/1/2010 22:00	7.18E-06
25	AmazonSimpleDB	DomainMetadata	DataTransfer-Out-Bytes	1/1/2010 21:00	1/1/2010 22:00	754
26	AmazonSimpleDB	Select	Requests	1/1/2010 21:00	1/1/2010 22:00	97
27	AmazonSimpleDB	DomainMetadata	BoxUsage	1/1/2010 21:00	1/1/2010 22:00	7.18E-06
28	AmazonSimpleDB	Select	DataTransfer-In-Bytes	1/1/2010 21:00	1/1/2010 22:00	88094
29	AmazonSimpleDB	ListDomains	Requests	1/1/2010 21:00	1/1/2010 22:00	1

Figure 7-2 CSV usage report displayed as a spreadsheet

```
<?xml version="1.0" encoding="UTF-8"?>
<ServiceUsage>
  <OperationUsage>
    <ServiceName>AmazonSimpleDB</ServiceName>
    <OperationName>StandardStorage</OperationName>
    <UsageType>EU-TimedStorage-ByteHrs</UsageType>
    <StartTime>01/01/10 00:00:00</StartTime>
    <EndTime>01/01/10 01:00:00</EndTime>
    <UsageValue>0</UsageValue>
  </OperationUsage>
  <OperationUsage>
    <ServiceName>AmazonSimpleDB</ServiceName>
    <OperationName>StandardStorage</OperationName>
    <UsageType>TimedStorage-ByteHrs</UsageType>
    <StartTime>01/01/10 05:00:00</StartTime>
    <EndTime>01/01/10 06:00:00</EndTime>
    <UsageValue>53294501327.8675</UsageValue>
  </OperationUsage>
  <OperationUsage>
    <ServiceName>AmazonSimpleDB</ServiceName>
    <OperationName>Select</OperationName>
    <UsageType>Requests</UsageType>
    <StartTime>01/01/10 14:00:00</StartTime>
    <EndTime>01/01/10 15:00:00</EndTime>
    <UsageValue>60</UsageValue>
  </OperationUsage>
  <OperationUsage>
    <ServiceName>AmazonSimpleDB</ServiceName>
    <OperationName>Select</OperationName>
    <UsageType>DataTransfer-Out-Bytes</UsageType>
    <StartTime>01/01/10 14:00:00</StartTime>
    <EndTime>01/01/10 15:00:00</EndTime>
    <UsageValue>426379</UsageValue>
  </OperationUsage>
```

report.xml

Figure 7-3 XML usage report opened in a text editor

Creating More Finely Detailed Usage Reports

Amazon usage reports provide detail down to the level of the hour, and this may be sufficient for your needs. If you desire a higher level of detail, you will need to track your own usage rather than relying on the AWS-provided reports. My recommendation for self-tracking SimpleDB usage is to have the SimpleDB client log the details of each request to a file. If there are multiple clients running, the files for all of them can be aggregated later based on timestamps. There are many different parsers available for parsing and reporting on web server-style log files. If your SimpleDB logs use a compatible format, this can be more convenient than using the AWS reports, since you don't need to log into your Amazon account on the AWS website and manually download the files.

In addition to mere convenience, you can get a much finer-grained reporting from your own custom logs. The most important place for this functionality is in the tracking of `Select` calls. The best you can tell by looking at the AWS reports alone is that `Select` operations are costing a lot of box usage. You cannot get any detail out of it, other than the cost breakdown by hour, and therefore there are no actionable insights. In fact, because it is probably common sense that the `Select` operations will cost a lot of box usage, you may end up gaining no insight of any kind from seeing the `Select` charges in the AWS report. If you log SimpleDB access yourself, you can include in the log files the actual select expressions being passed, along with the box usage, response size, and response time.

In addition, detailed logging enables a much more in-depth analysis into the true frequency of query use and the associated costs of each. This becomes more and more beneficial when you have various layers of caching in place. When that is the case, there is no other way to know how often you call a particular query. For a web application that already has web server log files, you may be tempted to use the existing web logs for this purpose, combined with an analysis of the code. This will provide more insight than the AWS usage reports alone, but unless the application is very simple, you cannot trust that it is giving you an accurate picture. What looks like the most-used query may end up being served from the cache most of the time, and multiple SimpleDB operations called from the same request cannot be differentiated.

The finer-grained reporting continues to add value beyond the identification of expensive queries. It can provide a wealth of information not available via any other means. Which queries are taking the longest to execute? This is not answered by the box usage; remember that the box usage is a synthetic estimate that is not based on the actual execution time. Why are these errors so expensive? One dimension of box usage that is not broken out at all on the Amazon reports is the box usage costs associated with the errors you receive. In the canned reports, these numbers are rolled into the totals for whichever operation generated the error. When you break out this data in your own report, you find out useful information. Sometimes the box usage for timeout errors and service unavailable errors is significantly higher than normal. Sometimes a query that normally returns in less than 200ms will take 5 seconds, return a `NextToken` with no results, and charge 20 seconds worth of box usage.

These things are rare, and as such, are merely interesting facts, rather than being necessarily actionable on an individual basis. However, if you have the means to do detailed reporting, you then also have the ability to determine if these aberrations correlate with higher-request volumes, large domain sizes, specific queries, and so forth. It may be something that needs to be dealt with by AWS support, or you may need to tweak the application-caching policies. If you don't have your own detailed reporting, you will never know.

Tracking Usage over Time

Although tracking usage can be beneficial during initial testing and deployment to verify costs and work out kinks, it is of particular value in the later phases of the application lifecycle. It is useful for running down issues that crop up, but more importantly, it allows you to plot the path that the application is taking in terms of growth.

Tracking growth across multiple dimensions is important when it comes to planning for the future. Different types of growth have different levels of impact on the application and on the database. For example, if a public web application experiences a spike in traffic from various sources, it may not have a large impact on storage if most of those new visitors either don't create an account and continue to use the site or if the usage is low. Another example is that a steady growth in data size could eventually cause a cascade of performance issues, even when there is not a significant increase in traffic.

Having the ability to plot different usage and growth trends over time can enable the types of planning that keep the application running smoothly. Either AWS logs or detailed logs can be used for this purpose. The detailed logging can lead to insights that are more actionable, but the larger trends will be present regardless and the added detail typically is not needed, except for purposes of drilling down into the data.

Storage Requirements

It is important to be aware of the SimpleDB performance characteristics compared to your other storage options. SimpleDB has significant differences from other types of storage you may use. When you compare SimpleDB to Amazon S3, at first glance you see that storage costs are more than 50% higher than S3 and the storage limits are much lower. In fact, despite the S3 limit on file size, the number of files you can store is actually unlimited. Although the data you store in both SimpleDB and S3 is replicated for high availability, there are many differences. One major difference is that S3 is optimized for accessing large files. This involves dense storage drives optimized for the cheap storage of those large files. SimpleDB, on the other hand, is not tuned for low cost, but for fast access to smaller chunks of data. This involves the use of storage drives that are less dense. Additionally, SimpleDB maintains indexes for every attribute name, to enable fast queries. These differences amount to very different sets of capabilities and a higher per-gigabyte storage cost for the additional SimpleDB features.

When comparing SimpleDB to other database products or services, it is good to keep in mind that, unlike a database running on a single server, SimpleDB is automatically replicated to multiple servers; thus, the storage costs may be higher. When comparing

SimpleDB to a relational database, it may be more accurate to compare costs based on a relational database cluster rather than a single database.

Computing Storage Costs

When computing storage costs, there is an additional charge for the storage of the index. The extra charge is assessed as the addition of 45 bytes added to the billable storage total for each entry in an index. These entries come in one of three forms: an item name, an attribute name, or an attribute value. For the majority of applications, the attribute name costs will be negligible, being dwarfed by the comparatively larger number of item names and values.

For the purposes of the storage cost billing, you can consider the item name to be just like any other attribute value being stored. As a result, the (simplified) formula for computing the billable per item storage is TotalBytesStored + NumberOfValues x 45. In this formula, each value of a multi-valued attribute, each value for a single attribute, and the item name each count once for the purpose of counting the number of values. These additional billable storage bytes are probably an accurate indicator of the index data that SimpleDB needs to store. However, the next section details some important implications of these costs related to the slack space in your data.

Understanding the Cost of Slack Space

The index storage cost can be a small part of your total storage costs, but depending on the data you store, it could also become larger than the raw storage numbers. This can happen if the size of the values you are storing is consistently less than 45 bytes. Some values are likely to be naturally small. A popular format of randomized UUID is frequently used for item names in the absence of an auto-increment feature. This UUID is 36 bytes long. User tags are frequently short in length, sometimes averaging only two to six letters long. 64-bit integers and floats can be stored in a string searchable format for 24 or fewer bytes. Sometimes there is a need to indicate that an item is one of a small number of types. For example, a user account could be active or suspended, a post could be open to comments or locked, or an event on a calendar could be pending, scheduled, or completed. These type fields can usually be stored with a single byte value.

Storing many small values has the effect of leaving a lot of slack space in attribute values, when you compare it to the size of what could be stored there. There is nothing wrong with this, and there is no extra charge for that slack space; you are charged for the actual bytes you store. However, you should be aware that there is also no discount on the index cost for small values. If you store an attribute value of only one byte, you still get charged for the additional 45 bytes for the index. Therefore, it is possible to store 2GB of values that average out to be 10 characters long and be charged for an additional 8GB worth of index.

Although the cost of storage is really not that high, it is still good to be informed about how the system works. You certainly won't benefit from storing your data in a more verbose format just to save slack space. That will reduce the percentage of your costs that come from index storage, but it will accomplish it by raising the overall cost, rather than reducing it. However, there is something you can do about it if it is a problem for you—you can store multiple logical values together in a single attribute value.

Evaluating Attribute Concatenation

Before you take that step, you should understand what you gain by separating out your data into naturally distinct attributes in the first place. You essentially gain three things. First, you can query for that attribute individually. Part of the benefit of using SimpleDB is the query capability, so there are probably values that you are required to include in queries. Others, however, may not need to be queried. The second benefit is the ability to have the equivalent of an array of values by using a multi-valued attribute. This can be very useful, and there is nothing special you need to do to enable this feature for any value of any item, other than keep it in its own attribute. The third thing you gain is the ability to update the value in isolation. This allows multiple clients to update different values within the same item without stepping on each other. If you concatenate values together, you lose this ability.

Knowing what you gain with separate attributes allows you to evaluate when it may be beneficial to combine attributes. If the values are small, are never queried, never contain multiple values, and are never updated independently by concurrent clients, it might be worth considering. To weigh the other side of the equation, here is what you will gain by combining attributes. First, you will save on the cost of index storage by having fewer attributes to index. Second, you will save on `PutAttributes` costs, which can be an issue because the box usage charge of `PutAttributes` is proportional to the number of attributes cubed. This is a surprising and extraordinary fact; however, you are not charged for box usage based on the size of the `PutAttributes` but instead on the number of attributes raised to the power of three. Anything over 53 attributes could be more cheaply stored with two separate calls.

One requirement this attribute-combining puts on the application is the ability to concatenate and parse these combined values in all situations. Ideally, this could be done automatically in a persistence layer, if at all. However, this does reduce flexibility for the future and thus should only be considered if storage costs are a serious issue.

Scalability: Increasing the Load

If you cannot get the throughput or performance you need from the initial number of domains for an application, it may be necessary to spread out the data across more domains. This can also be the case if the domain actually becomes full, but that is less likely. Performance tends to degrade faster as the domain fills up, so the need to expand will probably be felt before it is enforced. If your application is able to archive older items, if archiving fits into your application processing, that is something to consider before sharding. However, the primary unit of scalability in SimpleDB is the domain. This is true whether you are talking about scaling up the bandwidth, scaling up the storage, or scaling up the concurrency. Unfortunately, increasing the number of domains is seldom a simple matter. The data set must first support partitioning, and many types of data are not well suited to this.

There is a limit to how far you will be able to scale when the data cannot be split across multiple domains. This is something that needs to be considered upfront. In one respect, this may be easier than with the data in a relational database. Without the ability to create relations and perform joins, the data is naturally connected more loosely. If your data is structured such that the individual item forms the basis of unique data that must change together, as it ideally should, the process of splitting data may be easier.

One way to split the data is across a natural boundary. For instance, the data can be split across the natural categories already present, such as music, movies, and games or apparel for men, women, and infants. Other types of natural boundaries could be users, posts, and votes. If there are no natural boundaries, or if there are many but all are too small to warrant a domain, you are left with an arbitrary splitting. Moreover, this can also be the case if you have already split the data but still need the ability to scale more.

Splitting you data arbitrarily across domains will most likely involve using a hash function to assign each to one of the available domains. This is a straightforward process for all operations except Select. If you hash the items based on the item name, and if you perform `GetAttributes`, `PutAttributes`, and `DeleteAttributes` based on the item names, it is a simple matter of hashing the item name before each call to determine the proper domain.

The complication with data splitting and `Select` is a twofold problem that involves logistics and expense. On the logistics side, under ideal conditions, you will need to multiplex every query to each domain. For example, if you store metadata for videos in two domains, every time you perform a query to find videos with a specified tag, you will have to issue the query to both domains. This is not a problem from a performance standpoint—because you can call the queries concurrently, it will actually be faster. The multiplexing difficulty arises both from the need to have a mechanism in place to make the calls concurrently, which not every SimpleDB client supports, and from the standpoint of box usage. You will need some framework, or SimpleDB client extension to handle the concurrent calls, because there is some trickiness involved. The domain name will need to be substituted into the body of each `SelectExpression`, since it resides within the string and not as a parameter, like the other operations. The concurrency will need to be implemented, and this could mean multiple threads or asynchronous I/O. Scaling across domains will yield faster query times if done concurrently, but will lead to slower times if the queries are called sequentially. Additionally, the standard mechanisms of retrying the queries that experience a timeout or require the fetching of multiple pages will need to be in place. This is a more complicated affair because of the concurrency, and troubleshooting problems is more difficult.

The preceding discussion assumed that it is possible to multiplex `Select` calls successfully across multiple domains, but this condition is not always true. The factor to consider is the data model. If the logical unit of data that constitutes a query match can all be placed within the level of a single item, then this is ideal. But if you are not able to fit all the data into one item and make up for it by allowing that logical data to spill over into multiple items, there are going to be problems with multi-domain queries. It is easy to analyze how this will work for your application by taking a dozen sample items, splitting them across two domains and constructing the queries by hand. If you can make it work with two domains, it will work with any number of domains.

When the time comes to increase the number of domains in use, you have the same two options as when making other major types of SimpleDB maintenance. The two options are to either do it all at once during a period of downtime or update data during live usage of the application. These two options are explored in the next section.

Planning Maintenance

For simple applications or applications that do not need to undergo major changes, there may never be a need for large maintenance tasks. Nevertheless, there are many types of changes that may need to be made that would necessitate database-wide changes. SimpleDB maintains no schema requirements, but formatting is required to make numbers searchable; if you need to roll out a change in the format, you will need to deal with the SimpleDB equivalent of a schema update. Luckily, you should not need to take your application offline to implement the change. There are also other types of changes you may need to make on a large scale. The most convenient way to make any of these updates may be via a single blocking update procedure during a maintenance window, but read-repair updates are also a viable alternative.

Using Read-Repair to Apply Formatting Changes

Read-repair is a process that involves making changes incrementally over time to each item as an additional overhead at the time it is read. This is in contrast to stopping all access to the database and making all the changes in one large shot. If you primarily access data items using the item name, this technique can be effective. If there is a combination of item name and query access but the queries are mainly not sorted, read-repair could still work well. It is less suitable when sorted queries are continually being issued; it will require more work to accomplish.

The general technique first requires you to have a way to indicate what is changing. You will need to have the code to read both formats, old and new, and differentiate between them. Once you signal for the change to begin, the normal flow of your application should continue. Whenever the target of the change is detected on a read operation, an additional write operation is added that overwrites the old value with the new value. In the beginning, all the items that come back may need the repair. The popular items will be updated quickly, and the remainder will be the target updates over time in the order that they are actually accessed. In the end, you may need to clean up some items that were never accessed, but once you have the process working well, the cleanup may not be an issue.

An example of this type of change is if you have a certain count value stored in an attribute named "count." In the beginning, consider that you may have stored it in a format compatible with storing 32-bit integers. But now you find that you need to support larger numbers and need to move to a format capable of storing 64-bit integers. In this example, assume that this SimpleDB domain is being used as a key-value store, and there are no Select statements to consider. The steps you need to take, which should probably be a part of the persistence layer, are the following:

- Set the type information for this field to indicate the old format and the new format.
- Store the format information where the SimpleDB client can find it and use it for all subsequent calls to `PutAttributes`. The new format needs to be used for all subsequent writes of this.
- Access that stored format information from every call to `GetAttributes`. At the completion of each read where this attribute is present, the format of the value needs to be checked. If it is in the old format, a follow-up `PutAttributes` call needs to be made immediately with the single value in the new format, overwriting the old value. This call can be done asynchronously.

The reason the call needs to be immediately is so subsequent writes that update the value are not clobbered by the automatic format update.

When there are queries to consider, there is some additional work to do. There are basically three types of query handling to be done. The three cases cover the three levels of importance the attribute with the changing format can have to the query it is in.

In the first type of query, the attribute is present in the output selection clause but not in the `Where` clause. In this situation, the attribute is merely being returned as a value, and the format does not impact what the query returns. This case is very similar to the `GetAttributes` case. The query results need to be examined for items with the old format and a follow-up set of writes need to be made for those items. The writes can be rolled up into a `BatchPutAttributes` request for convenience, and depending on the size of the query results, more than one batch call may need to be made. This will also work for queries that use `count(*)` as the output selection parameter.

The second type adds an additional complication that may prevent read-repair entirely for the given attribute. These are the queries where the attribute in question is part of the actual search criteria. In this case, it is not always possible to use read-repair because it may not be possible to get correct query results back while values exist in two different formats. If the query uses equality via either the equals operator or the `IN()` function, it will be possible. Multiple queries will have to be issued for each query where the target attribute is in the Where clause, until such time as the read-repair is complete. If another type of comparison, other than equality, is used in the Where clause, it may not even be possible to match the criteria during a format change. It will depend on how the format is changing and what other criteria are in the query. You will need to analyze each query where this is the case to determine if it is possible.

The final case is when the target attribute is the subject of the `ORDER BY` clause. This case is similar to the previous case, except that because it is rare to sort on a value selected with an equality operator, it is almost certainly not possible to use read-repair in this situation.

Using Read-Repair to Update Item Layout

Adding new fields to items that already exist is especially easy in SimpleDB. Whether you use a batch process or make the changes more slowly over time is up to you. There are no schema changes to coordinate between clients or between domains. You are free to make just the changes as you need to. This can include the same read-repair style process as discussed previously with the format changes.

More simply, you may just be adding a new data field. If this is the case, you can just add the data when it is available. For example, if a user-tagging feature is being rolled out, you can just deploy the code responsible for storing the tags. The tags will be stored as they are created, and there is nothing special that needs to be done.

In a case where you already have the full set of data, you will need to put into place a mechanism to backfill the existing items in addition to adding the new values. Read-repair can work nicely for this in situations where an extended but incremental performance hit is more desirable than a short but full outage. An example is a count that is derived (and then cached) from a query, and now you want to store the actual count value in the item. Assuming it is a vote count, updating the vote count as votes are made will be part of the normal application code, but going back to update the older votes can be done as a special-case process while old-style items still exist. The read-repair can be done in the same steps as with a format change, transitioning between the old way and the new way. In this case, there is no need to run separate queries; it is the old vote-count query that must be run if there is no vote value in the item. Therefore, the code must be able to detect the old style items as they are read and make the change.

Using a Batch Process to Apply Updates

Updating the format or the layout of data items in SimpleDB has the benefits of speed and simplicity. The drawback is that you will need to prevent normal application access to the domain during the course of the update. If you are able to use a scheduled maintenance period to perform changes, using a batch update can be very convenient. The speed comes from the fact that you can submit updates as fast as SimpleDB will accept them without competing with normal application requests for domain bandwidth. This is how you would expect to apply an update.

The simplicity, compared to the read-repair approach, comes from the fact that you do not need to implement and test any special application logic. The expected application changes still have to be made surrounding the changes being applied, but nothing extra. Further, those changes may be confined to a persistence layer and only touch the application code via annotations or configuration. All of the data conversion logic remains neatly contained within the update utility, which can run to completion, enabling a nice clean end to the update activities.

Summary

If your application is one where growth is steady and performance is critical, it is wise to keep an eye on database usage and growth. Although rolling out synchronous schema updates is not typically part of SimpleDB usage, by design, some of the same issues can crop up and require some attention. In particular, you may need some form of limited and homegrown schema to manage object mapping, admin tools, or reporting tools in some combination. If you do, it is best to be informed about what a schema change rollout might look like.

8

Security in SimpleDB-Based Applications

A single secret key may be the only thing that stands between the public Internet and all the data you have in SimpleDB. Security is an important consideration during the development of any application. The use of web services in the cloud has the benefit of reducing maintenance costs, but it also serves to reduce the amount of control, and it can make security seem like more of an unknown quantity.

This chapter discusses security topics that apply to applications storing data in SimpleDB. The discussion includes many of the differences between applications running within the Amazon cloud and those using SimpleDB from the outside.

The three primary security areas covered are those pertaining to securing the AWS account, securing the service access keys, and securing the data.

Account Security

The safekeeping of your Amazon Web Services account is crucial. The account used to create a SimpleDB domain automatically has access to perform all operations on that domain. Anyone with access to that account will be able to view all the data, add to or update the data, and delete any or all of that data. The security and integrity of your data is at stake if you do not protect your account credentials.

Managing Access Within the Organization

Not only is your data at risk, your money is at risk too. The AWS account may also be tied to other services besides SimpleDB. An unauthorized user accessing a compromised account could also have access to run EC2 instances and use other resources that will end up costing you money and leave a mess for you to clean up. The first rule to follow is to limit access to the account credentials to only those people who actually need them. The primary use of the credentials is administrative. They are not required for day-to-day use by applications to access SimpleDB domains. Only trusted people playing the role of database administrator should have access to them.

Here is a list of the AWS tasks requiring account access:

- Downloading usage reports
- Signing up for any Amazon Web Service
- Viewing or modifying payment information
- Activating, deactivating, or creating access keys
- Consolidating billing
- Using the AWS management console

Limiting the access to account credentials in production to only those people required to perform the preceding tasks offers a first line of defense. Typically, these are the people in production support positions.

Although low-level software unit testing can be done using SimpleDB substitutes, other types of testing will require access to an actual SimpleDB account. This may not be an issue for small organizations and departments using the service in isolation. Larger organizations, however, can face a challenge when dealing with the need to use the service widely and safeguard account credentials.

The best solutions provide a way for each distinct group of stakeholders to maintain responsibility for their own account and account credentials. Remember that this concerns the AWS website login credentials and not the access keys used by applications. When there are database administrators and managers on staff tasked with handling database access and budgetary matters, the developers likely have no need for account credentials.

Also, remember that the AWS account is the management point for more than just SimpleDB. S3, EC2, RDS, and all the other services all require the same level of account handling. The challenge comes from trying to balance the separation benefits that come from multiple accounts with the headache associated with the need to deal with many accounts.

Consolidated billing offers a clean way to link AWS accounts and separate the technical concerns from the payment concerns. The feature allows the billing detail and payment responsibility for one account to be forwarded to a designated account, without granting any other privileges. At the end of the month, the billing account is charged instead of the account that accrued the charges. The billing account can see the breakdown of the charges but cannot manage or view resources or keys associated with the forwarding account.

This can work between any two AWS accounts and between multiple accounts. However, the primary intended configuration is to have multiple accounts that directly use Amazon services and forward the billing to a single account with no direct service access. This leaves one account to handle only billing and the remainder to handle only the technical matters. Figure 8-1 shows a graphical depiction of multiple accounts linked with consolidated billing.

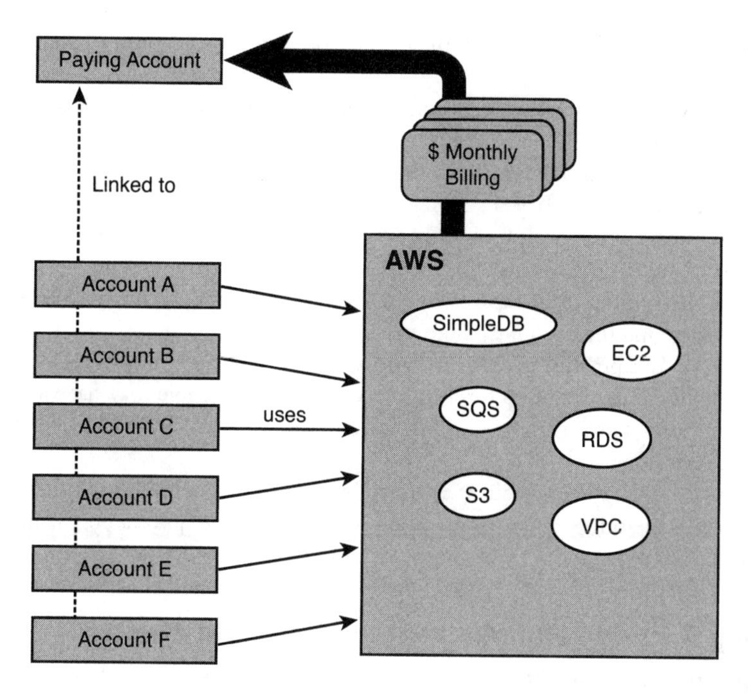

Figure 8-1 Multiple AWS accounts linked with consolidated billing

Account consolidation can be convenient if it fits well with your organizational structure. Better alignment can be achieved by mapping the accounts you need to the people or roles who manage them, as opposed to arbitrarily mapping accounts to departments or groups. Although different groups may have isolated needs, access to computing resources cuts across concerns.

However, the convenience of billing consolidation does not in any way lessen the need for security. Even though the billing for a given account is forwarded to an alternate account with no special access, the original account is no more secure than before. The risk of unauthorized access to the account is unchanged by the consolidation. The IT administration, DBA, or production support members with security responsibilities are the ones who ought to be handling the AWS account credentials.

Limiting Amazon Access from AWS Credentials

An AWS account is really a specific add-on or upgrade to a more general Amazon.com account. The Amazon.com account that exists behind every AWS account uses the same username and password, and grants access to the wide range of services available on the Amazon website. As a result, a raft of additional non-web service tasks can be performed with the Amazon account credentials. Those actions include placing product orders on the Amazon.com retail site and accessing an Amazon payments account or Amazon seller account.

All active AWS accounts must have valid payment information attached, so compromised accounts have the potential to be used for making direct purchases. This provides even more incentive to protect the account.

One area where unnecessary access can leak is with the AWS online support forums. Although the forums require you to login with an Amazon.com account, they do not require the AWS credentials you use for your production deployments. There is no special security risk when using these forums, and if the person posting to the forums is always the person managing the accounts, there may be no problem.

Nevertheless, this practice is not recommended. Access to the support forums are available to anyone willing to sign up for a free account. Various people may have a need to post on the forums, but it is unwise to pass around the AWS account login information for that purpose alone.

It is best to use the AWS accounts exclusively for web services and use other accounts to participate in the other Amazon programs, such as corporate purchasing, selling, shopping, product reviewing, fulfillment, and wish listing.

Boosting Security with Multi-Factor Authentication

One feature that can be used to boost AWS account security significantly is associating a multi-factor authentication (MFA) device with the account. By default, access is granted to the AWS account based on one factor. MFA requires an additional, unrelated factor to be supplied before allowing access to the account.

The default single factor authentication is a function of something you know: the password. In MFA mode, a second factor is added that is a function of something you have: an electronic device. AWS currently supports one specific device produced by Gemalto, Inc. Each device is unique, and you must have access to that one device each time you want to log in to the AWS account. To find out the specifics about this device and view the official information published by Amazon, open the web address http://aws.amazon.com/mfa/ in your web browser.

The device is the size of a small car-door remote and can fit on a key chain. The device has a single button and a numeric LCD display screen. Each time the button is pushed, a different number appears on the screen. On the back, a unique serial number is printed.

Before you can use the device, it must be associated to the account. This is done by selecting the option while logged into the AWS account. The serial number and consecutive number readouts are used for confirmation. Once the device is associated, the login process changes. After the normal username and password are verified, a new screen is displayed, prompting you to provide a current readout on the device. Only then is account access granted.

The added security is substantial; no one is able to log in to the account without the device and the password, for any reason. Employees or consultants who had access to the account credentials but have since left the company have no method of continued access. The account is also more secure against outside attack. Phishing scams, cross-site scripting attacks, and all other remote attacks are unable to supply account access in the absence of the physical device.

However, the security also applies to valid users. Administrators receiving a support call at home in the middle of the night cannot disable compromised AWS access keys without the device, even when they have full remote access to company systems. If the administrator carries the device home on a keychain, no one else is able to gain access to the account in its absence. Higher security involves a loss of convenience. If you have more than one account to manage, and you wonder if you can use the same device to secure multiple accounts, the answer is no. An MFA device can only be associated with a single account.

The actual content that remains locked behind MFA is limited to the AWS account and the Amazon Management Console. All other use of the account is still available to users with only the username and password. This includes access to shopping, the AWS support forums, and the other Amazon services.

Access Key Security

The AWS account credentials covered previously allow management of every aspect of the account. The Access Key ID and Secret Access Key, on the other hand, only permit access to the individual services and not the account management. These keys, however, are still important to keep safe.

Although very few people need access to the account credentials, the access keys will need to be distributed more widely. Each application using Amazon Web Services that you develop will need access to the keys during development, testing, and deployment.

Any tools you use will also need these keys. Common tools include S3 file transfer apps, SimpleDB query and backup tools, and EC2 launching and monitoring tools. In the midst of this wider distribution of credentials, it pays to guard them within a circle of trust.

Key Management

One good thing about key management in the AWS account is that it makes it easy to generate new credentials. Two sets of keys can exist for an account, and they can be disabled and deleted at any time. Generating a new set of keys requires nothing more than a button push on the AWS account page.

Once a pair of keys has been generated, the distribution of the credentials from the AWS website out to the applications is up to you. There are not any tools to automate the process of logging into your AWS account on the web and downloading the keys; someone has to do it manually. However, once that has been done, there is plenty of room for automating the process of key distribution. The keys are just text strings.

A very convenient arrangement is when a deployed application is able to detect a change in credential settings and switch to the new keys automatically. Another deployment option is for the application to look for new credentials in the event of a SimpleDB authentication failure. In both of these cases, the convenience comes from the elimination of an application restart to pick up new credentials.

The location of configuration files varies depending on the application and platform. For example, J2EE configuration might be in the web.xml file, whereas .NET settings might reside within the app.config file. Regardless of where the standard configuration is, if you want the ability to swap access keys without bringing down the application, it's best to store them in a file under your control. That frees you from reliance on another framework. For instance, if you place the keys within web.xml in J2EE, you won't have access to the updated keys until the application server decides to reload the web context.

In a situation where the access keys need to be replaced in a live running system, the benefits of this type of automation increase with the number of servers. However, even if there is not automation, the keys certainly should not be hard coded into the application; doing so would make it both brittle and insecure.

If you don't anticipate the need to change AWS credentials often, or if reloading the application is not a burden, then putting them where you would normally put the database credentials is probably a good idea. In a web application, that might mean putting it in a deployment descriptor or standard configuration file. For a stand-alone server application, it should go where the rest of the configuration goes.

Use caution when dealing with tools that need AWS access keys. There are an ever-growing number of tools to make your Amazon cloud deployment life easier. However, be careful that your credentials are being treated with adequate security precautions.

Secret Key Rotation

A general practice that can help limit your losses in the event of compromised keys is key rotation. When logged into the AWS account manager, you have the option to create a second set of keys. You have the ability to deactivate or delete the keys at any time.

To rotate the keys, you just log in, delete the old key, and generate a new key at regular intervals. As a result, you do not end up in a situation where an unauthorized user has access to the account over a long period using an old key.

There needs to be a process in place to distribute the new key each time it is generated. This is where there is room for some automation. The presence of two active keys is what makes the rotation work, even with large deployments. Both keys remain active during the distribution period, and the old one is deactivated only when it is no longer being used.

In addition to limiting your exposure, key rotation helps you clarify who has your keys and who really needs the keys. You can track who has them because it is part of the distribution process. As the rotation marches on, applications or projects no longer in need of the key may opt out rather than deal with unnecessary updates.

The key distribution will also need to include the tools you use, although this can be harder to automate. However, for third-party tool providers that hold a copy of your access keys, rotation is definitely a good thing. This is especially true for tools you merely evaluate, or tools that you no longer user. If you don't know how much care they take with your access keys, rotation makes it so you have nothing to fear from old credentials that were never properly purged.

A special case of key handling is to generate special-purpose keys. The key is then only used for the one database import, for example, and then deleted. This limits your exposure on a one-off basis, but is not a good substitute for a solid key rotation process.

> **Access Key Security in Desktop and Browser Applications**
>
> There is only one effective way to secure AWS access keys when used in applications that run on the user's machine, like desktop applications and JavaScript code running in a browser. The security technique is this: Do not put your keys there because it is not secure.
>
> Any time you put your access keys on a client machine, you open up a security vulnerability, because all SimpleDB operations are available for all domains in the account. The same is true for all of the other REST or query-based Amazon Web Services associated with your SimpleDB access keys. Key rotation will not help you because you will need to distribute the new keys out to the same clients.
>
> I have been making SimpleDB feature requests on the AWS support forums for several years now for S3-style access control lists, or SQS-style access policy language. A feature like this would allow keys to be distributed with strictly limited risk, or open the option for users to access your resources using their own keys. Because no such feature has emerged, the desktop and browser is not a safe storage location for your access keys. Applications in this space need to proxy calls through a server that holds the keys and signs the requests.

Data Security

Another aspect of security pertains to how you protect the sensitive bits of application data. Although account security is always important, the need for data security depends on the type of data being stored. Applications mashing up freely available information from the web, for example, have little need to protect it. Private enterprise data that provides a competitive advantage and personal user data both clearly require protection.

Regardless of the type of data in question, keeping it safe means examining the ways it could be compromised. Whether it is traveling across the open Internet or tucked away on a drive spindle in a data center, it does not become secure unless someone works to make it secure.

Storing Clean Data

One of the first things to think about with regard to collecting and transmitting user data is the possibility that the data you collect could include cross-site scripting (XSS) attacks. XSS is a website attack that, when successful, allows an attacker to execute malicious scripts from another site in the browsers of all the users visiting the infected page.

XSS is a serious threat. It can allow an attacker to steal the site-specific credentials of users and administrators, steal browser cookies, and automatically take actions with the user's session, like posting links or sending spam messages.

Although XSS should be a security concern for any site, it is most specifically a danger to those sites driven by a database. XSS attack vectors depend on pages that store data gathered from users and then display that data without the proper sanitization. If you store user-entered data in SimpleDB and then display that data to other users in a web page, your application could be just as vulnerable as any site that runs off database content.

The basis of the attack is that the attacker must find a way to inject script code that will intermingle with the HTML in the page. The key to preventing this is to sanitize all user-submitted data by stripping out the things that can break the HTML. In the case of user data that does not need to contain any HTML markup, sanitizing is very easy. Angle brackets, ampersands, and the various quote characters need to be encoded. This encoding alone will stop the vast majority of script injection attacks by blocking the insertion of malicious HTML tags. However, it has to be applied consistently to *all* user data, including links, images, usernames, and so forth, before it is stored in the database.

It is much more difficult to protect against XSS attacks when the user-entered data is designed to allow HTML tags. The same goals apply in trying to keep the data clean, but stripping out all the special markup characters is not an option. The best approach in this case is a comprehensive white list of the HTML tags that will be allowed along with the approved tag attributes, if any. For example, you may choose to allow only `<p>`, `<b>`, `<strong>`, `<i>`, `<strike>`, `<code>`, and `<a href= "">`. In this case, all tags and attributes need to be filtered out or encoded ruthlessly.

The white list approach of things to accept is far superior to a black list of things to ban. It is significantly more work to try to name all the bad things and also more prone to error. As a matter of computer security, an error of omission while black listing the malicious is called a vulnerability, whereas an error of omission while white listing the innocuous is called a feature request.

SSL and Data in Transmission

Data sent over the open Internet can be intercepted or observed. You do not have control over the systems between the endpoints, and one of those systems could be listening in.

At an application level, you need to decide what portion of the data should be encrypted over the wire and between which endpoints. If you want to use standard SSL encryption between the client and the server running your SimpleDB-based application, it may be a wise choice. However, that choice has nothing to do with SimpleDB.

The choice that is relevant to this discussion is whether to encrypt between the server and the SimpleDB endpoint. SimpleDB supports SSL encryption using HTTPS and port 443. All of the major SimpleDB clients support SSL.

The benefits of using SSL include security against data interception, packet replay attacks, and man-in-the-middle attacks. There is no real configuration downside, since it amounts to flipping a switch. However, there is additional latency in setting up each connection while the encryption is negotiated. None of the technical issues are a big concern; the two deciding factors should be 1) the location of the server and 2) the desired level of security.

Location, Location, Location

Endorsing server location as the primary decision criteria is for one simple reason. If the server is running within the Amazon cloud, in the same region as the SimpleDB endpoint, SSL is essentially worthless. It is true not because it has no effect, but because it provides no added benefits.

Amazon takes security seriously, and EC2 instances are well locked down by default. You cannot even SSH into your own instance without first specifically opening port 22. Moreover, network security is also very tight. Under no circumstances are network packets addressed to one instance delivered to a different instance. This is even true of multiple instances running on the same physical hardware with network adapters configured for promiscuous mode.

The result is that the EC2 to SimpleDB pipe is already well protected. Packets cannot be intercepted, so you are never subject to packet replay or man-in-the-middle attacks. The only additional protection you get from SSL is from Amazon employees listening in. However, this also is of no benefit since those few employees with physical access to the network also have physical access to the server before it encrypts the data and the SimpleDB replicas storing the unencrypted data. Therefore, it still provides a sum total of zero additional protection.

This does not mean that unauthorized physical access to your SimpleDB data should be a big concern. Amazon keeps the exact locations of the data centers secret, provides perimeter security around the buildings, and requires security credentials to be provided at multiple checkpoints within the building to get into the server rooms. Even then, only those who require access to those rooms are allowed in, and they are subject to a background check.

Of course, this is not a guarantee against unauthorized internal access, but it provides evidence of how important security is to Amazon and of how far they are willing to go in taking reasonable precautions to safeguard your data.

The bottom line is that SSL within the Amazon cloud is extra latency with nothing tangible to show for it. In addition, the added latency is particularly unwelcome with SimpleDB applications running on EC2 for several reasons. First, EC2 is presumably being used, at least partially, because of the reduced latency to SimpleDB. Second, high-volume SimpleDB access is heavy on the reconnects. Only the smallest requests can be pipelined; every medium-sized and larger request requires opening a new connection, and the initial connection overhead is the worst part of SSL latency.

Level of Security

For access to SimpleDB from anywhere else, the specific location makes no difference because the open Internet will be between the endpoints. If the need for connection security is there, SSL should be considered. The security benefits can be realized in this case.

The additional SSL latency is actually worse from outside the Amazon cloud. This is true because the inherently higher round-trip latencies are multiplied by the upfront SSL handshaking messages—the larger the base latency, the more pronounced the SSL overhead is.

Access to SimpleDB from other non-Amazon data centers in the same part of the country is not slow and can provide speed that is adequate for a variety of applications. SSL for these applications is not likely to be crippling. In fact, optimizing for this scenario can involve performing full `GetAttributes` calls and the use of `SELECT *` to facilitate caching and take advantage of the smaller incremental cost of pulling down more data per request. Both of these performance enhancers, fewer requests with more data and caching, also mitigate the SSL connection overhead. Fewer connections results in fewer handshakes, and effective caching results in even fewer handshakes.

The bottom line from outside the Amazon cloud is to let security considerations become the deciding factor for SSL use between the server and SimpleDB.

Data Storage and Encryption

Using SSL to encrypt data over the wire provides security against a narrow range of attacks. The threats are real; however, the focus is tight. A much broader security measure is to encrypt the actual data and not just the connection.

On the face of it, encrypted data storage prevents it from being read both during transmission and while it remains stored in the database. Unfortunately, just like SSL, the use case for data encryption from EC2 is completely pointless. To understand why, ask yourself from whom the encryption protects you.

The answer is not anyone on the open Internet, since the EC2 to SimpleDB pipe never leaves the Amazon cloud. The answer is not other AWS users, since they can access neither your network traffic nor your SimpleDB domains. The only conceivable protection you get is against Amazon staff members, either acting as lone attackers, or as part of an internal investigation of bad account behavior, or acting on behalf of law enforcement armed with a court order.

In all of those cases, the encryption has not helped you because you are keeping the decryption key on an EC2 instance. The EC2 instance is just as accessible to those people. It would be like locking your front door and leaving the key under the doormat: It may be convenient, but it is lousy security. Encryption for the purpose of security demands that you make the key difficult for an intruder to obtain.

On the other hand, the case for encrypting sensitive data on the outside and storing it in SimpleDB is easy to make. No one in the Amazon fold would have the ability to decrypt it, the brute-force capabilities of hundreds of thousands of commodity servers in close proximity not withstanding.

One thing to be clear about is the fact that although the case can be made for this encryption, it still offers protection only against the exact same group of Amazon employees and law enforcement officials but no one else. In order to make a rational case for data encryption, you need a real reason to protect against these threats. A false sense of security provides only imagined benefits.

The common reason for encrypting this data is in order to adhere to privacy regulations or policies. Certain rules apply when you need to store credit card data or patient health information. The accessibility of certain sensitive data to the IT personnel is one of the things for which an account needs to be made.

If you do decide to encrypt data before you store it, there are a few side effects. The biggest one may be that you lose the ability to do most queries against the attributes that are encrypted. The only comparison operator you can use on encrypted data is the equality operator. Even then, the data value within the query must be encrypted first. Sorting on any of those attributes will also be off the table.

If the data is fully encrypted, it essentially results in the loss of queries. Encryption also results in an increase in the number of bytes when the raw bytes are Base 64 encoded. Take care that the 1,024-byte limit is not exceeded. When data encryption is used, SSL will probably not be needed.

Storing Data in Multiple Locations

Another security option you have is to break down the data and store it in different locations. One example of this is patient health data. The individual bits of data are not as sensitive as the correlation between personally identifiable information and the procedures, treatments, and diagnosis information.

A large set of regulations govern the storage and transmission of protected health information in the United States. Data security is only one small piece of the puzzle. Organizational policies, procedures, training, and disaster recovery are just a few of the areas subject to audit. The Amazon cloud offers both the security controls and the privacy controls needed for the deployment of compliant applications.

In the context of database storage, the multiple location option allows for storing part of the data (procedures and billing, for example) in SimpleDB, with only a primary key to identify patients. The primary key references patient data, like name and contact info, stored at another location.

This arrangement prevents a security breach at one location from exposing usable information. As a practical matter, it results in a bifurcated system performing the same types of data storage in different ways. However, it can make full data encryption unnecessary, and it allows the smaller fraction of sensitive data to be stored with heavy security, whereas the remainder is unusable without the core and can be stored with less security and cost.

Summary

The bulk of security discussion in this chapter applies to services provided through a website or to SimpleDB access from beyond the borders of Amazon data centers. This is where the security weaknesses are.

Any part of your application that has to travel across the Internet or reside within a web browser is subject to attack. The Internet is not something to fear and avoid, especially in the era of web services and cloud computing. However, security remains as high of a concern as ever.

The most important steps you can take to secure your cloud-based applications involve a thorough evaluation of possible attack vectors. Consistency is required in the handling of credentials, in sanitizing user data, and in protecting sensitive information.

9

Increasing Performance

Concern for SimpleDB performance is expressed frequently and comparisons to standard database products are often made. There are many steps that can be taken to ensure the best possible performance when making calls into SimpleDB. This chapter explains these techniques in a practical way with code samples.

SimpleDB is fast—not super-fast, but fast. SimpleDB is not the king of total throughput or complex query speed. Nevertheless, for the simple cases, speed is probably not going to be one of your problems. How you use the service has important implications on how it will perform, however: If you use it in certain ways, it simply will not be fast.

Determining If SimpleDB Is Fast Enough

It is often said that everything is fast for small N. When applied to databases, this means that when the database is storing a small amount of data and the request volume is low, all the database functions will appear speedy. There is truth in this, and a few logical conclusions follow. The first thing this assertion implies is that when you use this service for small projects, it is going to be fast no matter what you do. All the operations are quick, and even complex queries return quickly without the need for optimization. This is not only true for permanently small projects but for projects that start out small and grow over time. In some quarters, this has become part of the standard advice; don't worry about optimizing your database when your current scale is small because it does not matter. The reason it is worth discussing here is the added benefits SimpleDB affords your project at a small scale.

Targeting Moderate Performance in Small Projects

It is easy to make accurate and precise comparisons between databases; anyone can do it, post a nice blog about it, and throw in a couple pretty graphs to go with it. The difficulty is in making valid comparisons. It's hard enough with installable, configurable databases competing in the same category. They have various options or storage engines, and even though you install them on identical hardware, there is still a need to find the most appropriate set of configurations. Valid comparisons are even more difficult for services like

SimpleDB, where the differences lie not only in the feature set but also in qualities of the service that are not addressed in other offerings. These difficult-to-measure aspects are what make the service so attractive.

SimpleDB is targeted at relatively small data sets, where modest query capability is needed. This should immediately eliminate comparisons to any sort of data warehousing or analytical database configurations. SimpleDB can scale up to medium-sized data, but only in increments of 10GB domains. The typical performance comparisons between databases today consist of benchmark operations against database tables measured in the hundreds of gigabytes if not terabytes.

This is where the interesting comparisons are for large-scale databases. Those comparisons are interesting because at that scale, you can really see the benefits of the performance optimizations. Conversely, at the small scale, benchmarking is less interesting because it is much harder to see the performance differences. Moreover, it is not even that the differences are harder to see; it is just that they are so small, it's harder to see them as important. This is no accident. At the small scale, the performance differences between databases may actually be unimportant, even order-of-magnitude differences. If a web page needs to be populated by data returned from a set of queries, a database that can return the data in two milliseconds is not significantly better than one that takes 20 milliseconds. The database time is dwarfed by the combination of times required for page building, internet latency, and browser rendering. Dropping the page load time for a web page from 1.540 seconds to 1.502 seconds is not an important accomplishment.

This is the territory where SimpleDB lives—fast, but not super-fast. Operations do not come back in the single-digit milliseconds (usually), but double-digit millisecond responses can be achieved. In addition, SimpleDB is excellent at handling concurrency, and so multiple requests can be made in parallel. This makes it possible to issue a handful of requests, each of which may take double-digit milliseconds and still potentially get all the responses back without breaking double digits. For small projects, the SimpleDB benefits can be much more important than the performance boost from fast to really fast that you might get by switching to a relational database.

Exploiting Advanced Features in Small Projects

At small scale, there are certain things that just are not worth doing with any database. These include things like engineering the application to handle thousands of transactions per second and optimizing queries that do not present performance problems until there are tens of millions of rows. Those efforts do not provide any value in the short term, if ever. However, there are also actions you can take that provide clear value, but the effort or expense is too high to justify at a small scale.

This category of valuable but expensive features includes implementing your database on a cluster of servers to mitigate hardware failures, spreading the cluster across data centers to mitigate catastrophic failures, and a custom replication protocol that tolerates network failures. Advanced features like these are difficult to justify for a small-scale application using a relational database product, even though they would provide value, potentially large value, to the small number of users. However, a database service that has already been engineered to provide these features serves as a small project enabler when it exposes those same features without the high upfront cost.

For this reason, everything being fast for small N is more beneficial for SimpleDB than for relational database products. With a relational database, the "everything" includes strong technical features like the optimized processing of complex relational queries, which a small project may not be able to use. Alternately, with SimpleDB, the "everything" includes strong service-level features like high availability and low maintenance. The latter features are immediately valuable to all small projects.

Speeding Up SimpleDB

A narrow focus on SimpleDB speed revolves around maximizing the performance of the individual operations. A broader view of performance examines how operations are composed and how data flows through an application to accomplish a given task. Across a different dimension, the application is scaled horizontally across servers and domains. However, tracking progress in any of these directions first requires the existing performance to be measured as a basis for comparison.

Taking Detailed Performance Measurements

Before you take steps to improve the performance of your SimpleDB access code, you need a way to measure that performance. It may seem obvious, but it is important for both knowing the source of any performance problems, as well as giving you the ability to observe the results of any changes you make.

If it is your only option, you can measure timings in your application code, but ideally, the SimpleDB client you use will expose it or log it for you. This is preferable when it has been done in a way that lets you view timings of individual operations, even when they are submitted to the client in batches, and when you can separate the response time from the connect time. The latter is beneficial because a long connect time indicates a different issue than a long response time. If they are measured together, it will increase the amount of guesswork you need to do.

Accessing SimpleDB from EC2

When you are concerned with performance, the first thing you should consider is running the application on EC2, if it is not there already, for an across-the-board speedup. In any multi-tier software architecture, it is advisable to locate the database tier as close as possible to any other tier that makes heavy use of that data. This is even more true for SimpleDB because of the way the service is optimized. SimpleDB is fastest and most scalable with small, concurrent operations. However, it is just this scenario, with many small service calls, that is most susceptible to the latency effects of the public Internet.

Optimizing for SimpleDB often involves trimming the fat from individual requests so you can make more of them. Optimizing for the Internet, in contrast, can mean loading up each request with as much data as possible to minimize the number of requests needed. The result is that optimizing for SimpleDB performance can be at cross-purposes with optimizing for the open Internet. This is not to say that you cannot get good performance from SimpleDB outside of EC2—you can, and there are many situations where it works well or where performance is not a big issue. If performance is an issue, EC2 can be beneficial, but in the end, most of the steps you take to ensure peak performance will work just as well from outside the Amazon cloud as from within.

> **Quoting Specific Performance Numbers**
>
> All the specific timings used as examples in this chapter are based on my personal experience with SimpleDB access code running on small EC2 instances accessing the SimpleDB endpoint in the same region. AWS does not guarantee any specific performance numbers, and this chapter does not make any promises either. What I am trying to do is relay my personal experiences and conclusions, and give you a starting point for looking into SimpleDB performance for yourself.
>
> I encourage you to take your own measurements and come to your own conclusions rather than merely relying on my numbers. Your results will depend on the details of your data and your requirements.

Caching

The use of caching has a lot of value in increasing performance and reducing both the load on SimpleDB and the resulting usage billing. Not only is this generally true of all database applications, but it is especially true when the database is a web service with no persistent connection.

Caching is most effective in a read-heavy environment. A large number of applications fit into this category, including most web applications and web services. In an application where the data access is dominated by writes, caching still may prove beneficial for the remaining reads, but more likely it will not make a significant difference. Consider the read-request volume and the likelihood of cache hits. If the application is write-heavy because the existing data is constantly changing, a cache is not going to help.

Another data access pattern that lends itself well to caching is the presence of a set of popular items that is accessed with greater frequency. For example, in applications where new data is constantly being added and queries that display the latest updates are invoked frequently, caching those query results can be a big win. When data access is more widely distributed, and there are neither popular queries nor popular data items, caching will not be very effective unless you cache the entire data set.

Local Caching

Given that SimpleDB is not designed to store large data sets, it is entirely possible to cache several domains full of data into the memory of a single beefy server. However, that would be an extreme case. A much more likely case is a local in-memory cache of limited size. You can get a lot of mileage out of a local cache in those read-heavy situations, even if it is small. You do not necessarily need to keep it small, but you do need to accommodate the memory needs of the application. A cache whose memory can be reclaimed as needed is ideal.

Distributed Caching

When your application spans multiple servers, local caches are still beneficial, but a distributed cache starts to become more attractive. With a distributed cache, you can spread the cached items across servers utilizing the unused memory. This can provide a very large cache. This is especially effective when your servers do not reside within the Amazon cloud. Caching products are typically light on configuration and setup when compared to other categories of server software like databases and application servers. However, be aware that there will be some configuration and maintenance involved. The benefit of running a distributed cache on your existing servers is that you already have a process in place to deal with configuration and problem resolution. Adding a caching service to an existing deployment should only incur a small incremental maintenance cost.

There is a host of caching options available from commercial and open-source products to pay-as-you-go services. Examples of distributed cache products include Memcached and Terracotta. An example of a distributed caching service is Cloud Cache.

The Dangers of Caching

One of the general dangers of heavy cache use early on in any project is that it can mask true performance problems. This can manifest in the form of unacceptable performance when the cache is empty. Caching is undoubtedly a powerful tool. Take care, however, not to over-rely on the cache too early. The performance of the system in the event of cache misses is important and not something to be merely glossed over.

SimpleDB is implemented with complex replication and failover behind the scenes. The hidden things going on in the background are what prevent SimpleDB from being super-fast. Putting a caching layer between your application and SimpleDB is all the more valuable because it can give you some extra speed on top of your availability and failover. In fact, it can be tempting to just cache the whole data set for fast access and use SimpleDB as a durable backing data store. There is nothing inherently wrong with this approach; however, trouble can arise when you expose a strongly consistent view of the data.

The trouble comes if the application relies on the strong consistency guarantee for proper function. SimpleDB is based on eventually consistent semantics for the express purpose of granting higher levels of availability. Any cache that fronts SimpleDB and relies on SimpleDB as the authoritative source of data can never guarantee stronger consistency without compromising the availability. Some people have expressed the sentiment that a strongly consistent cache backed by the highly available SimpleDB gives you the best of both worlds, but it simply does not. If your cache is hosted in a single data center and the data center experiences an outage, your cache is unavailable, whereas SimpleDB would not be. If your cache is distributed across multiple data centers and there is a network failure between them, you have to reject writes to the cache because you cannot guarantee consistency.

Just be aware that a cache in front of SimpleDB is not a silver bullet. You can string together cache servers and protocols in clever and useful ways. Nevertheless, as long as you use SimpleDB as the authoritative data source, no amount of cleverness will support a strengthened consistency guaranteed without weakening the availability. Of course, it is possible to assemble a system that provides strong consistency during normal operation and falls back to eventual consistency during periods where consistency cannot be reached. Nevertheless, that can only work when the application is designed to function properly with the weaker consistency.

This is not an indictment against caching or strong consistency. It may be perfectly valid for your application to have a super-sized cache with strong consistency. If this is the case, it ought to be the result of informed decisions about the service qualities you seek to provide your users. For example, if you cache the full data set in memory with strong consistency, you should have considered the actual benefits you derive from using SimpleDB versus an alternative like RDS.

Concurrency

Concurrency is one of the service features that let SimpleDB scale up so well. For the best performance, you clearly want to be able to take advantage of that concurrency. Unfortunately, it can be difficult for the application developer to take advantage of the concurrency support in a SimpleDB client, and it can be nearly impossible to achieve a high level of concurrency if the SimpleDB client does not explicitly support it.

Parallel Requests Using Threads

One of the ways to enjoy the benefits of SimpleDB concurrency is to make requests in multiple threads. Each thread can open a connection and make the web service request via a blocking I/O call. Each thread continues when the response comes back.

There are situations where this is a very natural solution; one of them is when the application is running in a naturally threaded environment like an application server. When a thread is used to service each incoming request, making SimpleDB requests in separate threads is almost a foregone conclusion. Other tasks that lend themselves to multi-threading include backup, restore, and import jobs. For these jobs, there is a large quantity of easily divided requests that can be queued up and a thread pool to make the service calls concurrently.

There are some problems with threads, though. The first is that not every situation is conducive to thread use. In truth, many are not. It is extremely common for a single unit of processing to require multiple calls to the database. Although multiple processes can easily take advantage of the concurrency in aggregate using threads, each individual process in a single thread can benefit greatly from concurrency. However, when the threading is not built into the SimpleDB client, each processing thread would need to coordinate with a pool of I/O threads to achieve concurrency.

Another problem with threads is shared state and synchronization. Each of the threads operates as independently as possible; however, coordination is needed. This coordination requires a shared state, which is not only difficult and error-prone to code, but also acts as a point of contention and a potential bottleneck. The most practical slice of shared state that needs to be coordinated is the information about 503 ServiceUnavailable errors and the subsequent backing off that needs to be done.

As an example, if you have 10 threads pounding out requests to SimpleDB, and one of them gets a 503, it is fine for that one thread to use a delay before retrying that request. Unfortunately, there are nine other threads humming along, happy to take up the slack, and the total request volume can remain just as high. Unless there is some shared state where the various threads can coordinate, the responsiveness to changing conditions is somewhat clumsy and lagging.

Asynchronous Requests in a Single Thread

There is a good solution for those situations where threading is awkward. A single-threaded solution can be implemented to manage a set of non-blocking SimpleDB requests. The state of each connection and the various error conditions is easily kept in one place without contention. Changes can be made across the board without delays or points of contention. For example, if the DNS entries for a SimpleDB endpoint change, it is easier for a single thread to accommodate the change than notifying a dozen threads each in various stages of execution and each vying for CPU time.

The problem is that managing queues of non-blocking I/O operations is even less approachable for application developers than threading is. As such, it is really in the purview of the SimpleDB client developer to handle the concurrency in a useful way.

Keeping Requests and Responses Small

The most universal performance advice for SimpleDB is to keep requests and responses small. The SimpleDB API gives us the first clues in this direction with a very strict set of limits on the size of items, attributes, requests, and responses and on the amount of time used to service a single request. This is for a good reason; the service is optimized to handle a high volume of small requests efficiently.

Small requests are easier to load balance across multiple back-end machines, providing the best utilization of heterogeneous hardware. Small requests are easier to handle concurrently within a single machine. The heavyweight, long-running tasks tend to monopolize resources.

Taking a cue from these limits, and from performance measurements of the service, leads you to keep the request and response sizes as small as possible. Across all of the operations, as you increase the quantity of data to process in a single request, there comes a point where the performance starts to degrade. There is no specific byte limitation in play. It's not like a line in the sand, which, if crossed, causes problems. It is more of a general trend. You'll have to test and see how much is too much in your own situation, but all things being equal, once the size of a single request or response starts to get large, performance will slowly being to decrease.

Operation-Specific Performance

Caching and concurrency are important, but no matter how much you employ them, eventually performance comes down to the speed of the actual SimpleDB operations. Knowing how to optimize each of them enables you to get the most out of your other performance measures.

In this portion of the chapter, we look at optimizing four of the most heavily used operations, beginning with `GetAttributes`.

Optimizing GetAttributes

The core functionality of reading data items via a primary key is the fastest and most scalable operation in SimpleDB. This is the most basic and foundational function of the database. `GetAttributes` scales predictably across most dimensions. A large part of this is that this predictability stems from the number of variables that have no noticeable impact on the time required to issue a `GetAttributes` call. The speed of a `GetAttributes` call is unrelated to the quantity of data stored in a domain. As a domain fills to capacity and even once it has become full, the `GetAttributes` calls do not begin to slow down. `GetAttributes` speed is also independent of the quantity of data stored in an item. Calls to read an attribute of an item storing 512KB of data need be no slower than if that item contained a single 10-byte value.

Those factors are not responsible for slowing down primary key reads; however, two factors do have an impact. One of these is request throttling that appears to be in effect on a per-domain basis. SimpleDB supports high levels of concurrency and this makes up, in large part, for individual request latencies. In my own testing, I have found that once I reach a level of about 1,000 to 1,200 `GetAttributes` requests per second, I begin to experience the effects of—what I have concluded is—throttling. The symptoms are a high level of network errors and a noticeable slowdown in the time required to open new HTTP connections to the service endpoint. While this is occurring, successful `GetAttributes` calls do not appear slower. Therefore, this is less of a slowdown and more of a limit.

The second factor is general traffic levels, and this is similar to the first. When you have a steady load of other request types, the number of `GetAttributes` calls per second will go down in the same way as with throttling. Combine this with the ability to realize higher requests per second during off-peak hours, and it points toward a general capacity threshold for internal SimpleDB nodes servicing domain requests.

Those factors indirectly affect `GetAttributes` responses by limiting the total request volume. The one remaining factor is the one that most directly controls the actual response time of the operation. This main factor is the size of the response, and it is important in terms of both the raw number of bytes returned and the number of attributes requested.

For each call, a base level of overhead determines minimum response time. This minimum response time is the time it takes for small requests to be satisfied. Typically, it is between 20 and 50 milliseconds for the vast majority of small requests. This base level is on the order of double-digit milliseconds, as a ballpark figure. In the world of sequential calls, waiting 50 milliseconds for a response is more than twice as bad as waiting only 20 milliseconds. However, when you are able to make the calls in parallel at a rate of more than 1,000 per second, the incremental cost of making additional requests averages out to be very small.

Figure 9-1 depicts the difference between sequential and concurrent calls. The upper portion represents the time taken by six calls that each return very quickly, but each does not begin until the prior call is complete. The bottom portion shows six calls that have more variability in response time and are all generally slower than the top depiction. However, the fact that the requests are all in flight at the same time makes up for both the variability and the speed of the requests.

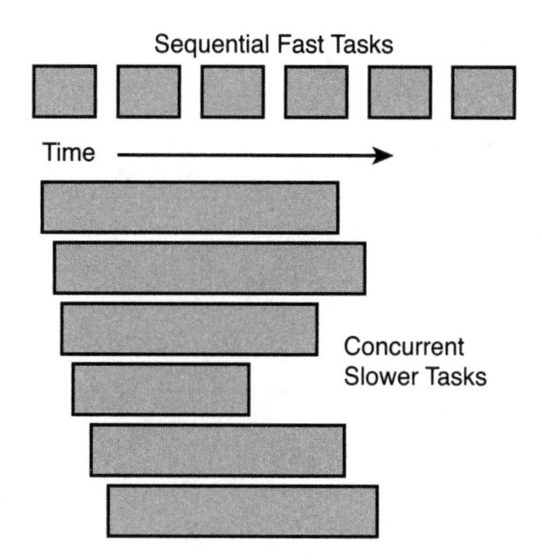

Figure 9-1 The time taken by sequential and concurrent calls

This approach scales differently than the sequential calls. The time taken by any individual call is much more important when there is no concurrency since the overall time taken is directly related to every individual call. In contrast, the response time of most of the concurrent calls does not change the total time taken since the total time is usually dominated by the longest request. As the number of calls increases for a given process, the total time taken increases much more slowly for concurrent calls compared to sequential calls. Figure 9-2 shows what happens when you double the number of calls shown in Figure 9-1.

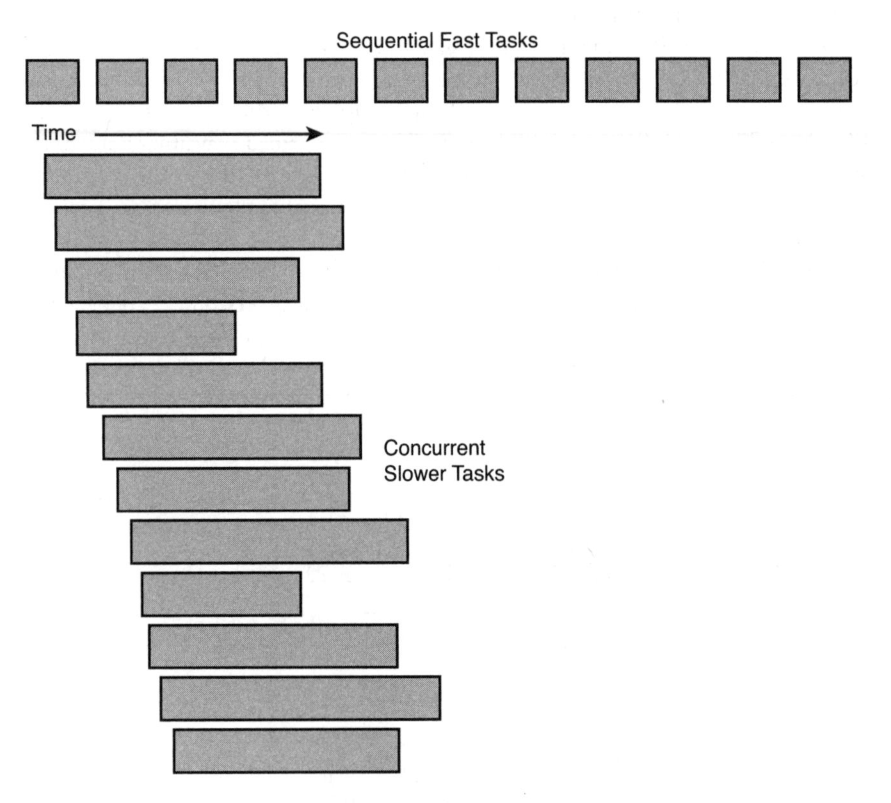

Figure 9-2 Scaling the number of calls sequentially and concurrently

Leveraging Concurrency

In order to take advantage of the concurrency that SimpleDB is optimized for, you have to have a client that supports it. Three of the common approaches taken by SimpleDB clients in exposing the concurrency are with futures, collections, and threads. At a basic level, a SimpleDB client can be implemented in a thread-safe way. This permits you to invoke operations on the client from different threads without breaking it. This can be awkward because it requires the application to handle all the threading issues properly.

A more friendly way for a SimpleDB client to expose the concurrency is with some form of API that allows requests to be submitted in collections. In the case of `GetAttributes`, the client may provide a get method that allows an arbitrary number of item names to be passed and returns all the results together as collection of results. In this scenario, all the concurrency is handled by the client behind the scenes, and the application does not have the need to implement or even be aware of the concurrency. The API method is called with a collection of item names, the caller is blocked until all the results have come back, and then those results are returned all together. The calling code is not required to know the details about the implementation used by the API to make the calls.

The approach of using futures as a placeholder for the results of a pending operation is becoming more common. When this is the case, the API methods will return immediately after the request has been queued, rather than waiting for the response to come back. Instead of returning the actual values, a wrapper object is returned. This wrapper object is initially empty, but behind the scenes, it will be updated with the response data once it has been received. The benefit of this pattern is that the application does not need to wait around in a blocked state for the operation to come back; it can continue with other work that must be done and retrieve the response data later. This permits the application to not only execute SimpleDB requests in parallel, but also execute application code in parallel without any explicit need to manage the threading or synchronization at the application level.

In a simplistic example, an application may need to fetch a dozen SimpleDB items to populate a web page that has been requested. Using a SimpleDB client with futures, the dozen requests can be made, and immediately a dozen empty futures are returned. The application can then proceed to the next stage of assembling the final web page, which may include tasks that do not depend on the responses from SimpleDB. This processing could consist of selecting an HTML template to use, building some HTML based on application-wide settings, and pulling in HTML page fragments from a cache. Once the application reaches a point where the data responses must be used, calls to get that data from the futures may already be populated. If any are not, they will block until the response comes back.

Having a client that supports asynchronous SimpleDB operations gets you part of the way there, but you must also have an application design that supports it. As a practical matter, there are usually some dependencies between data items. These dependencies prevent you from fully exploiting the available concurrency. When the data in one item determines what other items you need to get, it acts as a bottleneck, preventing concurrency until that first response comes back. This is something to keep in mind: The way data flows through your application will have an impact on the level of concurrency you can achieve. The degree to which performance might suffer from sequential access will depend on how much data you need to collect for a single process. If you only need to get a few items, it is unlikely to matter much.

Limiting the Use of Consistent Get

The ability to set the consistency flag on a `GetAttributes` request is an important feature. There are many situations where this is exactly what is needed. Another great aspect of consistent get is that frequently it is just as fast as the default eventually consistent get. However, be cautious about setting the consistent flag for all calls to `GetAttributes`, or even a majority of calls. The performance characteristics are less predictable; sometimes it will have higher latency and lower throughput. It could happen for a variety of reasons internal to the service, like network congestion.

The more heavily you use consistent get, the more at the mercy of failures you are. To ensure consistency, each replica currently accepting writes for your domain has to report back with the latest version of the data. If any of those replicas is having health issues, or if the network path to any of them is experiencing a slowdown, it will be reflected in your response time. Alternatively, a normal eventually consistent get should remain relatively unaffected by slow responses from a single replica. The most recent value from the replicas with a timely report will be returned.

Of course, it is entirely possible that you can write code to drop the consistent flag when there are either slowdowns or ServiceUnavailable errors. This is a wise thing to do in any case, especially when it allows the application to offer a useful, if degraded, level of service in the midst of an internal failure. The thing to realize is that the ability to drop the consistency flag presupposes that the application can function properly without it. Despite the stronger consistency, the application still needs to deal with the realities of an eventually consistent system.

That being said, you should consider using consistent get only when you have a good reason. This is not because it is always slower, but because the occasions when it does become slower are beyond your ability to control or predict.

Optimizing PutAttributes

There are two different ways to optimize SimpleDB writes. You will want to either minimize the latency for the most quickness, or maximize the throughput to push through bulky data at the highest rate. There are different operations to use depending on which of these you are trying to maximize. `PutAttributes` is the choice that gives you the best latency and `BatchPutAttributes` gives you the best throughput.

Minimizing Request Size

The best thing you can do to prevent `PutAttributes` performance from degrading is to keep the request size small. As a practical matter, you often cannot really reduce the size of individual data items that an application needs to store. However, what you can do is make sure to send only the data that has changed. This keeps your request sizes as small as possible, which will give you the fastest turnaround time on your writes.

Limiting Conditional Writes

Next, limit the use of conditional puts. Conditional writes make it easy to solve some problems that previously were very cumbersome to solve. Use them only when you actually need them. Setting a condition on every `PutAttributes` just to be safe will not have a huge impact on a small application; everything is fast for small N. However, fully "conditionalizing" all your writes is something that doesn't scale up well. If every write needs a condition check, why not just use a database with transactions?

One option that seems to have a slight impact on performance is the replace flag. Replacing a value seems to average out to be a little slower than adding a new value. Unfortunately, this is barely worth mentioning because most of the time, you will not have any choice in the matter. Application logic will dictate that certain attributes have multiple values and that others be limited to a single value. Therefore, any value that needs updating will have the replace flag set by necessity.

Optimizing BatchPutAttributes

`BatchPutAttributes` allows for optimizing the throughput side of the equation, accepting a good bit more data at speed than `PutAttributes` with additional latency. This operation is best used when the latency of any individual request is unimportant compared to the speed with which a large quantity of data can be shoveled into the service.

There is not much room to change the behavior of `BatchPutAttributes`; its use is straightforward. It handles up to 25 items at a time, but with much less concurrency than single-item puts. Batch puts per second in the double-digit range is common on items with 10 to 40 attributes. That rate is nearly triple the rate of normal `PutAttributes` throughput.

Consolidating Writes

Keep all the attributes for a single item in a single request. This rule could also be called, "don't use `BatchPutAttributes` to update existing items." Batched puts are reported to have a fast track-handling algorithm when the item does not yet exit and the replace flag is not set. This is the most natural way to handle an initial data import. It might occur to you to split the attributes of each item into multiple batch calls to keep request sizes low, but that only makes it slower. However, aside from a data import, there might be many occasions where you need to update existing items in batches. This is not something to avoid since it will still have higher throughput than individual puts, but be aware that the performance of batch updates will be lower than batch inserts.

Throttling Request Volume

The other thing to keep the batches flowing in as fast as possible is to mind the 503s. HTTP 503 errors with a SimpleDB `ServiceUnavailable` error code are what you get, in this situation, when SimpleDB wants to express to you its feelings about your request volume. Pay attention and ease back on the requests when you start to get a lot of 503 errors. Error rates can climb very quickly. A slight reduction in request volume can keep the data moving, whereas trying to maintain too high a rate could possibly result in 50% of your requests being rejected with ServiceUnavailable.

Optimizing Select

`Select` is really the operation that requires the most effort to optimize. If you use `Select` frequently in your application, you will find that a good deal of time is spent on that call in comparison to the other calls. There are many variables in play. There are a good number of principles and suggestions, but the best thing you can do is test for yourself using both nearly full and nearly empty domains, and compare the differences.

Focusing on a Single Attribute

In SimpleDB, there is an index for each attribute name in a domain. However, there are no composite indexes spanning multiple attributes. What this means to would-be query optimizers is that when SimpleDB executes your query, it will need to look at the criteria and the sort and determine a single best index to use. If the sort attribute is different from the attribute that is selected, the full result will need to be compiled before the first sorted result can be returned.

That fact can be a real killer for performance. As much as you can, you want to hone in on a poorly performing query with as few attributes as possible (ideally, a single attribute).

Being as Selective as Possible

Working within the single index that will be used for a query, you want to be as selective as possible. Limiting the number of criteria can be good, but you never want to eliminate a condition that only matches a small number of items. These highly selective conditions are what cause `Select` operations to return quickly despite there being tens of millions of items in the domain.

Using Parallel Range Queries

If you have trouble finding an attribute value that is selective enough, you might be able to create some artificial selectivity based on your knowledge of the data. For example, if the query matches hundreds of thousands of items, there may be no way to trim that down. However, if the item names are roughly sequential and you have a million of them, you may be able to break down the query by item name. As an example of how this is done, your single query might look like this:

```
SELECT * FROM songs WHERE tags = 'rock'
```

That query can be turned into, for example, five queries, each of which is more selective than the original, and all five can be executed in parallel:

```
SELECT * FROM songs WHERE tags = 'rock' AND itemName() < '0200000'
SELECT * FROM songs WHERE tags = 'rock' AND itemName() BETWEEN '0200000' and
'0400000'
SELECT * FROM songs WHERE tags = 'rock' AND itemName() BETWEEN '0400000' and
'0600000'
SELECT * FROM songs WHERE tags = 'rock' AND itemName() BETWEEN '0600000' and
'0800000'
SELECT * FROM songs WHERE tags = 'rock' AND itemName() > '0800000'
```

Limiting the Use of Consistent Select

Like the other calls with enhanced consistency guarantees, consistent `Select` is best used in moderation. It is highly useful in a number of situations, when you need to get an exact count or guarantee that you have all the most recent results. Over-reliance on the consistent `Select` can hurt performance more than with the other consistent operations because of the variability of the work you are asking the database to do.

Data Sharding

Sometimes streamlining your usage of SimpleDB leads to better performance and a lower bill. Alternately, other performance-improving measures result in more usage and a higher bill. The former improvements are a win-win, but the latter will cost you, so consider the costs and the benefits.

Partitioning Data

Sharding is important for scaling in SimpleDB. Because each domain has a limited throughput, the ability to spread your data across multiple domains becomes a fundamental requirement. Obviously, this only works when there is a way to partition the data, whether along some natural boundary or via consistent hashing. On top of that is a degree of complexity inherent in routing each request to the proper domain. Much of that complexity can be abstracted away.

Once you have a partitioning scheme in place and have dealt with the complexity, you have to decide how many domains to shard across. Because each domain affords additional throughput, you may want to shard across as many domains as possible so that the capacity will be available when you need it. In some situations, this may be a viable option, but usually it will not be cost effective. All things being equal, cost is the deciding factor.

The cost of most operations is actually unaffected by the number of shards. `GetAttributes`, `PutAttributes`, `BatchPutAttributes`, and `DeleteAttributes` will all need to be routed to exactly one domain for each request. As a result, the cost remains a function of request volume but not of domain count. The only operation that causes an issue is `Select`.

Multiplexing Queries

An application with data shards may need to issue queries across all domains. In the case where data shards are determined by hashing, every query will need to be issued to every domain. However, even when the data is partitioned along natural boundaries, queries to all domains may still be needed. For example, if product categories like Art, Jewelry, and Toys are stored in different domains, queries in a single category can be sent to a single domain, but cross-category searches will still need to be issued to multiple domains.

The query box usage costs that scale up with the number of domains is the single factor that will determine the cost effectiveness of sharding. Throughput is also a factor, to the degree that your throughput needs determine the minimum number of domains, whereas the box usage of `Select` calls determine the most cost-effective number of domains. The actual costs are different in every situation. The data is different, the complexity and selectiveness of the queries is different, and the number of attributes that must be returned as well as the number of items will vary.

In some situations, it can work out that sharding across more domains will actually reduce your `Select` costs. This is the case when queries are complex and you find that the number of items returned within the time limit drops below the number you need, forcing a follow-up query with the `NextToken`. A sharp increase in `QueryTimeout` responses is expensive, and when it happens, it also contributes to the cost savings of additional sharding.

In other cases, sharding will cost more in terms of `Select` box usage, and there is no way around it. In these cases, you want to have the minimum number of domains that will support your required throughput. Because it varies so much, the only way to determine that number is to test.

Accessing SimpleDB Outside the Amazon Cloud

One of the early suggestions in this chapter was to consider running your application on EC2 because of the low latency and the potential for free data transfer. If you decide against EC2 for whatever reason, you should be aware that there are some differences in the way you optimize performance.

The main difference is the latency, which will almost certainly not be as low. The additional request latency you see in practice will depend on the connection between your application and the Amazon data center servicing your requests. Much of the latency will be both beyond your control and more highly variable. As a result, it is less advantageous to optimize for latency and focus more on throughput and caching.

Working Around Latency

Caching is the first, and most obvious, thing to consider when optimizing SimpleDB performance outside the Amazon cloud. For those situations where caching is beneficial, as outlined previously, it will be doubly so from outside the Amazon data centers. The bigger the cache, the better.

The second action you can take to optimize around the latency goes hand in hand with caching: reading full items whenever possible. This is contrary to the best practice when inside the Amazon cloud; from the inside, you want to pull data chunks that are as small as possible. From the outside, the latency benefits from pulling the small chunks will be far less noticeable because of the Internet latency. Thus, the marginal cost of pulling full items is much smaller. This works well with caching because caching full items is more likely to maximize your cache hit rate. Because the cost of each additional request is higher, pulling the maximum data in each `GetAttributes` and `Select` call is beneficial whenever it results in subsequent requests.

Another consideration is that the additional variability and occasional slowdowns from consistent reads and conditional writes is less of a concern. You will still receive `ServiceUnavailable` when consistency is not immediately reachable. However, there will be a larger percentage of the time where a slowdown from the consistent call is observable. When you combine that with the fact that there is no additional box usage charge for the consistent calls, they become more attractive from the outside. Running a SimpleDB-based application from the outside means that you aren't going to have the absolute top-tier of database performance. Thus, these applications are most likely already tolerant of the incremental latency effects.

Ignoring Latency

One thing to consider is that there is a wide range of applications that can function very well from the outside with only minimal performance concerns. One of these categories is write-heavy applications with only minimal reads and queries. Think of applications that are primarily logging information from devices or websites. When write throughput dominates and reads and queries are more seldom, you are free to shard widely. If queries can be associated with reporting, and the reports can be generated by a scheduled batch process, any slowness or box usage concerns tend to fade. This is even true without the batch processing.

Another class of applications that can benefit from outside access to SimpleDB are small data-driven websites or blogs. These are usually read-heavy and respond well to caching. The low frequency of writes and low data storage requirements allows them to fit easily within a single domain. So, the only optimization that needs to be done is at the lowest level to make sure that the data for a page being built can be retrieved in a reasonable period of time. Caching may not even be necessary.

Summary

There are many steps you can take to improve the performance of an application based on SimpleDB. The important considerations include what level of performance to target. Caching yields great benefits to read access, but additional domains will be needed to scale write throughput. Queries are always fast for small quantities of data, but even when the domain is full, queries with selective criteria for a single attribute can be just as fast. Complex queries with criteria that span numerous attributes scale much more poorly. Simplifying them or breaking them down into multiple range queries may be necessary to minimize `QueryTimeout` errors and keep response times low.

Spreading data across domains also helps with slower query times, but often at an additional box usage cost. However, this additional cost applies only to Select and not to the other read and write operations. At a high level, this partitioning is important for scalability but comes with some cost in terms of application complexity.

The one thing that holds true for the entire realm of SimpleDB performance optimization is that you truly need to test and measure for yourself. Every situation is different, and what generally works for others may not work well for your specific situation. Be aware of the principles involved and think creatively, but realistically, about your options. Cloud computing and SimpleDB are not a panacea. Your scalability and performance problems do not get solved automatically, so consider what you give up and what you get by using SimpleDB.

10

Writing a SimpleDB Client: A Language-Independent Guide

This chapter covers the process of writing a client library from scratch. In addition to being a resource to client implementers, this chapter also affords the opportunity to go over the SimpleDB API calls again from a web service perspective. This chapter develops a full implementation of a new SimpleDB client geared toward simplicity and ease of use. The first portion of the chapter presents the client interface and uses that as a launching pad into a discussion about design choices and implementation considerations. The full implementation of the client is then presented in Java, tying the earlier discussion with the actual code. Even though the programming language used in this chapter is Java, both the design and the implementation issues addressed here exist in any language.

The SimpleDB client in this chapter implements all nine of the API operations. The goal is to raise many of the issues that crop up when working with this API and work through them. The design of this client makes a certain set of tradeoffs, which is a topic of discussion throughout the chapter. The coverage of these design decisions is meant to spur your own thought process. Think about how you might do it differently.

> **Note**
>
> Throughout this chapter, "this client" refers to the SimpleDB client software being presented here. Likewise, "the users" refers to all the people who may use a SimpleDB client that you write in the development of an application. The intentions and expectations of those who may use our software should be central to the design process, especially when they are other developers.

Client Design Overview

SimpleDB exposes a limited feature set with a simple, straightforward API. Functions that are more complex can be built using the small set of primitive operations. The most important considerations in the design of this client revolve around the users. The users of this client are developers using SimpleDB in applications. The service is simple, so the client should be simple to use. The API exposed to users needs to match up as closely as possible with the SimpleDB calls documented on the AWS website.

An important consideration is that the client should be as convenient to use as possible. One of the things that can make a client difficult to use is the requirement to write a lot of boilerplate code to set up service calls and to parse results. Another concern is the alignment with the expected use cases. For example, a client designed for use in mobile device applications may warrant a simpler interface that omits `CreateDomain`, `DeleteDomain`, and `BatchPutAttributes`. Alternately, a client embedded in a persistence framework may need much more complexity for the purpose of interfacing with exiting frameworks for object mapping, caching at various levels, and query manipulation.

The client developed in this chapter is intended for general-purpose use while maintaining as much simplicity as possible. The classes exposed to the user comprise three main abstractions, as follows:

- A `SimpleDB` class to act as the primary interface.
- An `Attribute` class to represent each instance of a name/value pair.
- An `Item` class to represent a named set of attributes.

From the user's perspective, this will be the full extent of classes in the interface, aside from the exception classes. That is about as simple as you can get. The role of the SimpleDB class is needed at some level, although you have more leeway when deciding how to represent items and attributes.

The item and attribute concepts are very simple. Depending on your programming language, you may have the option to use built-in language features to represent these abstractions. For example, PHP associative arrays might work, or a Python dictionary. A compelling reason for using dedicated classes to represent them is the fact that attributes need to also hold a replace flag in addition to the name and value, and no existing Java collection stands out as an obvious choice.

Public Interface

Let's take a stab at the primary interface for this client. Listing 10-1 shows ISimpleDB, a Java interface with abstract methods for all of the key functions. This interface is not intended as a necessary part of the client, although there is no reason why it could not be. Its purpose is to present the API of the client in a way that allows the initial discussion of the concepts without the cognitive load of the full implementation.

Listing 10-1 **ISimpleDB.java The Public Methods of the Client Interface**

```
package com.simpledbbook;

import java.util.List;
import java.util.Map;

public interface ISimpleDB {
```

```
    void createDomain(String domainName);

    void deleteDomain(String domainName);

    List<String> listDomains();

    Map<String, Long> domainMetadata(String domain);

    void batchPut(String domain, List<Item> items);

    void put(String domain, Item item);

    void putIfNotExists(String domain, Item item, String expectedName);

    void putIfExists(String domain, Item item, String expectedName,
        String expectedValue);

    void delete(String domain, Item item);

    void deleteIfNotExists(String domain, Item item, String expected);

    void deleteIfExists(String domain, Item item, String expectedName,
        String expectedValue);

    Item get(String domain, String itemName, String... atts);

    Item getConsistent(String domain, String itemName, String... atts);

    List<Item> select(String select);

    List<Item> selectConsistent(String select);

    boolean hasNextPage();

    List<Item> getNextPage();

    List<Item> getNextPageConsistent();
}
```

One thing you can see in this class is that built-in Java collections and types are returned from the methods in combination with the container class `Item` and its attribute children. This keeps the usage simple and minimizes the dependencies. One example of this is the `listDomains()` method that invokes the `ListDomains` operation. This method returns the list of SimpleDB domains, each in the form of a Java String.

A second example is the `domainMetadata()` method, which returns values in the form of a Java Map of String names to Long values. Custom classes could be added here to add another layer of API abstraction and allow more data to be returned—for instance, the box usage value contained in the SimpleDB response. That approach results in a more capable client by way of empowering the user with advanced features like the ability to track box usage. However, advanced features must be weighed against the extra complexity and boilerplate code it might require.

Providing a way for users to access everything that comes back in a response is important, but it doesn't need to be done at the level of the individual call. Logging to a file is one option; embedding the full response within an exception for error conditions is another.

Continuing to look down through the class, the next four methods make use of abbreviated naming. `put()`, `batchPut()`, `get()`, and `delete()` correspond to the SimpleDB operations `PutAttributes`, `BatchPutAttributes`, `GetAttributes`, and `DeleteAttributes`. This is done here to keep the line length down for the constraints of the printed page. It would be better to use names that match the operations identically, to avoid any confusion.

The remaining methods in this class expose the query functionality. Unlike the other operations, for which there is a one-to-one correspondence between operations and methods, this sample client defines four methods for `Select`. The first has a single parameter for the query expression, whereas the second adds an additional parameter for passing the `NextToken`. You will notice that the return type for both methods is an `Item` list and that no `NextToken` is ever actually returned to the caller. This design choice is justified in basic use cases, if not in advance situations. The caller has no use for a `NextToken` other than to pass it back to a subsequent call. It is purely a bookkeeping construct, and requiring callers to manage it explicitly is inconvenient.

The inconvenience can be understood considering any query in SimpleDB that runs too long can return with a `NextToken` along with as few as zero results. This means that proper handling of a query will require the user to code `NextToken` handling at the site of every `select()` call. The following chapter will present a more substantial solution to this problem. This chapter resolves it in a basic way, by implementing some rudimentary `NextToken` handling and providing a method to check for its presence called `hasNextPage()` and a method to resubmit the same query with the `NextToken` called `getNextPage()`. To support these methods, the class declares the private members `nextToken` and `select`. These store the values from the immediately prior call to `select()`.

Attribute Class

The basic unit of data in SimpleDB is the attribute, and having a structure to represent that data is fundamental. In addition to the expected name and value `Strings`, there is also a need for a boolean value to indicate replacement within requests. Listing 10-2 shows the full `Attribute` class.

Listing 10-2 **Attribute.java A Structure to Hold Named Values**

```
package com.simpledbbook;

public class Attribute {

  private String name;
  private String value;
  private boolean replace;

  public Attribute(String name, String value) {
    this(name, value, false);
  }

  public Attribute(String attName, String val, boolean repl) {
    name = attName;
    value = val;
    replace = repl;
  }

  public String toString() {
    return String.format("{%s:%s}", name, value);
  }

  public String getName() {
    return name;
  }

  public void setName(String n) {
    name = n;
  }

  public String getValue() {
    return value != null ? value : "";
  }

  public void setValue(String val) {
    value = val;
  }

  public boolean isReplace() {
    return replace;
  }

  public void setReplace(boolean repl) {
    replace = repl;
  }
}
```

The `Attribute` class is a very simplistic, JavaBean-like data structure. The three private members are exposed with three getter/setter pairs, the constructor comes in two variants, and a `toString()` method is thrown in for good measure. There should not be much surprising here.

Item Class

Because an item is nothing more than a named set of attributes in SimpleDB, the `Item` class has only two fields: a name and a collection of attributes. Listing 10-3 gives the code.

Listing 10-3 **Item.java A Named Collection of Attributes**

```
package com.simpledbbook;

import java.util.*;

public class Item {
  private final List<Attribute> atts = new ArrayList<Attribute>();
  private String name;

  public Item(String itemName) {
    name = itemName;
  }

  public Item(String itemName, List<Attribute> attList) {
    this(itemName);
    addAttributes(attList);
  }

  public String toString() {
    return String.format("\nItem: %s\n   %s", name, atts);
  }

  public String getName() {
    return name;
  }

  public void setName(String n) {
    name = n;
  }

  public Attribute[] getAtts() {
    return atts.toArray(new Attribute[atts.size()]);
  }

  public String getAttribute(String name) {
    List<String> values = getAttributes(name);
```

```
    return values.isEmpty() ? null: values.get(0);
  }

  public List<String> getAttributes(String name) {
    List<String> result = new ArrayList<String>();
    for (Attribute att : atts) {
      if (att.getName().equals(name)) {
        result.add(att.getValue());
      }
    }
    return result;
  }

  public void addAttributes(List<Attribute> newAtts) {
    atts.addAll(newAtts);
  }
}
```

The `Item` class starts out simple, declaring two constructor variants along with a matching pair of accessor methods, and ends with a twist, but not a complex one. The twist is the way the `Attribute` collection is exposed: Multiple getters are provided as a convenience, while the setter method is abandoned in favor of an add method.

Client Design Considerations

Every design decision comes with a tradeoff. Even before diving down into the details of the various operations, there are decisions to be made about a client of this nature. Let's begin with a discussion of the broader issues and then drop down to more specific concerns.

High-Level Design Issues

There are plenty of details to get hung up on when writing and debugging a SimpleDB client, but it's worth taking the time to consider those cross-cutting concerns that have an impact on the whole thing. These are the issues that come up repeatedly during development, and it's better to think about them ahead of time.

Simplicity vs. Feature Set

If you think of SimpleDB as a tool, then the client software can be considered the handle to that tool. There is value in choosing which parts to expose and which parts to keep hidden. The alternative is writing what merely works without giving the interface much thought. When designing an interface like this, it is useful to consider each concept in the underlying service and decide which ones to gloss over and which ones to emphasize.

Items, attributes, and domains are the core concepts, so they need to be well represented. Domains are just names, though; you cannot do anything with it but pass it around, so it probably does not need its own class. If it did have its own class, all that you could put in it is the name and the metadata, and the metadata would go unpopulated 99% of the time while domain objects are being passed around for virtually every operation. You could use a domain object as a front for operations on the data stored in that domain with calls like `media_domain02.getAttributes(item)`. This turns out to be a convenient way to decouple the calling code from the name of the domain. The problem is that it breaks down for `ListDomains` and `Select` calls where there are no domain parameters. `ListDomains` might be called infrequently, but you have to expect heavy Select use. You do not want to end up with confusion over where operations are called. It also hurts simplicity if you must pass multiple objects around. It is difficult to code enough usefulness into a domain class for it to pull its own weight, so in this client, it is represented as a `String` and kept simple.

Ease of Use

Exposing proper support for the underlying database is necessary. However, it is not sufficient. You need to think about the needs of the users and how they will use the client. If the attributes returned in an item are accessed via the attribute name, providing the attributes in the form of a list forces the user to loop and compare every single one. Alternately, if the attributes are being manipulated in bulk by code that has no knowledge of the attribute names, providing the attributes in map makes it more cumbersome.

When the user needs to drill down through three levels of object hierarchy to reach the data after each call, it results in boilerplate code. However, the other side of the coin is that you are simply unable to return that extra metadata about the operation when you have a bare data-only interface. Examining the raw request and response can be useful on occasion and can be crucial when there is an error, but are those occasions often enough to justify returning a wrapper object for every call? There is no one right answer, but if you don't think about it, you are more likely to go wrong.

More Methods vs. More Parameters

Sometimes you can do multiple things with the same operation, due to the underlying SimpleDB options. One example of this is the `GetAttributes` operation that can fetch a full item or fetch part of an item, and those can be done with either eventual consistency or read-your-writes consistency. When designing the client, you get to choose if you will mirror the web service verbatim with all the options or if you will create simpler, individual functions for each conceptual task. The verbatim approach suggests method signatures like the following:

```
Item getAttributes(String domain, String itemName, List attributes,
        boolean consistent);
```

This leads to a concise API, but long parameter lists with boolean and null value arguments obscure the intent to those reading the code. A more task-oriented AP leads you toward signatures like this:

```
Item getItem(String domain, String itemName);
Item getAttributes(String domain, String itemName, List attributes);
```

```
Item getItemConsistent(String domain, String itemName);
Item getAttributesConsistent(String domain, String itemName,
        List attributes);
```

In this case, you end up with a more bloated API, but the application code written against it is more readable. A balance needs to be struck between the two.

The choice you make also depends on where those parameters are going to come from. When users are going to be typing in the code to call the functions, the narrow functions with clear and distinct meaning can be easier to read. When the parameters are coming from another framework or interface, the comprehensive functions can be easier to interface while keeping excessive conditional logic in check.

Concurrency

SimpleDB is optimized for concurrency, and you cannot scale up the request volume without it. Writing a SimpleDB client that does not address the need for concurrency may significantly hinder its usefulness. Some applications, however, benefit from the inherent parallelism of networked platforms and require no client-level concurrency—for example, mobile device applications and browser plug-ins. Consider the expected use of the client when you make the concurrency decisions. The client presented here does not expose any explicit concurrency via the API; for example, there are no asynchronous methods or task queues. However, the design allows room for a thread-safe implementation. This supports the goal of having simple code for reference purposes without crippling all chances at scaling up the request volume.

Thread safety allows any number of threads to make concurrent calls into a single client instance without the corruption of internal state. Specific implementation steps have to be taken to realize actual thread safety, like minimizing contention for shared resources and synchronizing all access to mutable shared state. An alternative in one direction is to provide explicit concurrency controls, and in the other direction, the client can balk at thread safety and require each thread to use its own instance. Regardless of the stance taken, it is wise to document it for your users. It is difficult and error prone to write multi-threaded code. Isolating it into small and manageable constructs makes it easier to achieve correctness and reuse.

Operation-Specific Considerations

Basic operations should be simple. The two most basic operations in the SimpleDB API are `CreateDomain` and `DeleteDomain`. These operations accept a single parameter and return nothing. There is not much to them, and it is probably best not to overcomplicate their implementation. These functions are likely to be called rarely and in an administrative capacity. There are really no other considerations for these calls.

`ListDomains` and `BatchPutAttributes` also fall into the simple category. These operations don't force you to make any choices. `ListDomains` accepts no arguments and returns a list of names, whereas `BatchPutAttributes` takes a domain and a set of items and returns nothing. Both parameters are always required, and there are no other options. The considerations for these is also minimal.

Flexibility and DomainMetadata

`DomainMetadata` returns various named sizes and counts. The basic design choice is between returning the raw data and creating a custom type with named properties. The named properties are more convenient and relieve the application of the need to know the exact constant names. It also provides a nice place for convenience methods to calculate total storage, billable storage, and remaining space. When the client includes a domain class, it acts as a natural home for these responsibilities.

The client here does not have a domain class and instead returns a mapping of string names to Long values. The reasoning is that this function returns data that is as much as a day old, so it is not likely to see heavy use. It also would not illustrate anything interesting. However, as a practical matter, it would be easy to implement and is a useful addition to this client.

If you do implement a class to hold this data, it is best to make clear which functions result in the actual web service calls. When it is returned from a `getDomainMetadata()` call, it seems obvious that a fresh call is made. If it is returned from a call like `domain.getItemCount()`, the answer is less obvious. Does the call go over the wire at the time the domain is instantiated or when the method is called? If you call the method again, is it going to make more service calls? If the object is being reused and you call the method on the same instance tomorrow, will it make a new call? It is possible to answer these questions in the documentation, but making it clear via the API is preferable.

There is an additional consideration for this function regardless of the structure of the return type. A 32-bit integer will hold all the possible values when the domain is small, but once it grows larger, it will overflow. A 64-bit integer is needed to represent the metadata of a full domain.

GetAttributes

The `get()` method in this example client uses the Java varargs language feature for the optional attribute names. This helps resolve the more parameters vs. more methods question. Requests for the full item accept the domain name and item name, whereas requests for specific attributes can take a variable number of values or an array. Take advantage of the available language features available to keep the API clean and the intention of each method clear.

With regard to the SimpleDB option to attach a `ConsistentRead` flag to a `GetAttributes` call, for the client has separate methods: one for a normal read and one for a consistent read. For one thing, the difference in naming makes the intention clearer when reading the application code. Additionally, the choice in naming emphasizes the semantics that one call represents the standard mechanism and the other one has special consistency treatment. This choice aligns with the idea that the eventually consistent operations should be used unless there is a good reason to do otherwise. It also presents a uniform naming convention when you see the same naming used with the `select()` and `selectConsistent()` methods.

Conditional and Unconditional Writes

`PutAttributes` and `DeleteAttributes` are similar from the standpoint of both design and implementation. The basic forms are simple enough with only a domain and an item parameter. The addition of conditional writes based on the state of an expected attribute certainly adds a wrinkle.

The real issue is that there are three parameters used to expose two separate functions. On the one hand, you need to set `Expected.1.Name` and `Expected.1.Value` if you want to proceed based on a value that exists. On the other hand, you have to set `Expected.1.Name` and `Expected.1.Exists` when you want to proceed based on a value not existing.

You need to know how the conditional write system works, but there is no requirement for you to pass the parameter burden on to your users. If you pass all those arguments straight through your API, not only do you end up with a method with five parameters (which is bad enough), but it is also guaranteed that every call to that method will require the passing of unused parameters.

An even worse problem with that situation is the fact that the correctness of the request is at risk. For example, it is not valid to pass `Expected.1.Value if Expected.1.Exists` is set to false. And of course, you can validate the parameters before proceeding, but it is too late for the following reason: Giving the users of your client a method where each of the parameters can be correct individually but invalid together is a problem in itself. It's not going to matter to the user whether the runtime error comes from your client directly or from the SimpleDB response your client is parsing. Runtime is too late to catch this error, when it could be done in the mind of the developer while typing, or compile time at the latest.

This client declares three methods each for `PutAttributes` and `DeleteAttributes`, one method for each different type of action you would want to take, as shown in Listing 10-1. The `PutAttributes` methods are `put()`, `putIfExists()`, and `putIfNotExists()`. The naming of the "ifNotExists" is a little awkward as part of a method name, but it is in line with the type of phrasing used in other databases. Each of these methods has the exact number of parameters needed for the underlying action, with no optional parameters. It is still possible to pass bad data, as with any call, but it is not possible for the user to form an invalid request.

Hijacking the NextToken

Breaking down an operation into multiple methods is one thing, but a more drastic action has been taken with the `Select` operation. The design change to the select call revolves around removing all traces of the `NextToken`. Instead of returning the `NextToken` to users, it is stored for later use. Later use involves handling user calls to `hasMorePages()` and `getNextPage()`. The last `SelectExpression` is stored as well, for use in the follow-up calls.

Deviating from the base API is something to consider carefully when you are writing a client that other people will use. People who are familiar with SimpleDB and want to use your client will not be expecting substantial changes. Here is the reasoning behind this change:

- There is nothing productive the user can do with the token, except bear the burden of storing it and passing it back at the proper time.
- Any query can return the token, so every query may need to be wrapped in token-handling code.
- There is a strong mismatch between the meaning of `NextToken` and what users typically want to do.

From the standpoint of SimpleDB, the token always means the same thing, "Query execution stopped before exhausting the potential results; here's a token to resume the search." From the SimpleDB side, it does not matter why execution stopped, but from the user perspective, the "why" means everything. Was it because the specified limit was reached or the default limit, or did it run out of time? Determining the "why" requires looking at both the token and the result count, and that is confusing to users.

The mismatch really extends to the meaning of the `LIMIT` clause as well; you still get a `NextToken` when the `LIMIT` is reached. `LIMIT` is not expressive enough because you cannot say, "Give me the first 100 results." You cannot even say, "Give me the first 100 results, and if it takes too long, give me a token to fetch the remainder." What you end up saying is, "Give me the first 100 results; if it takes too long, give me a token. I'll check the result count to see if I got all 100, and if not, I'll check for a token just in case there aren't 100 matches. I'll then rewrite my query with a new limit to get the remainder."

`NextToken` and `LIMIT` are request-level parameters, while users have intentions that reach beyond one individual request. That is the source of the mismatch. The solution presented here is by no means an ideal solution. The biggest design flaw with the token hijacking attempt is the failure to address the `LIMIT` issue as well. This idea is rejected in the context of this chapter, because it involves rewriting select expressions, and that does not fit well in a chapter about a basic client. Another shortcoming of this approach is that the ability to fetch follow-up pages for a query is lost once a new query is issued.

Implementing the Client Code

With all the high-level considerations addressed, that wraps up the design discussion. What remains is to take the interface defined in Listing 10-1 and flesh it out into the implementation code.

Safe Handling of the Secret Key

Before the user can call the methods of this client, it must first be initialized. You may notice that the only constructor argument in this class is a service URL. Proper initialization also requires valid account credentials. An important consideration early in the development of this client is the safeguarding of the user's account credentials. First, we want to be careful how we store the Secret Access Key. It is impossible to predict where this client code might end up running someday. You do not want to be in a situation where you left a vulnerability in the SimpleDB client where some malicious code, perhaps running as a plug-in in the same process, might be able to gain access to the secret key. It may not be totally preventable, but there are some steps you can take to store only the minimum.

It is also beneficial to discourage users from hard coding credentials directly into source files. In keeping with this idea, keys will be loaded from the file .awssecret in the user's home directory. There are a number of other likely candidates for loading credentials. Web application containers define standard means to load configuration information, and a dependency injection framework would allow the credentials to be injected. Ideally, the client would have the ability to pull the credentials from any of these sources. For the purposes of this chapter, only the user home directory will be used.

The important thing is that database logon information needs to be externalized as configuration information. Giving the client code the ability to pull the credentials directly from the source has another nice side effect. It gives the client everything needed to look for updated credentials in the event of an authentication failure. The AWS website grants you the ability to activate and deactivate credentials as well as create new ones. Deleting old credentials may become necessary for a variety of reasons, not the least of which is compromised keys resulting from the lack of safe handling.

Having a SimpleDB client that can immediately refresh the credentials when needed, with no intervention from the application, can be very convenient. It is only a minor convenience when the client stores a small amount of state, as this client does. In a more sophisticated client handling thousands of simultaneous in-flight requests, the benefit of having a client capable of hot swapping credentials without an abrupt shutdown and re-initialization is much greater.

Implementing the Constructor

Listing 10-4 shows the implementation of the SimpleDB constructor. The full implementation is available for download from the book's website.

At the top of the constructor, a Java `Properties` instance is used to load the contents of the .awssecret file. The `AccessKeyId` is then stored in the final String member named `KEY`. Rather than storing the `SecretAccessKey` directly, it is used instead to initialize an instance of the javax.crypto.Mac class. The Mac provides an abstraction for the Message Authentication Code needed to compute the digital signature for each request.

The raw bytes of the `SecretAccessKey` along with the `String` name of a hash algorithm are needed for this initialization in conjunction with a `javax.crypto.spec.SecretKeySpec` object. Import statements have been added for these classes, and a constant has been added to hold the hash algorithm name. More details about the signature computation and options are covered later in the chapter in the "Computing the Signature" section.

Listing 10-4 **SimpleDB.java Implementation of the SimpleDB Constructor**

```
public SimpleDB(String serviceUrl) {
  try {
    Properties props = new Properties();
```

```
      String home = System.getProperty("user.home");
      props.load(new FileReader(new File(home, ".awssecret")));
      KEY = props.getProperty("AWS_ACCESS_KEY_ID");
      String secret = props.getProperty("AWS_SECRET_ACCESSS_KEY");
      HMAC = Mac.getInstance(ALORITHM);
      HMAC.init(new SecretKeySpec(secret.getBytes(), ALORITHM));
      URL = new URL(serviceUrl);
      CLIENT = new HTTPClient();
    } catch (Exception e) {
      throw new RuntimeException(e);
    }
}
```

The constructor ends with the creation of a URL object and some exception handling. Any problem with the file loading, Mac, or the URL will be caught here and rethrown as a `RuntimeException`. A `RuntimeException` is used because of the shortcomings of Java checked exceptions. In a nutshell, checked exceptions force both class dependencies and handling code at every level of the call chain, even those levels with no need to know. A better choice would be to define a custom exception class that subclasses `RuntimeException` type for convenient catching.

Implementing the Remaining Methods

Listing 10-5 shows a partial implementation of the SimpleDB class. The full implementation is available for download from the book's website.

Listing 10-5 **SimpleDB.java Partial Implementation the SimpleDB Client Class**

```
  public void createDomain(String domainName) {
    Request request = createNewRequest("CreateDomain");
    request.setDomain(domainName);
    CLIENT.fetch(request);
  }

  public List<String> listDomains() {
    Request request = createNewRequest("ListDomains");
    Response response = CLIENT.fetch(request);
    return response.extractDomains();
  }

  public Map<String, Long> domainMetadata(String domain) {
    Request request = createNewRequest("DomainMetadata");
    request.setDomain(domain);
    Response response = CLIENT.fetch(request);
    return response.extractDomainMetadata();
  }
```

```
public void batchPut(String domain, List<Item> items) {
  Request request = createNewRequest("BatchPutAttributes");
  request.setDomain(domain);
  request.addItems(items);
  CLIENT.fetch(request);
}

public void put(String domain, Item item) {
  Request request = createNewRequest("PutAttributes");
  request.setItemName(item.getName());
  request.addAttributes(item.getAtts());
  request.setDomain(domain);
  CLIENT.fetch(request);
}

public void delete(String domain, Item item) {
  Request request = createNewRequest("DeleteAttributes");
  request.setDomain(domain);
  request.setItemName(item.getName());
  request.addAttributes(item.getAtts());
  CLIENT.fetch(request);
}

public Item get(String domain, String itemName, String... atts) {
  Request request = createNewRequest("GetAttributes");
  request.setDomain(domain);
  request.setItemName(itemName);
  request.addAttributeNames(atts);
  Response response = CLIENT.fetch(request);
  return new Item(itemName, response.extractAttributes());
}

public List<Item> select(String select) {
  return select(select, "");
}

public boolean hasNextPage() {
  return lastToken.get().length() > 0;
}

public List<Item> getNextPage() {
  return select(lastSelect.get(), lastToken.get());
}

private List<Item> select(String select, String nextToken) {
  lastSelect.set(select);
  Request request = createNewRequest("Select");
```

```
    request.setSelectExpression(select);
    request.setNextToken(nextToken);
    Response response = CLIENT.fetch(request);
    lastToken.set(response.extractNextToken());
    return response.extractItems();
  }

  private Request createNewRequest(String action) {
    return new Request(HMAC, action, KEY, URL);
  }
}
```

All the methods in the `SimpleDB` class in this listing have a similar flow with only minor differences. They each take the following form:

1. Create a request.
2. Set parameters on the request.
3. Pass the request to the `HTTPClient` for transmission.
4. Optionally, extract a return value from the response.

Even though each method has slight differences, there is room in this class to refactor away some of the duplicated code. Nevertheless, it is arguable whether that is necessary. The current form of these methods allows them to remain below six lines in length while retaining a high level of clarity. Refactoring to eliminate this type of duplicate code style requires some type of new abstraction to be inserted into the clear flow of these methods.

Such a change would be an improvement if the abstraction makes the methods clearer rather than merely shorter. In order for this to be the case, there has to be some deeper, more basic, abstraction lurking in the code that is yet to emerge. Inventing one artificially to reduce line count is not an improvement.

In addition, three more classes in the client are used as part of the implementation but are not visible to the user. They are as follows:

- A `Request` class to handle the details of assembling a proper request.
- A `Response` class to hold the logic for parsing responses.
- An `HTTPClient` class to manage the connection specific code.

It could certainly be more complex; there are SimpleDB concepts that do not get classes. Nevertheless, simplicity has its own set of advantages. To maintain simplicity, each domain, `SelectExpression`, and `NextToken` is represented as plain string object.

Making Requests

Now that the basic structure is in place and a set of credentials have been loaded, let's work our way toward making requests. Creating a request involves the proper encoding and assembly of all the required parameters followed by a signature.

SOAP Requests vs. REST Requests

The SimpleDB web service supports requests in both SOAP format and REST format. There is no functional difference between the two, so the decision usually comes down to the technical differences. The SOAP format is more verbose and so to some degree consumes more memory and bandwidth. Because there are no benefits to be had from using that extra resource usage, the REST format is used for this client. The one situation where there are real benefits from using SOAP is when the developer of the client has web service tooling in place to generate the access code automatically. In this case, SOAP may be more convenient. Be aware, however, that convenience for the SimpleDB client creator is not the same as convenience for the client user. In my experience, code generation based on XML definitions has been awkward.

> **Merely a Wire Protocol**
>
> Across the Internet, battles have raged for years between the supporters of SOAP and REST. REST is the clear winner in the browser to server space but lacks the built-in features needed for robust enterprise web services.
>
> However, the SOAP vs. REST debate has zero bearing on the SimpleDB interfaces. First, the SimpleDB version of a REST interface is more of a HTTP query interface, and not RESTful at all. Second, and more importantly, SimpleDB is not a high-level service; it is a low-level database with only basic features. There is no service composition or grand web service activities going on here. It is just a wire protocol.
>
> If you want to feel the joy of using a RESTful service, go ahead: Write a proxy server that accepts a RESTful version of SimpleDB, and translates it into real SimpleDB requests. Then you can write a RESTful client and, in the end, what you'll find is that it didn't make the slightest bit of difference to real users who neither know nor care about the wire protocol. In the end, the only thing to be had is a little more overhead, which, incidentally, is what you would get from using SOAP.

Setting the Required Parameters

There are seven mandatory parameters required in every request. They are as follows:

- **`AWSAccessKeyId`**— A valid and currently active access key.
- **`Action`**— This is the name of the SimpleDB operation; for example: "DomainMetadata".
- **`SignatureMethod`**— The name of the hash algorithm; for example: "HmacSHA256".
- **`SignatureVersion`**— SimpleDB has supported three different methods of request signing over the years, named "0", "1", and "2". Version 2 is the most recent and the most secure, and is the one I recommend.
- **`Version`**— This is the published API version; the most recent is "2009-04-15".
- **`Signature`**— This parameter holds the final signature hash value of all the other parameters.

- **`Timestamp`**— A string that represents the request time in UTC; for example: "2007-01-31T23:59:59.645Z".

In addition to these, there are also request specific parameters that must be set for each operation. These parameters are discussed in detail in Chapter 3, "A Code-Snippet Tour of the SimpleDB API." However, for our purposes here, we need to collect all the parameters and sort them for the signature computation.

Listing 10-6 shows the start of a `Request` class to encapsulate the parameter holding, sorting, and signing. This class is declared in the package `com.simpledbbook.core`. In addition to `Request`, this package will also hold a `Response` class and an `HTTPClient` class. None of the classes in this package will be seen by users of the client; they are strictly for internal use.

Listing 10-6 **Request.java The Beginning of a SimpleDB Request Class**

```
package com.simpledbbook.core;

import java.net.*;
import java.text.*;
import java.util.*;

import javax.crypto.Mac;

public class Request {
  private static final SimpleDateFormat TIMESTAMP;
  private final SortedMap<String, String> PARAMS;
  private final Mac HMAC;
  private final URL URL;

  static {
    String format = "yyyy-MM-dd'T'HH%3'A'mm%3'A'ss.SSS'Z'";
    TIMESTAMP = new SimpleDateFormat(format);
    TIMESTAMP.setTimeZone(TimeZone.getTimeZone("GMT"));
  }

  public Request(Mac hMac, String action, String key, URL url) {
    URL = url;
    HMAC = hMac;
    PARAMS = new TreeMap<String, String>();
    PARAMS.put("Version", "2009-04-15");
    PARAMS.put("Timestamp", TIMESTAMP.format(new Date()));
    PARAMS.put("SignatureVersion", "2");
    PARAMS.put("SignatureMethod", HMAC.getAlgorithm());
    PARAMS.put("Action", action);
    PARAMS.put("AWSAccessKeyId", key);
  }
```

```
  public URL getURL() {
    return URL;
  }
}
```

A timestamp format is held in a class constant of type `SimpleDateFormat`; it can be reused for every request instance. The format is instantiated and initialized in the static block. The format string uses the special format defined by the `SimpleDateFormat` class. A notable modification to the format is that the ":" characters have been replaced with the final URL-encoded value '%3A,' making encoding unnecessary. Also, the GMT time zone is set, so the result will be compatible with UTC time.

In addition to the formatter, there are three final members, one each for Mac and URL passed into the constructor, plus a SortedMap to hold the parameters. The SortedMap is able to store all the parameter names and values in sorted order so that no explicit sorting needs to be done.

The constructor saves off the URL and the Mac, allocates a concrete instance of SortedMap, and proceeds to insert six parameters. Of the seven required parameters, these six are all known in advance, so they might as well be set immediately. The version and signature version are constant values. The timestamp is created by passing the current time to the formatter. The signature hashing method could conceivably change, so it is pulled directly from the Mac. The action and key are variable, but passed to the constructor.

The two remaining required parameters are the signature and the timestamp. The signature cannot be added until the request is complete, but the timestamp could be added now. The only concern is that the timestamp defines a window of validity for the request of 15 minutes. Even though it is unlikely that 15 minutes would elapse between request creation and transmission, sometimes the unlikely events occur, so the timestamp is set later.

Setting Optional Parameters

Because this `Request` class needs to handle all SimpleDB operations, it needs a way to accept all of the possible parameters. A simple way to do that is to create a method that can accept any set of parameters and add them to the sorted map. The method could look like this:

```
public void setParam(String name, String value) {
  PARAMS.put(name, value);
}
```

Then the SimpleDB class can set parameters with the following code:

```
request.setParam("DomainName", "users");
```

That approach will work, but when you start to think about it, you realize that seven of nine will need to set this domain name parameter. The inconvenience of having to repeat the hard-coded constant "DomainName" seven times suggests refactoring it into a class constant. However, it seems much more appropriate to make the `Request` class responsible for the names of the request parameters. So, let's move the parameter name into the `Request` class, as follows:

```
public void setDomain(String name) {
  PARAMS.put("DomainName", name);
}
```

Now it can be called as follows:

```
request.setDomain(domainName);
```

This conveys intent better and avoids the use of constants in awkward places. It also ends up requiring a separate method in the `Request` class for each optional parameter, but as you'll see, many of those parameters require special handling anyway.

Proper Request Encoding

One omission from the `setDomain()` method is the proper encoding of the domain name. The technical requirement for all SimpleDB requests is that all parameter names and values must be percent encoded in accordance with RFC 3986 section 2, commonly referred to as URL encoding. RFC 3986 defines the following set of unreserved characters:

```
A-Z, a-z, "-", ".", "_", "~"
```

These unreserved characters must not be encoded, whereas all other bytes must be percent encoded. However, there are a few situations where you can be certain that the value contains only unreserved characters and therefore skip the encoding step. The main case where this applies is to all AWS-defined constants. This includes all of the SimpleDB parameter names, all of the operation names, and a number of values. This is why no encoding was done in the `Request` constructor in Listing 10-6. In the case of the domain name parameter, the characters allowed in domain names are a strict subset of the unreserved characters. For all parameters other than domain name, however, all of the values need to be encoded.

Because `setDomain()` does not require encoding, let's add another parameter setting method to the `Request` class that does. Listing 10-7 shows setting the `SelectExpression` parameter and a method to implement the percent encoding.

Listing 10-7 **Request.java The Addition of Percent Encoding to the Request Class**

```
...
  public void setSelectExpression(String select) {
    PARAMS.put("SelectExpression", encode(select));
  }

  private String encode(String value) {
    String result = "";
    try {
      result = URLEncoder.encode(value, "UTF-8");
    } catch (UnsupportedEncodingException e) {
      e.printStackTrace(); // can't happen
```

```
    }
    result = result.replace("+", "%20");
    result = result.replace("*", "%2A");
    result = result.replace("%7E", "~");
    return result;
  }
...
```

The `encode()` method uses `java.net.URLEncoder.encode()` to do the actual encoding. It is crucial that the value first be converted to UTF-8 bytes before it is URL encoded and that is done here by passing the name of a character encoding along with the value. SimpleDB interprets all incoming data as URL-encoded UTF-8 bytes, so using any other encoding, including the platform-default encoding, can result in sending incorrect data. Storing improperly encoded data can be difficult to diagnose because usually you do not get an error at the time the data is written; the more common symptom is seeing incorrect characters coming back in a read.

It is also very important that every bit of data that needs encoding go through this process. It is possible to assemble all the parameters first and then encode the entire parameter list later, when it is used. The benefit of that approach is that you do not need to be vigilant about avoiding bugs of omission when encoding the parameter data coming into each method. You don't need to guard a dozen doors coming in when you are guarding the one door that goes out. However, the tradeoff here is with the number of times the parameters must be encoded. The parameter string is used multiple times: First to compute the signature, another time when the final request is sent, possibly a third to compute the content length, and maybe again for use in logging. Although it is possible to cache some of these, you cannot cache them all because the value changes once you add the signature.

The alternate tactic used here is to encode each piece of data, faithfully and fully, as it comes in to the parameter map. It leaves you exposed to potential bugs if you add new methods and forget to encode, but it obviates the need to encode the same data repeatedly. More than that, it lets you selectively encode the data that requires it while passing over the data that does not need to be encoded.

Looking back at the `encode()` method in Listing 10-7, URL encoding ought to be a straightforward task, but sometimes there are idiosyncrasies to deal with. In Java, you are forced to deal with an `UnsupportedEncodingException`, even though UTF-8 is always supported. More importantly, the Java implementation encodes spaces into the plus sign (+), fails to encode the asterisk (*), and encodes the tilde (~) unnecessarily. Listing 10-7 resolves these issues after the fact with string replacement.

Now that the encoding mechanism is in place, let's flesh out the rest of the parameter setting methods. Listing 10-8 displays the remaining eight methods needed for parameter settings, along with a private utility method. This listing is lengthier, but the methods are all quite small.

Listing 10-8 **Request.java The Remaining Parameter Setting Methods in the Request Class**

```
public void setNextToken(String nextToken) {
  PARAMS.put("NextToken", encode(nextToken));
}

public void setConsistentRead() {
  PARAMS.put("ConsistentRead", "true");
}

public void setItemName(String name) {
  PARAMS.put("ItemName", encode(name));
}

public void setExpectedAttribute(String name, String value) {
  PARAMS.put("Expected.1.Name", encode(name));
  PARAMS.put("Expected.1.Value", encode(value));
}

public void setExpectedToNotExist(String name) {
  PARAMS.put("Expected.1.Name", encode(name));
  PARAMS.put("Expected.1.Exists", "false");
}

public void addAttributeNames(String... atts) {
  for (int i = 0; i < atts.length; i++) {
    PARAMS.put("AttributeName." + i, encode(atts[i]));
  }
}

public void addAttributes(Attribute... atts) {
  addPrefixAttributes("", atts);
}

private void addPrefixAttributes(String prefix, Attribute... atts){
  for (int i = 0; i < atts.length; i++) {
    String finalPrefix = prefix + "Attribute." + i + ".";
    PARAMS.put(finalPrefix + "Value", encode(atts[i].getValue()));
    PARAMS.put(finalPrefix + "Name", encode(atts[i].getName()));
    if (atts[i].isReplace()) {
      PARAMS.put(finalPrefix + "Replace", "true");
    }
  }
}

public void addItems(List<Item> items) {
```

```
    for (int i = 0; i < items.size(); i++) {
      String prefix = "Item." + i + ".";
      PARAMS.put(prefix + "ItemName", encode(items.get(i).getName()));
      addPrefixAttributes(prefix, items.get(i).getAtts());
    }
}
```

The first three methods in Listing 10-8 are similar to those shown already; an entry is added to the parameter map and the value is encoded. The semantics of the second method, `setConsistentRead()`, are that it is called only to request the strengthened consistency. The SimpleDB API allows `ConsistentRead` to have a value of false, but since it is false by default, there is no reason to send the parameter at all in that case. The next two methods, `setExpectedAttribute()` and `setExpectedToNotExist()`, follow suit, only adding two parameter pairs instead of one.

These are followed by a method that starts us down the path of more complex attributes: `addAttributeNames()`. At this point, we must contend with adding a list of values rather than just a single value. This method is called as part of the `GetAttributes` process when the attributes to be fetched are listed by name. To adhere to the SimpleDB naming protocol, these parameters will take the following general form:

```
Attribute.Name.N=importantAttribute
```

In this form, `N` is zero for the first attribute name and increases by one for each subsequent attribute name. This form is realized via a simple loop and counter, culminating in the expected call to `PARAMS.put()`.

The final two public methods take that concept a step further. The `PutAttributes` and `DeleteAttributes` operations need the ability to set parameters of the form, as follows:

```
Attribute.0.Name=DisplayName
Attribute.0.Value=Mocky
Attribute.1.Name=ProfileLocation
Attribute.1.Value=NY
Attribute.1.Replace=true
```

Those parameters need to be created in a loop, with one iteration for each passed attribute. `BatchPutAttributes` requires the exact same treatment, the only difference being the need to add an item number to the front. The batch parameters look like this:

```
Item.7.Attribute.0.Name=DisplayName
Item.7.Attribute.0.Value=AnnikaHansen
Item.7.Attribute.1.Name=ProfileLocation
Item.7.Attribute.1.Value=UnimatrixZero
Item.7.Attribute.1.Replace=true
```

The parameter-building process for these two forms could easily be done in separate methods, but the differences are small enough to warrant a single method. Considering that the second form merely requires an extra item name prefix, this difference can be abstracted away by assigning a blank prefix to the first form.

This is done in the Listing 10-8 `addAttributes()` method. When this method is called, the attributes are forwarded to the private `addPrefixedAttributes()` method, along with an empty prefix. This method performs the work of looping through the attributes, building up the full parameter names based on the passed-in item prefix and a loop counter. The parameter values are all encoded before being set into the parameter map and the replace parameter is conditionally set.

The `addItems()` method fills in the last piece of the puzzle by looping through the items, setting the encoded item name parameter and calling `addPrefixedAttributes()` with an item prefix built from the loop counter.

Computing the Signature

The final bit of functionality missing from this `Request` class is the signature computation. The signature is merely another parameter that needs to be set, along with all the others. The difference, of course, is that it is a hash of the final request. Listing 10-9 shows the remaining methods in the `Request` class.

Listing 10-9 **Request.java The Signature Computation Methods in the Request Class**

```
void sign() {
  PARAMS.put("Signature", computeSignature());
}

private String computeSignature() {
  byte[] bytes = getStringToSign().getBytes();
  byte[] signature = null;
  synchronized (HMAC) {
    signature = HMAC.doFinal(bytes);
  }
  return encode(Base64.encode(signature));
}

private String getStringToSign() {
  StringBuilder toSign = new StringBuilder("POST\n");
  toSign.append(URL.getHost()).append("\n");
  toSign.append(URL.getPath()).append("\n");
  toSign.append(getParamString());
  return toSign.toString();
}

String getParamString() {
  StringBuilder result = new StringBuilder();
  for (Map.Entry<String, String> p : PARAMS.entrySet()) {
    result.append('&').append(p.getKey());
    result.append('=').append(p.getValue());
```

```
  }
  return result.substring(1); // omit the leading '&'
}
```

Computing the Signature Hash

Reading through the Listing 10-9 methods in order, first we have `sign()`. The single-line implementation is a concise description of the two actions taking place: `computeSignature()` is being called, and the result is stored in the parameter map.

In order to perform the actual signature computation, we need to obtain the final string to sign and convert it into a byte array. A call to the Mac is needed to get the hash of those bytes. The result of that hash is a byte array that must be first Base64 encoded and then percent encoded before it can be returned. Those are the steps taken in `computeSignature()`, but let's take a closer look at each of them.

The astute reader may notice that the string to sign is converted into bytes with the no-arg version of the `getBytes()` method that uses the platform-default encoding. Although it is crucial that the UTF-8 encoding be used, it is not needed at this stage; this string has already been through character encoding and percent encoding.

You may also have noticed that the same Mac instance is being passed to the constructor of each request. The call to `doFinal()` here presents the lone thread-safety concern for this instance. To protect the Mac from simultaneous calls to `doFinal()` from different threads, it is wrapped in a synchronized block, where only one thread at a time can get in.

The byte array containing the signature hash is just that: a set of bytes. Because these bytes represent binary data and not character data, the Base64 encoding is used to make them transmittable over HTTP. A follow-up encoding is needed, however, because there are three characters in the output of Base64 that require percent encoding: plus (+), forward slash (/), and the equals sign (=).

Building the Sorted Parameter String

Assembly of the string to sign occurs in `getStringToSign()`. The string takes the following form for REST requests:

```
HTTPVerb<newline>
HTTPHost<newline>
HTTPRequestPath<newline>
SortedParameterString
```

In this form, `<newline>` is the ASCII newline character and `HTTPVerb` is either GET or POST. `HTTPHost` and `HTTPRequestPath` are the host and path in the HTTP request and `SortedParameterString` is the culmination of all the parameter handling up to this point.

The `getStringToSign()` method mirrors this format. The verb POST is here. The main difference between POST and GET for SimpleDB purposes is the limit on the maximum size of a GET URL. The limit does not apply to POST, since the parameter string is sent as content and is not part of the URL. The limit is easily reachable with

`BatchPutAttributes` calls that use GET, so this client uses POST for all requests for consistency.

Parameter Ordering

The final method in Listing 10-8, `getParamString()`, wraps up the signature code by providing the base value upon which the others operate. The format for the parameter string is the familiar series of name/value pairs, separated internally by an equals sign (=) and delimited with an ampersand (&):

```
param2=value2&param3=value3
```

The `getParamString()` method loops over each map entry, building up the result. The most important part of this process does not appear in this code: the sorting. When computing the signature, the parameters must be put into a canonical order so that SimpleDB is able to compute an identical signature. The ordering that SimpleDB requires is an ascending lexicographic sort, which is commonly the natural sort order for strings. This is exactly the key ordering that `SortedMap` uses when it returns the list of map entries.

The keys, in this case, are the parameter names, and only the parameter names need to be sorted. Because they are all unique within a request, the variation in parameter values will never affect the order. The `SortedMap` is convenient, but there is nothing special about it. You can use whatever data structure is convenient for you.

Sorting the Parameters Properly

The final ordering of the parameters as they are sent across the wire is irrelevant because SimpleDB reconstructs the canonical order to verify the signature. Nevertheless, the ordering at signature computation time is the difference between success and a 403 `SignatureDoesNotMatch` error code.

The signature code seems pretty cut and dried, in the sense that it always fails until you get it right and then it always succeeds. However, there are conditional errors that occur due to sorting bugs that only manifest once you have enough parameters.

The classic case is when the parameter string is built on the fly without an explicit sort. If the request has nine attributes, you can get by without a data structure to hold the names and values. You can loop through the attributes, appending values to the result:

...Attribute.0.Name=color&Attribute.0.Value=red...

However, as soon as you try it with 10 or more attributes, you are hosed:

...Attribute.9.Value=red&Attribute.10.Name=...

With a string-based sort, `Attribute.10` comes before not only `Attribute.9`, but before `Attribute.2` as well.

Making the Connections

With a `Request` instance populated with parameters and ready to sign, it is time to start opening HTTP connections. There are various HTTP client options available, from writing your own to using full-featured third-party library code. The approach taken for the SimpleDB client in this chapter is to make use of the humble `java.net.URLConnection` that comes standard with Java. As a result, there are not any advanced features available, and neither do you get much fine-grained control. However, you get to see how to make things work simply and without having to spend the time hunting for a third-party download and learning yet another API.

Like the `Request` class, the `HTTPClient` class that encapsulates all the network I/O is in the `com.simpledbbook.core` package. The SimpleDB class instantiates an instance of `HTTPClient` in its constructor and uses it for all subsequent requests. Listing 10-10 gives the full implementation of the class.

Listing 10-10 **HTTPClient.java A Class to Handle All the Network I/O to SimpleDB**

```
package com.simpledbbook.core;

import java.io.*;
import java.net.*;

public class HTTPClient {
  private static final String CONTENT_TYPE =
    "application/x-www-form-urlencoded; charset=utf-8";

  public Response fetch(Request request) {
    request.sign();
    URLConnection con = getConnection(request);
    writeRequest(request, con);
    String body = readInput(con);
    int code = getResponseCode(con);
    Response result = new Response(body, code);
    return result;
  }

  private URLConnection getConnection(Request request) {
    try {
      URLConnection con = request.getURL().openConnection();
      con.setRequestProperty("Content-Type", CONTENT_TYPE);
      String contentLength = request.getParamString().length() + "";
      con.setRequestProperty("Content-Length", contentLength);
      con.setDoOutput(true);
      con.connect();
      return con;
    } catch (IOException e) {
      throw new RuntimeException("Error opening connection", e);
    }
  }

  private void writeRequest(Request request, URLConnection con) {
    try {
      OutputStream outputStream = con.getOutputStream();
```

```
      OutputStreamWriter wr = new OutputStreamWriter(outputStream);
      wr.write(request.getParamString());
      wr.flush();
    } catch (Exception e) {
      e.printStackTrace();
    }
  }

  private String readInput(URLConnection con) {
    InputStream in = null;
    try {
      in = con.getInputStream();
    } catch (Exception e) {
      HttpURLConnection http = (HttpURLConnection) con;
      in = http.getErrorStream();
    }
    return readFully(in);
  }

  private String readFully(InputStream in) {
    try {
      BufferedReader br = new BufferedReader(
          new InputStreamReader(in));
      StringBuilder page = new StringBuilder();
      String line = null;
      while ((line = br.readLine()) != null) {
        page.append(line);
      }
      in.close();
      return page.toString();
    } catch (IOException e) {
      throw new RuntimeException("Error reading from stream", e);
    }
  }

  private int getResponseCode(URLConnection con) {
    try {
      return ((HttpURLConnection)con).getResponseCode();
    } catch (IOException e) {
      return -1;
    }
  }
}
```

Instances of `HTTPClient` maintain no state and have a single public method: `fetch()`. It is designed to be thread safe. With no shared state and each call to `fetch()` operating in isolation, multiple threads can be performing I/O concurrently.

The body of the `fetch()` method is a high-level overview of what needs to be done. All the remaining methods in the class play a support role. The first thing that happens is the request signing. It can be done here because it is now clear that no more parameters are being added to the request.

After that, a connection is opened, the data is written out, the XML response is read back, and then a new `Response` object is returned, holding that XML and the HTTP response code. All of it is straightforward, with the exception of two points that apply specifically to SimpleDB.

When using POST, you have to be sure to set the headers correctly. This is done within `getConnection()`, and there are two headers to be set. "Content-Type" must be set to "application/x-www-form-urlencoded; charset=utf-8" and the "Content-Length" must be set to the length of the parameter string, which is all that is being sent.

The second thing to notice is the way errors are handled in `readInput()`. An exception thrown while trying to retrieve the `URLConnection` input stream indicates an abnormal response. At this point, attention is shifted from the input stream to the error stream and the code continues as if nothing happened. This is because a proper XML response is being returned regardless of the source; it is just a matter of reading it in at this point.

The need to switch to reading from a different stream is an idiosyncrasy of the underlying URL connection; however, the concept applies to all languages and libraries. You must handle any errors in such a way that processing can continue and the full error response can be retrieved.

This type of handling can be seen in the `writeRequest()` method. If an exception is thrown during the write, the stack trace is printed, but it is otherwise ignored. This is not an oversight; the error message needs to be read, and that happens in the very next method call.

Checking the HTTP Response Code

When everything is successful with your SimpleDB requests, the response code will always be 200. When there is a problem, a different code is returned. The type of code returned can give insight into the type of problem, and it is a good practice to make these codes available to your users. Codes in the 400s indicate a problem with your request that retry attempts do not fix. This includes signature problems, invalid `SelectExpression` issues, and conditional check failure, just to name a few.

Alternately, response codes in the 500's indicate an issue on the SimpleDB end that is not the result of a client error. These requests can be retried later. This includes the indeterminate `InternalError`, as well as the Service Unavailable error.

Although the 500 class codes indicate a retry, the specifics depend on the situation. 503 Service Unavailable in response to a `BatchPutAttributes` hints at an overloaded service with a prescription for a dose of exponential back-off. However, 503 Service Unavailable from a `ConsistentRead` or conditional write hints at a rare failure scenario or outage that may take time to repair.

There is not much else that is interesting in `HTTPClient`, other than some Java-specific blocking I/O. So, let's turn our attention to the final class in the SimpleDB client.

Parsing the Response

With the network I/O complete, the last step is to take the XML response and parse out the appropriate data. This functionality is the responsibility of the `Response` class, which stores the raw XML and HTTP response code, providing methods to extract every possible piece of data.

The best way to parse XML is with an XML parser; in addition, XPath can also be a very nice solution. The data extraction in this chapter is not done with any of the powerful XML tools, though. It is done with regular expressions. There is no design justification for going this route. In fact, XML is not a regular language, and so it is not possible to construct regular expressions to parse XML in provably correct ways. Regular expressions are used here because the XML is simple, the parsing requirements are simple, and the expressions are all simple. Moreover, it just works. If XML comments or CDATA sections start to come back from SimpleDB, this class could have some issues with it. This chapter does not endorse regular expressions as a superior or desirable XML parser; the only endorsement is that it can work with just as little effort as the other uninteresting XML parsers options.

Listing 10-11 gives a partial implementation of the `Response` class as part of the user-hidden `com.simpledbbook.core` package. The full code is available for download from the book's website.

Listing 10-11 **Response.java A Class to Extract the Data from SimpleDB XML Responses**

```
public class Response {
  // single group expressions passed to matchSingles()
  private static final Pattern DOMAIN_REGEX = Pattern.compile(
    "<DomainName>(.*?)</DomainName>");

  private static final Pattern TOKEN_REGEX = Pattern.compile(
    "<NextToken>(.*?)</NextToken>");

  // double group expressions passed to matchDoubles()
  private static final Pattern ATTRIBUTE_REGEX = Pattern.compile(
    "<Attribute><Name>(.*?)</Name><Value>(.*?)</Value></Attribute>");

  private static final Pattern ITEM_REGEX = Pattern.compile(
    "<Item><Name>(.*?)</Name>(.*?)</Item>");

  public List<String> extractDomains() {
    return matchSingles(DOMAIN_REGEX);
  }

  // returns a list of all single group expression matches
```

```
private List<String> matchSingles(Pattern pattern) {
  Matcher matcher = pattern.matcher(body);
  List<String> result = new ArrayList<String>();
  while (hasMoreMatches(matcher)) {
    result.add(matcher.group(1));
  }
  return result;
}

private boolean hasMoreMatches(Matcher matcher) {
  return matcher.find() && matcher.groupCount() > 0;
}

public String extractNextToken() {
  List<String> token = matchSingles(TOKEN_REGEX);
  return token.size() > 0 ? token.get(0) : "";
}

// Select returns Items with nested Attributes
public List<Item> extractItems() {
  List<Item> items = new ArrayList<Item>();
  for (Attribute row : matchDoubles(ITEM_REGEX, body)) {
    Item i = new Item(row.getName());
    i.addAttributes(matchDoubles(ATTRIBUTE_REGEX,row.getValue()));
    items.add(i);
  }
  return items;
}

// returns a list of double group expression matches
// with group 1 in the name and group 2 in the value
private List<Attribute> matchDoubles(Pattern pattern, String s) {
  Matcher matcher = pattern.matcher(s);
  List<Attribute> result = new ArrayList<Attribute>();
  while (hasMoreMatches(matcher)) {
    String attrName = matcher.group(1);
    String attrValue = decodeXMLEntities(matcher.group(2));
    result.add(new Attribute(attrName, attrValue));
  }
  return result;
}

public List<Attribute> extractAttributes() {
  return matchDoubles(ATTRIBUTE_REGEX, body);
}
```

```
private String decodeXMLEntities(String str) {
  String result = str.replace("&", "&");
  result = result.replace("&lt;", "<");
  result = result.replace("&gt;", ">");
  return result;
}
```

At the top of the class are static constants for all expression patterns. The first section of patterns is made up of expressions with a single group, and the second section expressions contain two groups.

Although there is a swarm of `extractXXX()` methods, the lion's share of work is done by two matching methods, which are called by everything else: `matchSingles()` and `matchDoubles()`. The `matchSingles()` method simply returns a list of strings from the XML body matching the passed expression. The `matchDoubles()` method returns a list of `Attribute` objects, where the attribute name is the content of a group one match and the value is the content of a group two match.

The only SimpleDB specifics are that even though you were careful to percent encode all the outgoing data, none of it comes back percent encoded. However, there are three characters in the response XML subject to encoding, and all three of them are XML entities. The less-than sign (<), greater-than sign (>), and ampersand (&) embedded within your data come back encoded as <, >, and & and need to be decoded.

Summary

Writing a SimpleDB client does not require six classes—it can be done with one class and with fewer than 200 lines of code. However, writing one that is well suited to its purpose takes some thought. You have to get a handle on the technical details of HTTP requests and XML parsing, but none of it is inherently more difficult than what you find with other web services.

There are weaknesses in the client presented here. A better, perhaps more scalable `HTTPClient` could be built using a library more advanced than the `URLConnection`. A proper XML parser could be substituted, and it would probably add clarity and reduce the quantity of code needed. The metadata could be enhanced with some nice methods to get at the values. The beauty of a design with a separation of concerns is the ability to vary one part independently of the others. A new HTTP class that honored the `fetch()` method would be a drop-in replacement. An alternate `Response` class with the same extract methods would have the freedom to implement the XML parsing in any conceivable way.

Instead of improving what already works, in the next chapter, new and advanced client functionality is discussed.

11

Improving the SimpleDB Client

Simplicity is one of the main characteristics of SimpleDB, but achieving simplicity does not guarantee convenience. The SimpleDB operations provide an excellent set of primitives, and there are many useful and creative ways to assemble those primitives.

Some of the most common usage patterns of SimpleDB involve a degree of awkwardness when the underlying abstractions do not fit the task you want to accomplish. It is in these areas that the SimpleDB client can be enhanced by adding the conveniences and the abstractions that fit better.

This chapter provides ideas, suggestions, and, in some cases code, as part of a discussion on where the future of SimpleDB clients could be. The overall viewpoint is the practical day-to-day use of the service. The goal is to address a wide variety of topics, all of which apply in some way to practical enhancements of SimpleDB clients. The themes include user convenience, avoidance of pain points in the pricing structure, and the development of a new level of primitives to support the enablement of better clients and better tooling.

The ideas here can be used directly by client implementers or by the users of clients when designing applications or requesting features.

Convenience Methods

If you spend much time writing application code that uses SimpleDB, you start to run into situations where you need the same small bits of extra functionality throughout your code. These convenience methods can exist as part of the application, but since they typically have feature envy of the SimpleDB client, the client is a better home for them. When developing a client, consider adding these.

Convenient Count Methods

One of the annoyances of using `count(*)` in a query is that you do not just get a number back. The response includes a fake item with one fake attribute that holds the number. This is a good thing from the standpoint of having an operation that always returns consistent responses. The response XML has the following format:

```
<SelectResult>
```

```
    <Item>
        <Name>Domain</Name>
        <Attribute>
            <Name>Count</Name>
            <Value>2</Value>
        </Attribute>
    </Item>
</SelectResult>
```

In addition, if there is a `NextToken` included in the response, this count will need to be added to all subsequent counts to get the final count. At the application level, frequently you just want the count as a number without the fake item and without the loops and the math. Placing the loops and the math within the client makes it more convenient.

Listing 11-1 shows convenience methods for obtaining a query count based on the client developed in the last chapter.

Listing 11-1 SimpleDB.java Additional Convenience Methods for Counting

```
...
  public long count(String domain) {
    return count(domain, "");
  }

  public int count(String domain, String whereClause) {
    return count(domain, whereClause, Integer.MAX_VALUE);
  }

  public int count(String domain, String where, int limit) {
    String query = "SELECT count(*) FROM `" + domain + "` " + where;
    List<Item> items = select(query);
    int count = 0;
    count = extractCount(items);
    while (hasNextPage() && count < limit) {
      items = getNextPage();
      count += extractCount(items);
    }
    return count;
  }

  private int extractCount(List<Item> items) {
    int result = 0;
    if (items.size() > 0) {
      Item item = items.get(0);
      result = Integer.parseInt(item.getAttribute("Count"));
    }
```

```
    return result;
  }
...
```

The first three methods provide the option to count all the items in a domain, only those matching a WHERE clause, and finally specifying a limit. The first two forward the call along to the third, where the work takes place. This code builds the final `SelectExpression` from the component parts. In all cases, the limit parameter is left out of the actual expression. Using a limit is not required when selecting a count because the default limit of 100 does not apply.

Typically, you will not get back counts of more than 120,000 to 200,000. If the final count number is in the millions, multiple follow-up selects will be necessary. The count method in Listing 11-1 performs an initial query, and if there is a NextToken and the limit has not been reached, it continues to query in a loop. The final method, `extractCount()`, provides the code to turn the resulting item into the numeric count.

Select with a Real Limit

Another frequent need is to get the results of a query that returns a NextToken and loop until the final desired limit is reached, as opposed to intermediate limits during the loop. This better serves the user intention of fetching the desired number of results. Listing 11-2 shows the implementation of a method that handles the looping and the limit checking internally. This method is based on the SimpleDB client developed in the last chapter.

Listing 11-2 **SimpleDB.java Additional Convenience Method for Querying with a Limit**

```
...
  public List<Item> selectWithRealLimit(String select, int limit) {
    List<Item> result = select(select);
    while (result.size() < limit && hasNextPage()) {
      result.addAll(getNextPage());
    }
    return result;
  }
...
```

The method `selectWithRealLimit()` builds up a list of matching items by calling the query in a loop until the query returns all matching items or the limit is reached. The final collection is then returned.

Custom Metadata and Building a Smarter Client

The operation built into SimpleDB that reports domain metadata gives you the basic counts and sizes required to see how close a domain is to the limits. There are limits on the number of attributes and bytes a single domain can hold.

This metadata is a description of the domain that represents the key information from the perspective of account billing and database administration. There is additional information, however, that is important to the application, which is usually stored in configuration files.

It can be convenient to use a configuration file for an application running on a single machine. However, the more machines in a deployment, the more of a task it becomes to distribute these files. Automation works well, but for applications using SimpleDB, there is another option.

There are trade-offs when you choose to use a database service instead of a database product. One of the benefits of this service, in particular, is the high availability and the fact that it always runs on a well-known host. Treating the configuration like a combination of database metadata and application metadata with storage directly in SimpleDB becomes a viable option.

Obviously, you cannot store the entire configuration in SimpleDB because the application at a minimum needs the database credentials. Nevertheless, it may be possible to keep the remainder of the configuration in the database.

Maintaining a single authoritative copy of the configuration not only makes it easy to administer; it also allows changes to propagate quickly and acts as an enabler for dynamic application features.

Justifying a Schema for Numeric Data

SimpleDB does not have a schema feature. However, if you store and query numeric data, special formatting is required. That format has to be stored in at least two locations: in the code that calls the format encoder/decoder at the right time, and in the queries.

The well-understood problem with storing information twice is that neglecting to make the change to all copies causes things to break. Another problem with the number formatting is that all queries written by hand must have any constants written in the target format. The format is most certainly not human readable.

A big step forward is the elimination of handwritten queries in favor of prepared statement style queries. Implementing this requires you to write code that manipulates the query string, building it from parameters. Passing parameters into a query is more convenient and less error prone. It also opens the door to other advanced features that require query string rewriting. One example is query execution in an environment of domain sharding; each query must be sent to each domain.

At some point, it becomes necessary to extract the type information about those numbers to a single location. Persistence frameworks commonly use a configuration file or source code annotations. Wherever it is stored, having a simple, declarative means to define types is convenient.

Whether it is declared formally or not, the schema types for numbers exist if you query them. Because you already have a schema, you might as well make it explicit and get the benefits of tooling.

Database Tools

The required schema in relational databases makes tool integration a breeze. That does not mean the tool is easy to develop, but the part of the tool that pulls the type information from the database is never the difficult part.

SimpleDB tools exist, but they suffer from some common problems. Running queries in a query tool never gives you a readable format for your numeric data, and if you want to run queries against numeric data, you have to manually convert the numbers in the query into the offset and padded format. Import and export tools also need to be told what to do with those numbers, as do reporting tools.

Storing a limited schema in a single, easily accessible location allows a greater degree of automation in the application and in tools.

Coordinating Concurrent Clients

A schema is not the only thing you can store as part of your custom metadata. Applications that use multiple servers generally need to coordinate in some way. Whether the servers need to share a common resource or a common workload, they frequently need to know about each other.

It can be beneficial to use SimpleDB as the well-known point of contact between individual servers in a deployment. This protects them from needing to have preconfigured information about the other servers. Preconfigured information can go out of date as soon as one of the servers needs a reboot.

Each server can keep its status updated at a configurable interval and use the database to discover both needed application settings as well as details about other servers.

Storing Custom Metadata within SimpleDB

Custom metadata could be stored anywhere, but the more universally accessible it is the better. Possibly the most accessible place to keep it is in the SimpleDB domain to which it applies. Any application or tool with access to the domain will also have access to the metadata. This also takes advantage of the high availability of the SimpleDB service.

However, storing metadata in the same domain as data could cause a problem. The issue is that you do not ever want metadata to come back from a data query. You can name the metadata attributes using a naming convention that prevents any conflicts with data attributes, but data queries will always exist that will match these items. It is the negation and `IS NULL` queries that do not really have a workaround.

Another option is to store the data in a separate SimpleDB domain dedicated solely to metadata storage. The domain can store all the metadata for domains in the same account. Access to this domain will be available to any client or tool with the credentials to access the account.

A naming convention can be used for the domain name, and because domain names only need to be unique per account, the same name can be used for the metadata domain in every account. Using multiple accounts became more convenient with the release of

AWS consolidated billing. Consolidated billing allows AWS accounts to be linked together for the purpose of billing. This makes it easier to manage the billing of multiple accounts associated with individual projects, departments, or clients.

Storing Custom Metadata in S3

A different option for the storage of custom metadata is to keep it in S3. It would be stored as a file and would not have the same query capabilities as SimpleDB, but it is unlikely that those will be needed. S3 also provides high availability.

On the plus side, there are more access controls available in S3. As a result, the metadata could be made publicly readable or only readable by specific AWS accounts. Additionally, versioning can be turned on to make all previous versions of the metadata available.

On the negative side, there is more latency when reading a file from S3 than a SimpleDB `GetAttributes` request. Also, the accessibility will have to be managed since S3 has to be signed up for separately from the SimpleDB sign-up. The S3 Access Control List will need to be updated to grant each account access, if you go that route.

The final problem is that S3 bucket names must be universally unique. As a result, you cannot select a single bucket name and use it to store metadata for every account. Each account would need its own, unique bucket name. The effect of this is that clients and tools cannot know ahead of time the exact name of the bucket to examine when fetching the metadata. A workaround for this is to use a naming convention and append unique characters at the end to create a bucket name that is both unique and identifiable.

Automatically Optimizing for Box Usage Cost

The pricing model for SimpleDB is straightforward. There are data transfer charges for moving data in and out of Amazon's cloud, frequently with discounts on inbound data. There are storage charges, currently at $0.25 per GB-month ($0.275 for Singapore, N. California and Ireland). Finally, there are charges for the box usage of each operation. Each SimpleDB response includes a number indicating the fractional hours to be billed. Box usage charges stand at $0.14 per hour ($0.154 for Singapore, N. California and Ireland), with the first 25 hours free (at the time of this writing).

Data transfer usage is measured directly. Data storage is measured at intervals throughout the month. Box usage, however, is not measured; it is assigned for each request based on formulas and variables. Formula-based assignments eliminate the variability that might otherwise be present across SimpleDB replicas running on heterogeneous hardware. It also obviates the overhead of measuring every operation.

Although the box usage is computed and not measured, the pricing turns out to be reasonable. There are, however, two noteworthy exceptions to that reasonableness. The first exception includes certain forms of `PutAttributes`/`DeleteAttributes`/`BatchPutAttributes` and the second is the cost of `QueryTimeout`.

The Exponential Cost of Write Operations

Back in June of 2008, Colin Percival broke down the SimpleDB box usage formulas in a post on his blog at www.daemonology.net/blog. He reported that the formula for `PutAttributes` and `DeleteAttributes` box usage was as follows:

0.0000219907 + 0.0000000002 N^3

In the equation, N is the number of attributes passed to the operation. The important fact is that the operation cost rises proportionally to the attribute count cubed. I verified the accuracy of the formula when it was posted, and it is still accurate at the time of this writing. The numbers are the same whether you pass single-valued attributes or multi-valued attributes, and the formula holds true for `BatchPutAttributes` as well.

What this means is that the cost of these write operations grows outrageously fast at the top end of the range. Figure 11-1 shows a graph of the cost of SimpleDB write as the number of attributes in the request grows.

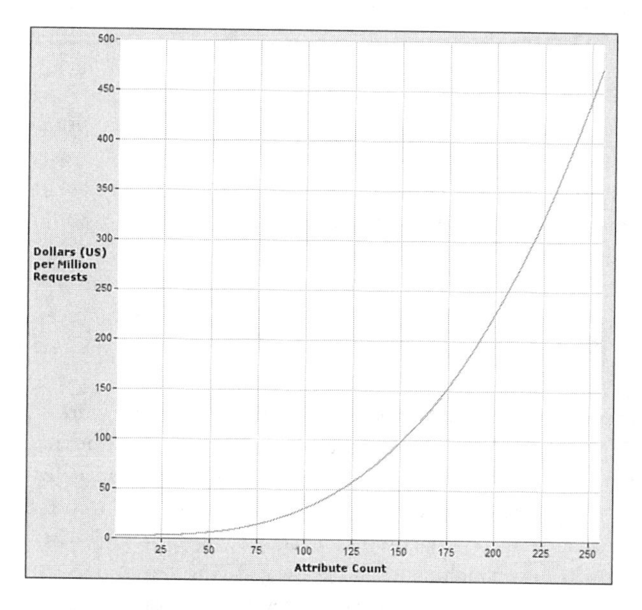

Figure 11-1 The charges for write operations as a function of attribute count

The x-axis in Figure 11-1 is the number of attributes, from 1 to 256. The y-axis is the box usage charge per million requests, in dollars.

There is a base charge for the operation, independent of the data you pass, of slightly more than $3 per million. At the bottom end of the graph, where the number of attributes is small, the base charge dominates the total charge. In fact, as you increase the number of attributes in a request up to 32, the charge per million never exceeds $4.

At this point, the incremental attribute cost begins to rise quickly. By the time you get to 53 attributes per request, the cost is above $7 per million, and it would actually be cheaper to write the data using two requests.

The remainder of this graph has charges rising fast enough to make your head spin. At 120 attributes, you pay above $50 per million. Add 50 more attributes, and the charges triple to above $150 per million. At the per-item limit of 256 attributes, the charge is a mammoth $472.84 per million.

What this all means is that if you have 256 attributes to put into an item, and you do it in a single request, you will pay a charge an order of magnitude higher than if you sent the exact same data in five smaller requests. To make the point in dollars, imagine that you have an application that sends data to SimpleDB at an average rate of two writes per second. If those writes each contain 2KB of data in 20 attributes, the monthly box usage charges will be roughly $34, or about half the cost of a small EC2 instance. If, however, those writes contain the same 2KB of data, but in 256 attributes, the charges will be about $4,902, which is enough to run 80 small EC2 instances all month long.

Attribute Counting

Applications that naturally have 50 or fewer attributes per item are not going to suffer from those punitive box usage charges. There are a wide variety of applications in this group. For applications writing larger quantities of attributes, there are a few workarounds to reduce the cost. However, there are tradeoffs with each choice, so none of them can apply to every situation.

The first thing to realize is that using SimpleDB for some applications would be prohibitively expensive. If 256 attributes per item feels restrictive for a given project, and you need to use the full 256 to make it work, SimpleDB may not be the best choice. This is especially true if none of the workarounds is suitable.

For those applications that fall somewhere in the middle, one workaround is merging values into composite attributes. With attribute merging, multiple attributes values are appended together and stored in one attribute. This was discussed in the context of query performance, and it can be used here as well. The benefit comes from reducing the number of attributes that need to be written. One drawback is the 1,024-byte limit on attribute values that limits how much data can be merged. Another drawback is that you only have the ability to query efficiently the first of the merged attribute. Subsequent attribute values stored within the composite can only be queried by combining the prior values as query constant, or using LIKE. Since using LIKE to match the end or middle of a value cannot use an index, the query can be done, but it will require a table scan and will not be efficient unless there are other criteria that limit the items that must be scanned.

A different option is to write all the attributes that you normally would, but write them in multiple requests, each with 52 or fewer attributes. The benefit is the significant reduction in cost by avoiding the high-attribute count in any single request. However, there are two downsides. The first is the loss of atomicity. When you perform a write of any kind in SimpleDB, the change is applied atomically. This is true for both normal writes and conditional writes. With eventual consistency, you may not see the change immediately, but subsequent reads always reflect the update either fully or not at all; it is never seen partially. When splitting a write across requests, each partial write remains atomic, but the write as a whole is not. The loss of atomicity should be carefully considered.

The other downside to request splitting is the impact on request volume. If you are able to maintain 100 writes per second normally, splitting each write into four smaller writes quadruples the request volume, and you may only be able to write data at a net rate of 25 items per second. This can be alleviated in the same way as throughput issues, spreading the data over multiple domains.

Avoiding high-attribute counts are more likely to be an issue for inserts. Updates and deletes frequently do not require passing as many attributes. When `PutAttributes` is used to update an item, only the changed attributes need to be passed. There is no reason to pass the unchanged values, and high cost is a good reason not to.

Deletes are typically rarer than inserts and updates, and it is, in fact, difficult to rack up high charges using deletes. If you want to delete specific attributes, those attributes must be passed specifically, and deleting the whole item is done by passing the item name and no attributes. The main thing that can get you in trouble with deletes is deleting items by passing every attribute.

Automatic Attribute Merging and Request Splitting

The one drawback that applies to all of these workarounds is the fact that you have to somehow code the knowledge of when to do them and when not. It is undesirable to write a lot of application code just to get around the database pricing. This is something best done declaratively in the application, in combination with a smart client providing the implementation.

This declarative information is just the sort of thing that fits into application-level metadata. Having a way to declare an attribute as an integer could allow a smart SimpleDB client to read, write, and query for it using a format suitable to the task. In the same way, a mechanism could be provided to specify which attributes can be merged and which attributes cannot be split up among multiple requests.

The value of having a way to define this information declaratively and then storing it somewhere accessible is that tools will also be able to use this information.

QueryTimeout: The Most Expensive Way to Get Nothing

Sending a write to SimpleDB with 256 attributes is expensive at upwards of $472 per million. It is especially expensive compared to writing one attribute for $3 per million. However, it isn't nearly as expensive as getting back a `QueryTimeout` response.

A `QueryTimeout` can come back as a response from any query. Complex queries are more likely to experience this, but it can happen with queries using a single comparison. It is difficult to predict when they will happen, but often they are easy to reproduce once they do happen.

One example is a domain I have that is close to the 10GB limit with 12.4 million items in it. Each item has an attribute named "tags" containing one or more tag values. A frequent query for this domain fetches the 20 most recently created items for a given tag. The query looks like this:

```
SELECT title, description, dateCreated, userCreated, tags
FROM `domain_024`
WHERE tags = '%s' AND dateCreated IS NOT NULL
ORDER BY dateCreated DESC
LIMIT 20
```

To run the query, I replace `%s` with the name of the tag I want to query. This query runs all the time, each time with one given tag. Some tags are very common, being present in more than 200,000 items. Other tags are much more rare.

Initially, I expected the popular tags to be most likely to have problems, because of the combination of a sort and a where clause that is not very selective. However, this did not turn out to be the case at all.

Popular tags like "family" matching 203,878 items, "travel" matching 201,416 items, and "friends" matching 37,699 items had no problems at all. Performance is always good, and they never see `QueryTimeout`. At the other end of the spectrum are the tags set in very few items. These rare tags also have flawless performance and no `QueryTimeout` errors, from tags with only one match up to tags like "autumn" with 544 matches.

However, some tags in the middle almost always return with the `QueryTimeout` error. From "party" matching 11,694 items to "dance" with 5378, all of the problem tags are middle of the road with regard to selectivity. I have been unable to discern any pattern to it, other than that they mostly happen in domains with millions of items.

When you get the `QueryTimeout`, it is bad in many ways. First of all, it takes the full five seconds to return, which is far too long to wait when building a web page, for example. Then when it finally does come back, you get an error message and no data. You don't even get a `NextToken`; you get nothing. Well, you don't get nothing—you get the maximum box usage charge of all operations.

The box usage charge for a `QueryTimeout` is a constant value of $778.26 per million, or $856.09 for Singapore, N. California and Ireland. That is 65% higher than a fully loaded write operation, and equal to the two rightfully expensive operations `CreateDomain` and `DeleteDomain`. When creating and deleting domains, at least you know ahead of time that they will be expensive and can use them in a strictly administrative capacity. `QueryTimeout` error could come back from any query.

If you have millions of attributes in a domain that gets regular use, you will want to have something in place to alert you to a high incidence of these errors. If you get 42 of them per day, it adds $100 to your monthly bill. This is a useful feature in a smart SimpleDB client—the ability to track `QueryTimeout` errors. The seriousness comes from the fact that the same queries tend to bring out that error at a high rate.

To fix the problem, I implemented a solution of adding a new set of attributes that contained the same information as the "tags" attribute, but the names and values inverted. So, for example, an item with the following attributes:

```
"tags" = "birthday" and "tags" = "party"
```

gets the additional new attributes:

```
"birthday" = "tags" and "party" = "tags"
```

The point of this is that the new attribute names get their own index, so I am able to change my query to use these new smaller indexes, where every attribute in the index is a match.

Now, in the worst case, these extra attributes could conflict with existing attributes, but even if they don't, it is desirable to be able to distinguish between the natural attributes and the synthetic ones. To resolve this, I prefixed each of these inverted attributes with "tags_". This eliminates the possibility of name conflicts and makes it easy to tell the purpose of the attribute.

The next step is to incorporate the new attributes into the query and see if it performs better. As you look at that initial query, you may notice that a descending sort was being done on "dateCreated" to display the newest items first. Because these new attributes all have the redundant value "tags", I decided to put the value of "dateCreated" into the new synthetic attributes instead. Therefore, those additional new attributes look like this:

```
"tags_birthday" = "2009-12-24T17:20:54.893"
"tags_party" = "2009-12-24T17:20:54.893"
```

It is still redundant, but now that query can be written to use only one attribute:

```
SELECT title, description, dateCreated, userCreated, tags
FROM `domain_024`
WHERE `tags_%s` IS NOT NULL
ORDER BY `tags_%s` DESC
LIMIT 20
```

In this query, `%s` still needs to be replaced with the tag name for each query. Notice that the attributes being selected in this query have not changed. The synthetic attributes are used to find matches, but "dateCreated" and "tags" are still the values returned.

I expected the new query to be faster than the old one because there is only one attribute in it. As it turns out, it is not faster at all, on average. Sometimes it is slightly faster, and other times it is slightly slower. However, one thing was unquestionably improved: The new query never returns a `QueryTimeout`, running in the same domain as the initial query.

The inverted attributes addition was an adequate solution for this project due to the complete elimination of the `QueryTimeout` errors. One reason this turned out to be an option is that the number of existing attributes in the target items was already low, with none above 30. If the attribute count had been high, adding additional attributes may not have been a good solution because of the exponential write costs.

It would be a useful feature of an advanced SimpleDB client to allow the application developer to specify declaratively which attributes to invert. The client would then automatically handle creating, updating, and deleting the synthetic attributes. This would also require integration with some advanced query functionality to rewrite conditions and sorts.

Automated Domain Sharding

You can get a good performance boost for read operations by using a cache, but for increased write throughput, you need to scale up the number of domains. Queuing up writes above the throughput limit can allow requests to be serviced quickly but does not solve the problem.

Domain Sharding Overview

Sharding data across domains, as discussed near the end of Chapter 9, "Increasing Performance," can be tricky. If the data is split on natural criteria, finding further ways to split it can be difficult. If the data is split based on a consistent hash function, it's better not to shard until you need the throughput, because all queries need to be multiplexed to every domain.

Sharding only when you need the throughput means you have to shuffle the data around to new domains after it has been stored in one domain. A common approach is to rehash the data based on the new number of locations.

The best approach might be to keep the same hash values, but use a configurable number of the hash bits to determine the location. If the application is configured to look at the last one bit of the hash, each item will have a value of either 1 or 0. A domain must be assigned to store the each of those—for example "users_0" and "users_1".

When the time comes to expand, the application can be reconfigured to look at the final two bits of the hash, which doubles the number of possible values to four. Two new domains would need to be created: "users_2" and "users_3". This can continue as needed, each time looking at an additional hash bit, and doubling the number of domains.

Put/Get Delete Routing

When the data is sharded across multiple domains, each call `PutAttributes`, `GetAttributes`, and `DeleteAttributes` will need to be routed to the proper domain. Each of these operations requires an item name and exactly one of the domains will be the proper location.

To find that location, the item name must be run though the hash function and then mapped to the domain responsible for that hash.

The implementation of the domain routing requires the hash function, the number of bits to examine, and the name of the domains in use. The domain names can use a naming convention as in the example of "user_0" and so on. However, it is better not to depend on a naming convention and instead use configuration. The domain names may need to change for administrative reasons like the restoration from a backup. Explicitly configured domain naming is more flexible

The code that implements the routing will need to stand between the application and the normal SimpleDB client. It could be a wrapper class for the client, selecting the domain before passing the data onto the client code. This wrapper code requires access to the application configuration that specifies the parameters of the hashing and domain mapping. Listing 11-3 shows what a class might look like that holds this configuration data.

Listing 11-3 **AppConfig.java A Class to Hold the Application Configuration**

```
package com.simpledbbook.metadata;

import java.util.*;

public class AppConfig {

    private List<String> domainList;
    private int bitCount;
    private int bitMask;
    private String serviceURL;

    private AppConfig(String appName, int bits, String... domains) {
        bitCount = bits;
        bitMask = (int) (Math.pow(2, bitCount) - 1);
        domainList = Arrays.asList(domains);
    }

    public String getDomain(int hash) {
        return domainList.get(hash & bitMask);
    }

    public String getServiceURL() {
      return serviceURL;
    }
}
```

The configuration would need to be stored somewhere accessible to the application and be loaded upon initialization. The data is passed into the constructor and consists of an application name, the number of hash bits to use, and an ordered list of domains for the mapping.

A derived field named `bitMask` is created in the constructor. The purpose of the bit mask is to encode the number of bits currently in use into a mask that easily allows a hash value to be converted into a list index.

The `getDomain()` method demonstrates the use of the bit mask. The hash value is passed into the method as an argument. Within the method, the hash value is combined with the bit mask using the Java bitwise AND (&) operator. The result of this operation is a numeric index corresponding to a domain in the list. The index is used to look up and return the name of the domain.

Listing 11-4 shows the implementation of a sharding wrapper class for the client developed in the last chapter. The wrapper class uses the AppConfig from Listing 11-3 to route all the gets, puts, and deletes to the proper domain.

Listing 11-4 **ShardingClient.javaA SimpleDB Client Wrapper Class for Sharding**

```
package com.simpledbbook.metadata;

import com.simpledbbook.*;

public class ShardingClient {
  private final SimpleDB sdb;
  private AppConfig config;

  public ShardingClient(AppConfig appConfig) {
    config = appConfig;
    sdb = new SimpleDB(config.getServiceURL());
  }

  public void put(Item item) {
    sdb.put(domainForItemName(item.getName()), item);
  }

  public void putIfNotExists(Item item, String expectedName) {
    String domain = domainForItemName(item.getName());
    sdb.putIfNotExists(domain, item, expectedName);
  }

  public void putIfExists(Item item, String expectedName,
      String expectedValue) {
    String domain = domainForItemName(item.getName());
    sdb.putIfExists(domain, item, expectedName, expectedValue);
  }

  public void delete(Item item) {
    sdb.delete(domainForItemName(item.getName()), item);
  }

  public void deleteIfNotExists(Item item, String expectedName) {
    String domain = domainForItemName(item.getName());
    sdb.deleteIfNotExists(domain, item, expectedName);
  }
```

```
  public void deleteIfExists(Item item, String expectedName,
      String expectedValue) {
    String domain = domainForItemName(item.getName());
    sdb.deleteIfExists(domain, item, expectedName, expectedValue);
  }

  public Item get(String itemName, String... atts) {
    return sdb.get(domainForItemName(itemName), itemName, atts);
  }

  public Item getConsistent(String itemName, String... atts) {
    return sdb.get(domainForItemName(itemName), itemName, atts);
  }

  private String domainForItemName(String itemName) {
    int hash = ConsistentHash.hash(itemName);
    return config.getDomain(hash);
  }
}
```

This sharding client takes an AppConfig instance in the constructor and initializes a SimpleDB object for use in request forwarding. Notice that each put, get, and delete method from the original client is present and that the method signatures are identical except that the domain name parameter is absent.

Each method makes an initial call to `domainForItemName()`. The bottom of Listing 11-4 shows the implementation of that method. First, a consistent hash value is computed for the item name and then the corresponding domain name is looked up and returned using the saved `AppConfig` instance. The referenced class `ConsistentHash` is fictitious and not provided. All that is needed is the implementation of a hash function that returns values that are well distributed.

With the appropriate domain name in place, each of the public methods has all the necessary parameters to call the underlying SimpleDB client. An instance of this class would be initialized and used instead of the vanilla SimpleDB client.

Query Multiplexing

The queries in a sharded application need to be sent to every domain. The results from all domains must then be merged together and returned. Because the data is evenly distributed across the domains, potential matches exist in all locations. Identical `Select` calls to each domain are the only way to gather all the matching results.

The process of taking a single input request and splitting it to multiple destinations simultaneously is called multiplexing.

This multiplexing of `Select` operations is implemented in a similar way as the routing of item-specific requests. The difference is that when selecting all of the application's domains, the query string has to be modified with the updated domain name, rather than passing it as a parameter.

The code to implement this is not as straightforward as the routing code, and this is not only because of the domain replacement. It is also necessary to honor the sort if one is present and within the limit. On top of that, a count request has to be handled appropriately.

Summary

Some of the ideas in this chapter are more practical, and some are more conceptual. Any of them may be needed or beneficial for a given project. Any of the tooling, convenience methods, or sharding support that you may need requires code to be written. Where you put that code is up to you, but much of it can be rolled into SimpleDB client advancements.

12

Building a Web-Based Task List

In this chapter, you create a web application where users can log in and enter to-do items into a task list. The user interface is simple and easy to use; all of the list management is handled via Asynchronous JavaScript and XML (AJAX) calls, so the web page does not need to reload each time.

In this project, you get a chance to see a diverse set of SimpleDB usage scenarios. The goal of this chapter is to take a top-to-bottom walk through the process of writing the application in Java. This includes full source code for the implementation and the necessary artifacts to deploy and use the application with minimum effort.

Application Overview

The application presents a very simple interface. After logging through a web page, a list of all the day's tasks is presented. At the top of the list is a text field to enter additional items. There are no buttons or checkboxes; the user just types in new items and hits the Enter key to save it.

Requirements

Through the course of this example, you implement the following features:

- Authenticating users through a login page
- Providing a means to log out of the application
- Displaying error messages in the case of an incorrect username or password
- Presenting the list of task items
- Storing newly added task items
- Allowing multiple task items with the same name, to accommodate cases where the same action needs to be taken multiple times
- Updating the list immediately as new items are saved without reloading the page

On the back end, SimpleDB is used for all of the data storage. This includes the following:

- User accounts with configurable authentication groups
- The hashes of user passwords for authentication
- Each of the task items
- The proper order of task items
- A key for each user session

The inclusion of authentication groups allows for the existence of more privileged classes of users (site administrators, for example), and leaves the door open to use the stored user data for different applications entirely.

Passwords need to be stored securely. Storing the passwords in plain text is a bad idea. Anyone with access to the database, the SimpleDB credentials stored with the application, or any administrative tools will have full access to all the passwords—this is not secure. The secure way to store them is to take a one-way cryptographic hash and store that value instead of the password. Checking the password is then a matter of performing the same hash function on the password the user supplies and comparing the two hashes. You then have the ability to authenticate users without keeping clear-text password data.

The Data Model

It is probably obvious that each task item needs to be stored in the database. The more difficult aspect of this, however, is storing the proper order. There are multiple ways to accomplish that goal, but most of them are difficult to update consistently.

Remember that in SimpleDB, the item is the unit of consistency. Any time you call `PutAttributes`, those values are applied atomically. This is not the case, however, when you update multiple items at once. As a result, when you need to keep multiple chunks of data in sync with each other, it leads you toward putting those chunks into the same item.

In this case, the chunks of data are the sequence of items. When the order of tasks in the list is changed, you want that to be reflected consistently. You do not want a user to move an item and see it disappear from the old location but not show up at the new location for a while because of eventual consistency.

In keeping with this idea, the data model for the task list is as follows. Each task is stored in a separate item. These items are lightweight, consisting of a unique ID and the text of the task. It is necessary to put each task in its own item to accommodate tasks with the same text. Because the text does not uniquely identify each task, another identifier is needed and an item is the logical choice.

It is possible to store the tasks as individual attributes of a larger item; however, space in an item is limited. It would be easy to run out of space in an item for all the tasks. In addition, it becomes awkward to try to store both a unique ID and the text in a name/value attribute pair. You end up with an item filled with unique attribute names.

This makes it more difficult to read, and it completely prevents queries. Using `Select` effectively requires consistent attribute naming.

The remainder of the task data that needs to be stored consists of the date, the order of items on the list, and a session ID. All of these are stored in a single item associated with the user. The dates and task sequences are stored together, where the date is used as the attribute name, with a prefix, and the task IDs for that date are the attribute value in the form of a comma-separated list.

In a way, it feels awkward to store a list as a comma-separated string. However, this is one of the idiosyncrasies of SimpleDB: You can easily store an array of values in a multi-valued attribute, but there is no easy way to maintain the sequence.

User data is the final piece of the data puzzle. This is stored in a different domain with the user ID as the unique item name. The hashed password and an 'enabled' flag are stored as single-valued attributes, and a multi-valued attribute holds the names of the authority groups.

Implementing User Authentication

The first set of Java classes here form a small API for managing users and tasks. These classes are the ones that deal directly with SimpleDB and handle all the details of mapping items and attributes to instance fields.

Let's begin with the `UserService`, which is shown in Listing 12-1.

Listing 12-1 **UserService.java A Utility Class for Managing Users**

```
package com.simpledbbook.tasklist;

import java.nio.charset.Charset;
import java.security.*;
import java.util.*;

import com.simpledbbook.*;
import com.sun.org.apache.xerces.internal.impl.dv.util.Base64;

public class UserService {
  private static final String SALT = "Salting-Thwarts-Rainbow-Attack";
  private static final Charset UTF_8 = Charset.forName("UTF-8");
  private static final String AUTH_GROUP = "AUTH_GROUP";
  private static final String PASSWORD = "PASSWORD";
  private static final String ENABLED = "ENABLED";
  private MessageDigest MD5;
  private SimpleDB sdb;
  private String domainName;

  public UserService(SimpleDB simpleDB, String domain) {
    sdb = simpleDB;
```

```
    domainName = domain;
    try {
      MD5 = MessageDigest.getInstance("MD5");
    } catch (NoSuchAlgorithmException cannotHappen) {}
  }

  public String createUser(String name, String pass, String... group){
    Item item = new Item(name);
    item.addAttribute(PASSWORD, hash(pass));
    item.addAttribute(ENABLED, Boolean.TRUE.toString());
    item.addMultiValuedAttr(AUTH_GROUP, group);
    try {
      sdb.putIfNotExists(domainName, item, PASSWORD);
    } catch (RuntimeException e) { // condition failed
      throw new UserNameUnavailable();
    }
    return item.getName();
  }

  public void deleteUser(String name) {
    sdb.delete(domainName, new Item(name));
  }

  private String hash(String pass) {
    byte[] salted = (SALT + pass).getBytes(UTF_8);
    byte[] hash;
    synchronized (MD5) {
      hash = MD5.digest(salted);
    }
    return Base64.encode(hash);
  }

  public List<String> authenticate(String userName, String password) {
    Item user = sdb.get(domainName, userName);
    String suppliedCredential = hash(password);
    String storedCredential = user.getAttribute(PASSWORD);
    if (! suppliedCredential.equals(storedCredential)) {
      throw new AuthenticationFailure();
    }
    return user.getAttributes(AUTH_GROUP);
  }

  public void addAuthGroup(String userName, String group) {
    Item item = new Item(userName);
    item.addMultiValuedAttr(AUTH_GROUP, group);
    sdb.put(domainName, item);
```

```
  }

  public void removeAuthGroup(String userName, String group) {
    Item item = new Item(userName);
    item.addMultiValuedAttr(AUTH_GROUP, group);
    sdb.delete(domainName, item);
  }

  public List<String> listUsers(String group) {
    String query = "SELECT itemName() FROM `" + domainName +
      "` WHERE " + AUTH_GROUP + " = '" + group + "'";
    List<Item> items = sdb.selectWithRealLimit(query, 100000);
    List<String> result = new ArrayList<String>();
    for (Item item: items) {
      result.add(item.getName());
    }
    return result;
  }
}
```

There is a lot to look at in Listing 12-1, but the following quick summary of the public methods should bring it into sharper focus:

- `createUser(String name, String pass, String... group)`
- `deleteUser(String name)`
- `authenticate(String userName, String password)`
- `addAuthGroup(String userName, String group)`
- `removeAuthGroup(String userName, String group)`
- `listUsers(String group)`

These are all the basic management functions for user accounts. This is a thread-safe class with a SimpleDB client instance passed into the constructor.

The user creation method does a conditional write of the requested username that only succeeds when that item name is not yet taken. This lets you guarantee unique names. When the name is taken, an exception is thrown back to the caller.

In addition, this is where the password is salted and hashed before storage. This is the only place where it appears in plain text. The remainder of the methods in this class are straightforward.

The two exception classes defined for this package are shown next. First is `UserNameUnavailable`, as follows:

```
package com.simpledbbook.tasklist;

public class UserNameUnavailable extends RuntimeException {}
```

The other exception represents a bad username/password combination as an `AuthenticationFailure`:

```
package com.simpledbbook.tasklist;

public class AuthenticationFailure extends RuntimeException {
  public AuthenticationFailure(){}

  public AuthenticationFailure(String message){
    super(message);
  }
}
```

There is not much to these exception classes; they serve two purposes. First, they perform the normal exception function of giving an easy-to-understand name to place in a catch block for readable code. The other function is merely to extend `RuntimeException` rather than a checked exception. This enables exception handling to be placed where it belongs without unnecessary dependencies where it does not.

Implementing a Task Workspace

Having handled the users, we need a class to convert between our big SimpleDB item that is storing all of the task list dates and sequences. Listing 12-2 shows a TaskWorkspace class that encapsulates these responsibilities.

Listing 12-2 **TaskWorkspace.java A Class to Hold All of the Workspace Data**

```
package com.simpledbbook.tasklist;

import java.util.*;

import com.simpledbbook.*;

public class TaskWorkspace {
  public static final String REVISION = "workspaceRevision";
  private static final String NEXT_TASK = "nextTaskId";
  private final String name;
  private Item originalItem;
  private HashMap<String, List<String>> calendar;
  private int nextTaskId = 0;
  private int revision = 0;
  private String sessionId;

  public TaskWorkspace(String workspaceName) {
    name = workspaceName;
    calendar = new HashMap<String, List<String>>();
  }
```

```
public int getNextTaskId() {
  return nextTaskId;
}

public void setNextTaskId(int nextTaskId) {
  this.nextTaskId = nextTaskId;
}

public int getWorkspaceRevision() {
  return revision;
}

public void setWorkspaceRevision(int rev) {
  revision = rev;
}

public String getSessionId() {
  return sessionId;
}

public void setSessionId(String sessionId) {
  this.sessionId = sessionId;
}

public List<String> getDay(String day) {
  List<String> list = calendar.get(day);
  List<String> result = new ArrayList<String>();
  if (list != null) {
    result.addAll(list);
  }
  return result;
}

public void setDay(String day, List<String> values) {
  calendar.put(day, new ArrayList<String>(values));
}

public Item toItem() {
  Item item = new Item(name);
  item.addAttribute(NEXT_TASK, nextTaskId + "", true);
  item.addAttribute(REVISION, revision + "", true);
  item.addAttribute("sessionId", sessionId, true);
  for (Map.Entry<String, List<String>> day: calendar.entrySet()){
    String serializedDay = serializeDay(day.getValue());
    item.addAttribute("date_" + day.getKey(), serializedDay, true);
```

```
    }
    return item;
  }

  public static TaskWorkspace fromItem(Item item) {
    TaskWorkspace result = new TaskWorkspace(item.getName());
    result.nextTaskId = Integer.parseInt(item.getAttribute(NEXT_TASK));
    result.revision = Integer.parseInt(item.getAttribute(NEXT_TASK));
    result.sessionId = item.getAttribute("sessionId");
    result.originalItem = item;
    result.calendar = toCalendar(item);
    return result;
  }

  private static String serializeDay(List<String> values) {
    StringBuilder result = new StringBuilder();
    for (String s : values) {
      result.append(',').append(s);
    }
    return result.substring(1); // omit the leading ','
  }

  private static HashMap<String, List<String>> toCalendar(Item item) {
    HashMap<String, List<String>> result;
    result = new HashMap<String, List<String>>();
    for (Attribute attribute: item.getAtts()) {
      String name = attribute.getName();
      if (name.startsWith("date_")) {
        String date = name.substring(5);
        List<String> tasks = parseTasks(attribute.getValue());
        result.put(date, tasks);
      }
    }
    return result;
  }

  private static List<String> parseTasks(String value) {
    String[] values = value.split(",");
    return Arrays.asList(values);
  }

  public String toString() {
    return originalItem.toString();
  }
}
```

The first half portion of the class is devoted to getter and setter methods. Two of the important ones are the workspace revision number and the next task ID. The revision number is used to keep the item from falling victim to destructive writes.

It is true that each call to `PutAttributes` is applied atomically. However, two calls to the same attribute can be made at nearly the same time, and the last write wins. It is consistent with the last write, but the first write gets clobbered. We do not want this to happen to the sequence info we are storing, so we can use the revision attribute as an optimistic lock with conditional writes. The revision number is incremented each time the workspace is updated with new sequences.

Something similar is being done with the next task ID. The actual task text is kept in separate items. We could use UUID values to get unique item names, but since we are keeping the list sequence data in a comma-separated list, smaller values are better.

To meet these requirements, the `nextTaskId` attribute is used in the workspace item. The value is incremented with a conditional write, and if it is successful, the value can then be used as the primary key of the next task item.

The code in Listing 12-2 does not show the mechanics of how these processes are implemented. Instead, it is the class that holds the data and provides access for the service class that performs the actual work.

Implementing a Task Service

Listing 12-3 shows the actual work behind managing the tasks in the workspace with a partial implementation of TaskService.java. The full implementation is available as a download on the book's website.

Listing 12-3 **TaskService.java A Class for Managing Tasks**

```
public class TaskService {
  private UserService userService;
  private SimpleDB sdb;
  private String domain;

  public TaskService(SimpleDB sdb, String userDomain,
      String appDomain) {
    this.sdb = sdb;
    this.domain = appDomain;
    this.userService = new UserService(sdb, userDomain);
  }

  public String registerNewUser(String name, String password) {
    if (! validateUserName(name)) {
      throw new InvalidParameterException(name);
    }
    if (! validatePassword(password)) {
      throw new InvalidParameterException(password);
```

```
    }
    userService.createUser(name, password, USER_GROUP);
    TaskWorkspace workspace = new TaskWorkspace(name);
    workspace.setSessionId(randomSessionId());
    sdb.put(domain, workspace.toItem());
    return workspace.getSessionId();
  }

  public String addTask(String user, String date, String value,
      String sessionId) {
    TaskWorkspace workspace = validateSession(user, sessionId);
    int taskId = incrementTaskId(workspace);
    int revision = incrementRevision(workspace);
    addTaskIntoWorkspace(date, workspace, taskId);
    sdb.putIfExists(domain, workspace.toItem(),REVISION,revision +"");
    storeTask(user, value, taskId);
    return taskId + "";
  }

  private TaskWorkspace validateSession(String user, String sessionId){
    Item item = sdb.getConsistent(domain, user);
    String storedId = item.getAttribute("sessionId");
    if (storedId == null || ! sessionId.equals(storedId)) {
      throw new AuthenticationFailure();
    }
    return TaskWorkspace.fromItem(item);
  }

  public List<String> getTasksForDay(String user, String date,
      String sessionId) {
    TaskWorkspace workspace = validateSession(user, sessionId);
    List<String> taskIds = workspace.getDay(date);
    String queryString = String.format(TASK_SELECT, domain, user, "%");
    List<Item> items = sdb.select(queryString);
    List<String> result = new ArrayList<String>();
    for (Item i: items) {
      String taskId = i.getName().substring(user.length() + 1);
      if (taskIds.contains(taskId)) {
        result.add(i.getAttribute("text"));
      }
    }
    return result;
  }

  public TaskWorkspace logIn(String user, String password) {
    List<String> groups = userService.authenticate(user, password);
```

```
    if (! groups.contains(USER_GROUP)) {
      throw new AuthenticationFailure();
    }
    Item item = sdb.get(domain, user);
    TaskWorkspace workspace = TaskWorkspace.fromItem(item);
    workspace.setSessionId(randomSessionId());
    sdb.put(domain, workspace.toItem());
    return workspace;
  }

  public void logOut(String user, String sessionId) {
    TaskWorkspace workspace = validateSession(user, sessionId);
    workspace.setSessionId("");
    sdb.put(domain, workspace.toItem());
  }

  public List<String> listUsers() {
    return userService.listUsers(USER_GROUP);
  }
}
```

This class is the analog to `UserService`, providing methods to perform all the management functions, but for the workspace rather than for users. In fact, it actually makes use of `UserService` to do many of these things. As a result, managing the Task List application mainly involves interactions with this one class.

This class holds the real meat of dealing with SimpleDB. It is a hefty class, but many of the methods are private utility methods. The primary methods of the class are as follows:

- `registerNewUser(String name, String password)`
- `logIn(String user, String password)`
- `logOut(String user, String sessionId)`
- `getTasksForDay(String user, String date, String sessionId)`
- `addTask(String user, String date, String value, String sessionId)`

The method `registerNewUser()` combines the functionality of creating a user account, creating the workspace, as well as initializing the sessionId. The sessionId is a random number stored in the SimpleDB workspace item for each user. This number is matched against a web browser cookie to grant access to users who have already logged in. For this application, no other session state is being stored, so simply matching the ID is done.

As with any cookie-based session management, stolen cookies could cause a security issue. The solution is to store additional data along with the ID so that the cookie alone does not grant access. However, since this application is not storing sensitive data, extra precautions are not really warranted.

One thing that is different about this style of session is that it is stored in the database rather than in memory on the web server. The lack of state on the web server allows the application to scale horizontally across many servers without the need to route users always back to the same server they first hit.

Another interesting side effect of this arrangement is the speed with which you can get the sessionId. It is certainly true that data stored in server memory will be accessed with much lower latency than a call to SimpleDB. However, that does not tell the whole story. The real situation is that each of these calls has to pull a SimpleDB item by primary key anyway. Fetching one extra attribute does not add a statistically significant latency to the existing call, on average. This essentially means that storing the sessionId in an item you have to fetch anyway makes it a freebie.

Finishing up the discussion of the primary methods from Listing 12-3, `logIn()`, `logOut()`, and `addTasks()` are fairly self-explanatory. The method `getTasksForDay()` takes the workspace object and gathers all of the tasks marked with the chosen date. A Select is used against SimpleDB to fetch the text for all of those tasks; remember that the workspace only stores the task IDs in sequence. This query is highly selective and runs very quickly even when the domain contains many users. However, it is still more work than most of the other methods do, but this only gets called when the full page loads. AJAX calls are used for all of the list manipulation, and so the processing occurs without a page reload.

Adding the Login Servlet

Now that we have worked through the primary business logic workhorse, let's turn our attention to web interface. Listing 12-4 shows the super class servlet that defines the commonality between all of the web interface servlets.

Listing 12-4 **BaseServlet.java Abstract Parent Servlet with Cookie Management**

```
package com.simpledbbook.servlet;

import java.io.IOException;

import javax.naming.*;
import javax.servlet.ServletException;
import javax.servlet.http.*;

import com.simpledbbook.SimpleDB;
import com.simpledbbook.tasklist.TaskService;

public abstract class BaseServlet extends HttpServlet {
  private static final long serialVersionUID = 1L;
  private static final int ONE_WEEK = 1000 * 60 * 60 * 24 * 7;
  public static final String USER_DOMAIN;
  public static final String TASK_DOMAIN;
```

```
public static final String SESSION_COOKIE_NAME = "tasksession";
public static final String USER_COOKIE_NAME = "taskuser";
protected TaskService app=
  new TaskService(new SimpleDB(), USER_DOMAIN, TASK_DOMAIN);

static {
  String userDomain = "users_01";
  String taskDomain = "tasks_01";
  try {
    Context ic = new InitialContext();
    Context context = (Context) ic.lookup("java:comp/env");
    userDomain = (String) context.lookup("userDomain");
    taskDomain = (String) context.lookup("taskDomain");
  } catch (Exception e) {
    e.printStackTrace();
  }
  USER_DOMAIN = userDomain;
  TASK_DOMAIN = taskDomain;
}

protected void doPost(HttpServletRequest request,
    HttpServletResponse response) throws ServletException,
    IOException {
  doGet(request, response);
}

protected String getSessionCookie(HttpServletRequest request) {
  return getCookie(request, SESSION_COOKIE_NAME);
}

protected String getUserCookie(HttpServletRequest request) {
  return getCookie(request, USER_COOKIE_NAME);
}

private String getCookie(HttpServletRequest request,
    String cookieName) {
  if (request.getCookies() != null) {
    for (Cookie cookie : request.getCookies()) {
      if (cookie.getName().equals(cookieName)) {
        return cookie.getValue();
      }
    }
  }
  return "";
}
```

```
  protected void deleteSessionCookie(HttpServletResponse response) {
    response.setContentType("text/html");
    Cookie cookie = new Cookie(SESSION_COOKIE_NAME, "");
    cookie.setMaxAge(0);
    cookie.setPath("/");
    response.addCookie(cookie);
  }

  protected void setCookies(HttpServletResponse response,
      String session, String user) {
    response.setContentType("text/html");
    Cookie cookie = new Cookie(SESSION_COOKIE_NAME, session);
    cookie.setMaxAge(ONE_WEEK);
    cookie.setPath("/");
    response.addCookie(cookie);
    Cookie cookie2 = new Cookie(USER_COOKIE_NAME, user);
    cookie2.setMaxAge(ONE_WEEK);
    cookie2.setPath("/");
    response.addCookie(cookie2);
  }

  protected boolean empty(String value) {
    return value == null || "".equals(value.trim());
  }
}
```

There are a number of methods to look through, but they all have pretty cut-and-dry purposes. The constants at the top are immediately followed by a static initializer block. This initializer is loading the domain name settings from the web application deployment descriptor file, web.xml. Those constants are made available to all of the subclasses that we will look at next.

Following that block is a single `doPost()` method, as a convenience that forwards the request on to `doGet()` in the subclass. The class winds down with four protected cookie management methods. These are also used by subclasses to fetch and manage this little bit of state.

Listing 12-5 shows the first concrete servlet: a humble login servlet.

Listing 12-5 **Login.java A Servlet Providing Login Functionality**

```
package com.simpledbbook.servlet;

import java.io.IOException;
import javax.servlet.ServletException;
import javax.servlet.http.*;

import com.simpledbbook.tasklist.*;
```

```
public class Login extends BaseServlet {
  private static final long serialVersionUID = 1L;

  protected void doGet(HttpServletRequest req,
      HttpServletResponse resp) throws ServletException, IOException {
    String userId = req.getParameter("userId");
    String password = req.getParameter("password");

    // handle direct navigation
    if (empty(userId) || empty(password)) {
      if (empty(getSessionCookie(req))) {
        req.getRequestDispatcher("index.jsp").forward(req, resp);
      } else { // redirect for the logged in
        resp.sendRedirect("tasks");
      }
      return;
    }

    // login
    try {
      TaskWorkspace workspace = app.logIn(userId, password);
      setCookies(resp, workspace.getSessionId(), userId);
      resp.sendRedirect("tasks");
    } catch (AuthenticationFailure af) {
      req.setAttribute("message", "Invalid Credentials");
      req.getRequestDispatcher("index.jsp").forward(req, resp);
    } catch (Exception e) {
      e.printStackTrace();
      req.setAttribute("message", "Error: " + e.getClass().getName());
      req.getRequestDispatcher("index.jsp").forward(req, resp);
    }
  }
}
```

The real purpose of this class is to authenticate users who are coming from the login JSP, and redirect them to the main part of the application. That happens in the lone method in this class, but not until the end; some other things need to be handled first.

It is possible that a user arrives at this URL from direct navigation, for whatever reason, and does not have a username and password in the request. If this is the case, but a cookie has been set, they can be sent to the main application. If the cookie is missing too, the only alternative is to send them to the logon page.

If we get past that part of the code, we know there is a username and password, so go ahead: Put the workspace to good use, and log in. The result of the login is the actual workspace object. Because the password hash is stored right in the SimpleDB workspace item, it is convenient to return it from the login so we can prepare and store the authentication cookie.

Listing 12-6 shows the index.jsp page that collects that login data in the first place.

Listing 12-6 **index.jsp A JSP Logon Page**

```
<%@ page pageEncoding="UTF-8"%>
<%@ taglib prefix="c" uri="http://java.sun.com/jsp/jstl/core"%>

<!DOCTYPE html PUBLIC "-//W3C//DTD HTML 4.01 Transitional//EN"
    "http://www.w3.org/TR/html4/loose.dtd">
<html>

<head>
<meta http-equiv="Content-Type" content="text/html; charset=UTF-8">
<title>Login to Task List</title>
</head>

<body>
<form action="login" method="post" name="Login">
<div><c:if test="${not empty requestScope.message}">
   <div><c:out value="${requestScope.message}" /></div>
</c:if>

<div>Username <input type="text" name="userId" size="14"
   maxlength="20" /></div>

<div>Password <input type="password" name="password" size="14"
   maxlength="32" /></div>

<div><input type="submit" name="Login" title="Login"
   value="Login" /></div>

</div>
</form>
</body>
</html>
```

There is not much special going on here, other than a simple HTML form. At the top of the form, a message is conditionally written into the output. When present, this is the error message you may have noticed being set in the first catch block of Listing 12-5, surrounding the appearance of an `AuthenticationFailure`.

Adding the Logout Servlet

Logging out of the application is a simple matter, as shown in Listing 12-7. The browser cookie is deleted, the client is redirected to the logon page, and an attempt is made to clear the sessionId stored in the SimpleDB workspace item.

Listing 12-7 **Logout.java A Servlet Providing Logout Functionality**

```
package com.simpledbbook.servlet;

import java.io.IOException;
import javax.servlet.ServletException;
import javax.servlet.http.*;

import com.simpledbbook.tasklist.AuthenticationFailure;

public class Logout extends BaseServlet {
  private static final long serialVersionUID = 1L;

  protected void doGet(HttpServletRequest request,
      HttpServletResponse response) throws ServletException,
      IOException {

    deleteSessionCookie(response);
    response.sendRedirect("./");
    try {
      app.logOut(getUserCookie(request), getSessionCookie(request));
    } catch (AuthenticationFailure af) {
    } // ignore
  }
}
```

Displaying the Tasks

Now we come to the heart of the user interface: the code that fetches the tasks in Listing 12-8. The first thing that happens in the `doGet()` method is a check to verify that the session cookie is set. All that really remains after that is to pull today's tasks and set them in the request object where the JSP page can pick them up.

Listing 12-8 **Tasks.java A Servlet to Fetch the Task List**

```
package com.simpledbbook.servlet;

import java.io.IOException;
import java.util.List;
```

```
import javax.servlet.ServletException;
import javax.servlet.http.*;

import com.simpledbbook.tasklist.*;

public class Tasks extends BaseServlet {
  private static final long serialVersionUID = 1L;

  protected void doGet(HttpServletRequest req,
      HttpServletResponse resp) throws ServletException, IOException {

    String session = getSessionCookie(req);
    if (empty(session)) {
      resp.sendRedirect("./");
    } else {
      try {
        String today = TaskService.today();
        String user = getUserCookie(req);
        List<String> tasks = app.getTasksForDay(user, today, session);
        req.setAttribute("tasklist", tasks);
        req.getRequestDispatcher("tasks.jsp").forward(req, resp);
      } catch (AuthenticationFailure af) {
        af.printStackTrace();
        deleteSessionCookie(resp);
        resp.sendRedirect("./");
      }
    }
  }
}
```

Listing 12-9 shows this follow-up JSP that performs the actual HTML presentation. Notice that a reference to the jQuery JavaScript library is present in the HTML head. This is used as the basis of the AJAX functionality.

Beneath that is a logout link and a single text field for entering new tasks. An unordered list follows that with a loop that emits a list item tag for each task present in the tasklist variable.

Listing 12-9 **tasks.jsp A JSP to Display the Task List**

```
<%@ page pageEncoding="UTF-8"%>
<%@ taglib prefix="c" uri="http://java.sun.com/jsp/jstl/core"%>
<!DOCTYPE html PUBLIC "-//W3C//DTD HTML 4.01 Transitional//EN"
              "http://www.w3.org/TR/html4/loose.dtd">
<html>
<head>
<meta http-equiv="Content-Type" content="text/html; charset=UTF-8">
```

```
<title>Task List</title>
<script src="http://code.jquery.com/jquery-latest.js"></script>
</head>

<body>
<div><a href="logout">Logout</a></div>
<div>
<form action="add" name="form">
<div><input id="input_field" name="task" type="text" size="20"
   maxlength="140" /> <input type="hidden" name="date"
   value="20100315" />
<ul id="list_">
   <c:forEach items="${requestScope.tasklist}" var="task">
      <li><span><c:out value="${task}" /></span></li>
   </c:forEach>
</ul>
</div>
</form>
</div>

<script>
      $("form").submit(function() {
              $.post("add", $("form").serialize(), function(data) {
                     $("#input_field").val("");
                     $("#list_").append(data);
              });
              return false;
      });
</script>

</body>
</html>
```

Listing 12-9 wraps up with a script tag. Within that script tag is the jQuery code necessary to send new tasks back to the server when the user presses enter in the text field.

After the call to serialize the HTML form, a callback function is declared. The callback first clears the text field, and then appends the data from the server to the end of the unordered list. This callback function is declared at the time the user presses Enter, but does not get called until the round trip between the server and SimpleDB is complete and the response comes back from the servlet.

Adding New Tasks

When the Enter key is pressed, the jQuery code specifies that the form data be posted to the URL named "add." "Add" maps to the AddTask servlet, shown in Listing 12-10.

Listing 12-10 **AddTask.java A Servlet for Handling New Tasks via AJAX**

```
package com.simpledbbook.servlet;

import java.io.IOException;
import javax.servlet.ServletException;
import javax.servlet.http.HttpServletRequest;
import javax.servlet.http.HttpServletResponse;

public class AddTask extends BaseServlet {
  private static final long serialVersionUID = 1L;
  private static final String TASK_HTML =
      "<li><span id='%s'> %s </span></li>";

  protected void doGet(HttpServletRequest request,
      HttpServletResponse response) throws ServletException,
      IOException {

    String session = getSessionCookie(request);
    String user = getUserCookie(request);
    String date = request.getParameter("date");
    String task = request.getParameter("task");
    String taskId = app.addTask(user, date, task, session);
    String result = String.format(TASK_HTML, taskId, task);
    response.getWriter().write(result);
  }
}
```

The server-side function of this call is simple. All of the parameters are gathered and then passed to `workspace.addTask()`. Once that call returns, the data has been stored in SimpleDB. The only thing that remains to do is format the HTML tag with the new task and ship it back to the jQuery callback handler patiently waiting in the browser.

Deployment

This last file shown in Listing 12-11 is the web application deployment descriptor. It provides all the mapping between URLs and servlets.

Listing 12-11 **web.xml The Web Application Configuration File**

```
<?xml version="1.0" encoding="UTF-8"?>
<web-app id="WebApp_ID" version="2.4">
```

```
<display-name>Chapter12</display-name>
<servlet>
   <display-name>Login</display-name>
   <servlet-name>Login</servlet-name>
   <servlet-class>com.simpledbbook.servlet.Login</servlet-class>
</servlet>
<servlet>
   <display-name>Tasks</display-name>
   <servlet-name>Tasks</servlet-name>
   <servlet-class>com.simpledbbook.servlet.Tasks</servlet-class>
</servlet>
<servlet>
    <display-name>Logout</display-name>
   <servlet-name>Logout</servlet-name>
   <servlet-class>com.simpledbbook.servlet.Logout</servlet-class>
</servlet>
<servlet>
    <display-name>AddTask</display-name>
   <servlet-name>AddTask</servlet-name>
   <servlet-class>com.simpledbbook.servlet.AddTask</servlet-class>
</servlet>
<servlet-mapping>
   <servlet-name>Login</servlet-name>
   <url-pattern>/login</url-pattern>
</servlet-mapping>
<servlet-mapping>
   <servlet-name>Tasks</servlet-name>
   <url-pattern>/tasks</url-pattern>
</servlet-mapping>
<servlet-mapping>
   <servlet-name>Logout</servlet-name>
   <url-pattern>/logout</url-pattern>
</servlet-mapping>
<servlet-mapping>
   <servlet-name>AddTask</servlet-name>
   <url-pattern>/add</url-pattern>
</servlet-mapping>
<welcome-file-list>
   <welcome-file>Login</welcome-file>
   <welcome-file>index.html</welcome-file>
   <welcome-file>index.htm</welcome-file>
   <welcome-file>index.jsp</welcome-file>
   <welcome-file>default.html</welcome-file>
   <welcome-file>default.htm</welcome-file>
   <welcome-file>default.jsp</welcome-file>
</welcome-file-list>
```

```
  <env-entry>
    <env-entry-name>userDomain</env-entry-name>
    <env-entry-type>java.lang.String</env-entry-type>
    <env-entry-value>users_01</env-entry-value>
  </env-entry>
  <env-entry>
    <env-entry-name>taskDomain</env-entry-name>
    <env-entry-type>java.lang.String</env-entry-type>
    <env-entry-value>tasks_01</env-entry-value>
  </env-entry>
</web-app>
```

This xml descriptor has a lot of boilerplate to it, but at the very bottom, you can see the environment entries for our SimpleDB domains: "users_01" and "tasks_01". When you need to set the names for the domains, this is the place to do it.

Summary

In this chapter, you have gone through the full cycle with this simple application. A number of additional features could usefully be added to this tool. The display can be enhanced to show a full week's worth of lists. Support can be added to rearrange the items on the list.

There are many things that could be done. This is one of the types of basic applications that can benefit from SimpleDB. The application is rudimentary, but it never touches a web server session object. Clients could bounce around from one web server to another and never know the difference.

Storing a session key in the database is not really anything special, and it is not specific to SimpleDB. You could do it with any database. The part that is specific to SimpleDB is the availability and automatic replication. You can store session data in a database without SimpleDB, but you cannot as easily deal with database failures.

Index

A

B

C

D

E

F

G

H

I

J

Q

R

S

V

W

X

A Developer's Guide to
Amazon
SimpleDB

FREE Online Edition

Your purchase of **A Developer's Guide to Amazon SimpleDB** includes access to a free online edition for 45 days through the Safari Books Online subscription service. Nearly every Addison-Wesley Professional book is available online through Safari Books Online, along with more than 5,000 other technical books and videos from publishers such as Cisco Press, Exam Cram, IBM Press, O'Reilly, Prentice Hall, Que, and Sams.

SAFARI BOOKS ONLINE allows you to search for a specific answer, cut and paste code, download chapters, and stay current with emerging technologies.

Activate your FREE Online Edition at www.inform

STEP 1: E

STEP 2: New Safari users, complete the brief registration form. Safari subscribers, just log in.

If you have difficulty registering on Safari or accessing the online edition, please e-mail customer-service@safaribooksonline.com